THE FACE IN THE
SHADOWS

WENDY JANE COLLINS

authorHOUSE®

AuthorHouse™ UK
1663 Liberty Drive
Bloomington, IN 47403 USA
www.authorhouse.co.uk
Phone: UK TFN: 0800 0148641 (Toll Free inside the UK)
        UK Local: 02036 956322 (+44 20 3695 6322 from outside the UK)

Published by AuthorHouse 10/05/2020

ISBN: 978-1-6655-8075-5 (sc)
ISBN: 978-1-6655-8076-2 (hc)
ISBN: 978-1-6655-8074-8 (e)

Print information available on the last page.

Any people depicted in stock imagery provided by Getty Images are models, and such images are being used for illustrative purposes only.
Certain stock imagery © Getty Images.

This book is printed on acid-free paper.

I'd like to dedicate this book...to the two people in my life
that have kept me going through some very tough times...
My daughter Courtney-Lee. You are my driving force, my rock and
quite simply my best friend. Nothing is ever too much trouble for you
and your every thought is always for others. You are a true inspiration.
My daughter Kacey-Lee. Despite all your own difficulties,
in a non verbal world of autism. You never fail to make
me smile...you are the sunshine in my day.
I love you both with all my heart Xxx

ABOUT THE AUTHOR

Wendy Jane Collins was born in Orsett, Essex on June 12th 1968. She was an only child, but went on to have six children of her own. She has four daughters, but sadly her identical twin sons were born early at 26 weeks and only survived a short time. Wendy has been blessed with three beautiful granddaughters.

Today, Wendy lives in Aveley, Essex with her husband and two youngest children and spends her time organising charity events with her family, donating to many worthwhile causes thanks to the support of generous people far and wide and volunteering her time whenever possible to help and befriend those in need.

Wendy has always had a love of writing, starting at a young age and enjoys writing both stories and poems. She really hopes you enjoy her first mystery novel, The Face In The Shadows.

CHAPTER 1

GOODBYE PRIMROSE HILL

"Ben, will you be much longer? Jake and Emily are getting restless" Lucy Reid called to her husband. "Yeah, I'm coming Lucy" Ben replied, taking one last look around Number 7 Primrose Hill. Ben had been born there and spent many, mostly happy, years growing up in that house. It seemed so empty now that the removal men had taken the last of their belongings. The rooms, once filled with the sound of children's laughter, seemed to echo an eerie silence. Primrose Hill, in its day, had been an extremely sought after area, full of very affluent people, seemingly leading very comfortable lives. All had nice cars and lavish houses, full of all of the latest mod cons. When Ben was born, the house had been owned by his late Great-Aunt Maud, an elderly spinster, set very much in her own ways. Maud never made any secret of the fact that she had no time for her flighty neighbours. She would often watch the 'goings-on' of the street, as she called it, tut-tutting at how, if one neighbour got a new car, the others would soon follow suit.

Ben remembered, one weekend, the Baileys over the road held a big party, and the very next weekend, every other family in the cul-de-sac had a party, apart from his great-aunt. She would watch from behind the curtain, chuckling to herself about them being sheep and having to follow the flock. Ben had only fond memories of his great-aunt, from when she used to chase him round the table leg on her hands and knees when he was small, to playing darts in the back garden just weeks before she died. Great-Aunt Maud clearly declared, often to her neighbours' faces, that they had far too many airs and graces and that life was for living to the full, not wasting time pretending to be someone you're not.

When Maud passed away, the house remained the Reid family home.

Ben had chosen to stay put when his parents had decided to take early retirement, to run Maud's shop, over 100 miles away. It came as quite a shock when Mr Benson, Great-Aunt Maud's solicitor, told them about it, because they didn't even know she had one! The appearance of the shop seemed very odd, but all questions about it were met with his mother doing everything possible to stop the conversation flat. She would quickly change the subject, whilst his father shifted uncomfortably from foot to foot in the background.

That was 6 months ago, and it should have been a happy ending, but it was far from that. Frank and Janet Reid had decided to take a last minute holiday. Ben didn't know too much about it, just that it was a deal 'too good to be missed', offered to them by a customer at the casino where his father worked. Ben had waved his parents off from the private airstrip a few miles from his home, but they had never returned. His father had just gained his pilots licence and said it was part of the fun, being able to fly to the destination himself.

The first Ben had heard of his parent's disappearance was while watching the television one night with Lucy. The newsreader had announced that a light air-craft had come down in the trees just after takeoff, and the bodies of a male and female had been found nearby. Frantically, Ben had continually rang the incident line number provided, until he eventually got through to the police control room. Once he had explained who he was, and that he suspected that the stricken plane may have been carrying his parents, he was told to hold the line. The operator returned seconds later, saying that they would need to arrange for a car to come and collect him. As much as Ben tried to ask questions about the accident, the operator calmly kept telling him to try not to worry, only serving to make him worry more.

While Ben had been on the phone, he had been watching his wife gather a few things together for the children, who were going to stay with Bob and Sue next door, and their two children Adam and Laurel. Jake loved Adam, he was 8 and played for the local under 9s football team and according to Jake, Adam was 'way cool'. Emily was equally smitten with

Laurel, who even though turning 13 this year, spent ages trying to teach her ballet steps in the garden. She and Laurel were going to dance on the stage together one day, Emily often declared.

A short while later, Ben carried the children next door, both still sleeping soundly, then joined Lucy in the waiting police car for the short journey to the station. The two officers barely said a word in the car and once there, lead them to a small room just off to the left at the bottom of the main corridor. The elder of the two policemen told them someone will be with them shortly and quietly shut the door. The room was sparsely decorated with a small sofa at one end and coffee machine and tv at the other, but strangely enough it still had a homely feel.

After a few moments, a tall, slim man with dark hair greying at the temples entered, introducing himself as Chief Superintendent Rob Jeffers, one of the senior officers on the case. Chief Superintendent Jeffers explained that the male and female occupants of the plane were in no fit state for their bodies to be viewed. Lucy squeezed her husband's hand, she had visibly seen the raw pain in his eyes at that comment.

Rob Jeffers showed them a small silver tobacco case, although well worn and battered, they could still make out the faint initials 'B.D.R' on the lid. The case had been found on the body of the plane's male occupant. Although the last initial was correct, Ben was certain that it didn't belong to his father as he had never smoked. All the officer could tell them about the lady was that she had deep blue eyes. Lucy heaved a sigh of relief as she knew that her mother in law had the darkest chocolate brown eyes that she had ever seen. All this had still left one very important question unanswered. If this couple were not Ben's mum and dad, who were they, and where were his parents? They seemed to have disappeared without a trace.

As the weeks passed with still no news, crash investigators were at a loss as to what had happened. The only vague explanation they could offer was, as the accident had happened near a river, Ben's parents' bodies had been washed out into the open sea. But that didn't explain to him why they hadn't been found. The bodies found near the plane had been identified as a middle-aged Swedish couple, who had gone missing from a cruise liner some weeks earlier, and had been washed ashore. A guy called Tom Baker was running the shop, which Ben and Lucy found out was called Bartons, during the weeks when Ben's parents were arranging their relocation. Tom had become his father's right hand man. Ben knew that with his parents not being able to take charge of the business someone had to, and he was equally aware that the responsibility lay with him. Bob next door had suggested rather tentatively, only yesterday, that maybe they should consider selling the shop, but Ben wouldn't hear of it. He would not even entertain the thought that his parents would not be returning and always positively insisted to Lucy that it was a matter of when they returned, not if. He and Lucy had talked long into the night and eventually made the decision to move to Blackville Meadows to run Bartons. The house was a lot bigger, with far more space for the children to play, and with the business, at least there would be a regular income.

They also needed an extra bedroom, as Nick, Ben's 18 year old son from a previous relationship was moving in with them. Nick's mother had remarried and he didn't get along with her new husband very well it seemed. Ben had thought this quite odd as Nick was such a happy-go-lucky lad. Nick and Lucy, on the other hand, were very close and shared a love of art. Both were very competitive, each always choosing things to draw in the hope that the other one couldn't. Lucy treated Nick like her own and despite the age gap between herself and Nick's mother, he clearly thought of her like a second mum.

"Ben," came Lucy's voice again from the driveway. "Are you ready chip?" Ben smiled at his wife's pet name for him, she always called him that when she was worried about him. As Ben took a final glance around his parent's bedroom, he recalled how he had gained his nickname 8 years ago. The new fish bar opened in town and the first time Ben went in there with his friends after work, he was smitten. The pretty redhead with the gorgeous eyes behind the counter took his breath away. For the next 3 weeks, Ben became an avid chip fan, until one night when he was sitting at the table, staring wistfully at the assistant, his friend Nigel could take no more. He walked over to the girl behind the counter and asked if she had a pen and paper. She obliged, smiling, and Ben watched as Nigel began scribbling something. When he had finished, he handed back the pen and then the paper, informing her that this was his friend on table 5's number and to please put him out of his misery, then promptly turned and walked out. Ben was horrified, he hid his head in the menu, even though he had finished eating over an hour ago. "Err, excuse me, can I get you anything else?" Said a voice, and Ben looked up into those deep brown eyes he had spent so long admiring. "I'm Lucy," the girl said, holding out her hand and then sitting down. "I'm Ben" he replied, smiling broadly. At that moment, Ben was hooked, and he and Lucy had been together ever since.

Ben closed the front door with a heavy heart, and turned to face his future. His new life with his wife and children. Jake was 5 with blonde cropped hair, that he insisted on having spiked on top like his dad. Emily was almost 4 with emerald green eyes, blonde curls tumbling down onto her shoulders and tiny pink rosebud lips. Lucy couldn't help but smile every time she looked at them, both children had her mother's beautiful blonde locks. Ben and Lucy had only been married 6 years, but they had been the best 6 years of his life.

As their old home disappeared from view, Ben settled back in his seat and closed his eyes to think as Lucy drove. He missed his parents so much. His mum was a really down to earth woman deep down, she was everybody's friend and couldn't walk down the road without being stopped at least half a dozen times, he remembered fondly. His father, on the other hand, was totally different, kept himself to himself and only seemed to go out when he went to work. He started late and returned home well into the small hours. This caused numerous problems between his parents, and apart from not being able to see them as much, this move would probably have been a good thing.

Ben must have drifted off to sleep as he woke to the sound of the engine being switched off. "I'm sure this is the place that Nick wanted us to meet him," said Lucy. Ben looked around, they appeared to be stopped at some sort of road side cafe. "This place looks like one of those American diners you see in the films" Lucy laughed, voicing what he was thinking. Ben turned to look at the children in the back seat, who were starting to get very restless. "Shall we take the kids in for a drink while we are waiting? Nick will see the car anyway" he asked Lucy. "Yes!" Came a chorus of little voices from behind him. "Okay" he laughed, as him and Lucy got the children out of the car.

Just as they reached the door of the diner, "Nick!" Screamed Emily excitedly, trying to wriggle free from her father's grasp. Ben turned to see Nick running towards them, Emily flew into his arms with Jake not far behind. Nick hugged them both tightly to him, he hadn't seen them since his grandparents were reported missing. "Let's go inside and you can tell us what you've been up to" said Lucy, smiling warmly. Ben grabbed Nick's rucksack while he carried Emily and Jake, one in each arm.

The inside of the diner had booths along each wall, just like they had imagined, and at the far end above the bar, a large neon sign flashing 'Pineapple Diner' in a vivid purple glow. They all sat in a booth, Emily and Jake on one side with Nick, and their parents on the other. "How come you chose here for us to pick you up Nick?" Lucy asked. "It's on route to Phil's mum's, so they dropped me off on the way" Nick replied. Phil was his mother's new husband. "How does your mum feel about you moving out now?" Ben asked his son. "She seems okay as long as I promise to visit often" Nick said quietly. "Are you sure?" Ben pressed. "Ouch!" He said, stopping suddenly as Lucy had just given him a swift kick in the ankle. As he glanced in her direction, her look said everything he needed to know to warn him to shut up. Luckily, the waitress arrived at that point, which broke the rather strained silence. Something was clearly bothering Nick, but this just as clearly wasn't the right time for him to want to talk about it. Nick was a lovely lad, bright, honest and hard working. He done well at college, gaining high marks in maths and science, and he was now taking some time out before he began university. Everyone made small talk whilst waiting for the food to arrive, discussing everything possible apart from the two people foremost in their minds.

"Ooo, look!" Squealed Emily, as the waitress returned carrying a tray laden with juicy looking burgers and chunky chips. Everyone tucked in hungrily. "Can I have ice cream with chocolate sauce please?" Asked Jake when he was finished. "Of course you can mate" laughed Ben, reaching over and ruffling his son's hair playfully. "Do you want the ice cream with marshmallows honey?" He said, smiling at Emily, who was busy trying to wipe a dribble of thick red tomato ketchup off her chin with a tissue. "Yes please" she nodded happily. Half an hour later, everyone sat back in their seats sighing contentedly. "I think everyone should use the toilet before we leave, as there is still a fair way to go" said Ben. "I don't need to go" said Jake. "Try anyway" said his mother, expertly leading a protesting Jake off by the hand, with Emily skipping along behind.

A short while later, Lucy returned with the children. "He wouldn't go", she said. Once everyone was loaded back into the car, with Ben taking the wheel, they set off. They had only been travelling for about 10 minutes when a little voice piped up, "I need a wee!". "Oh Jake," sighed Lucy, "are you sure?". "Yes" he replied, squirming in his seat. "We're going to have to stop again Ben," she told her husband, "but I don't know where". "There's a store just up here," said Nick. "It has a toilet as we have stopped there before". "Right, hold on mate" said Ben, as he pulled into the parking area and they all piled out again. Ben had thought it was a good idea to get some milk and bread, as they didn't know what was going to be at the house when they got there. Tom had told them he would get a few things in, but he didn't want to take any chances.

"Where's Milky?" Said Emily. Milky was Emily's cuddly toy, a grubby looking white rabbit with the longest ears imaginable. Emily never went anywhere without him. "Has he fallen on the floor sweetheart?" Asked Ben, bending down to look under the seats. "Oh no!" Exclaimed Lucy. "What's up love?" Ben inquired, looking at his wife questioningly. "She put him down to wash her hands at the diner, and what with all the fuss Jake was making about not wanting to use the toilet, I don't remember her picking him back up again" Lucy said. "I want Milky!" Said Emily, starting to wail. "I'll have to go back and get him" said Ben. "You go in with Nick and I'll be back before you know it, it's not far" Ben said, giving Lucy a reassuring hug. Before Lucy had time to answer, Ben was back in the car driving out of the carpark, waving out of the window as he drove away.

Lucy, Nick and the children went into the store to get a few essential items, then came out to sit on the grass and wait. "I want Milky," said Emily sadly. "I know princess, daddy should be back at any minute" said Lucy. "He has been gone a while hasn't he?" Said Nick uncomfortably. "Yes," Lucy replied, looking her watch and frowning, "nearly an hour". "I'll try ringing him," said Nick, reaching for his mobile. "hmm, it says his phone's switched off" "Ben never turns his phone off," said Lucy, her voice anxious, "try it again please". "Just the same" said Nick, putting his phone back in his pocket. "I'm going back into the shop to see if they might have the number to the diner, you hang on here with the kids for a minute". Lucy nodded, cuddling Jake and Emily to her, she had a really bad feeling something was wrong, very wrong indeed.

When Nick didn't return after 10 minutes, Lucy took Jake and Emily back inside to look for him. Nick was on the phone at the counter. "Are you sure?" He said in a strange voice. "Okay, thank you. We'll come and pick it up as soon as we can." Nick replaced the receiver and turned to Lucy with unmistakable fear in his eyes. "What's going on Nick?" She asked, her voice trembling. "I spoke to the manager at the Pineapple Diner. He remembers dad coming in and asking if anyone had handed in Emily's toy. When they hadn't the manager sent a female staff member off to check the toilet while dad waited at a nearby table. The manager said three men in suits approached dad, and after a brief conversation they all got up and left. He said he couldn't hear what they were saying, but he saw through the window that all four men drove off in dad's car. What he did say though is two things struck him as very strange, dad didn't wait for the toy, and one of the other men drove dad's car while he got in the back." Finished Nick. "Oh my god" said Lucy, sitting down hard on the chair by the counter. "What on earth is going on and who were those men Nick?" "I'm calling the police." He said, picking up the phone again.

"Come through to the back room lovey, you don't want to be sitting out here." Lucy looked up into the kindly face of the store owner. "Thank you" she said, taking the children through the hatch after her. "You look after the lady and the nippers, I'll be fine here" said the elderly man behind the counter. Lucy sat on the sofa in the cosy living room, with Jake and Emily playing by her feet. "I'm Gladys," said the lady. "Please try not to worry too much, I'm sure your husband will be fine" "I hope so" Lucy whispered. 20 minutes later, the door opened and Nick walked in, followed by two policemen. "This is Sergeant Walker and PC Jenkins" he said. "I've told them everything we know and now they would like to speak to you. They've sent colleagues back to the diner as well." "Hello Mrs Reid, we've heard from your son what's gone on, but could you tell us again in your own words please?" Said Sergeant Walker. Lucy told them what she knew, she just couldn't believe what was happening, couldn't take it in. It was as if it was happening to someone else. The radio crackled and PC Jenkins went to the far side of the room to take the message. "Err, I'm sorry to interrupt but I think you should take this" he said coming back over to the chair where Sergeant Walker was sitting. "Okay, please excuse me" said Sergeant Walker.

As he walked away Lucy watched him, listening intently to whoever was on the radio. A couple of minutes later he came and sat down opposite her again, his face grave. "I don't want to alarm you Mrs Reid, but my colleagues have found your husband's car abandoned just down the road from the diner. His doors were all open, so we suspect the occupants left in a hurry", he said. "Oh no..." said Lucy, her face crumpling as she promptly burst into tears. Nick put his arm around his stepmother in an attempt to comfort her as she sobbed. "CID officers are on the way to talk to you Mrs Reid" said the sergeant softly. "Shall I take the children into the garden?" Asked Gladys. "Yes please," replied Sergeant Walker, "You go with them please PC Jenkins, we don't know what we could be dealing with here yet". "What do you mean?" Asked Lucy, "You think something bad has happened to Ben, don't you?" She said, looking at Sergeant Walker. He was spared having to answer that question, as the door opened again and two men entered the room.

"I'm DCI Fields, Mrs Reid, this is my colleague DS Roach" the taller man said, "We've just come from the Pineapple Diner and having reviewed the CCTV footage, it certainly appears your husband left of his own free will. You hadn't had a row or anything, had you?" He questioned. "Mr Reid seems to have been under a lot of pressure lately. Is there any way he may have wanted to get away and take a break?". "No!" exclaimed Lucy, horrified, "Ben and I rarely argue, we're very happy together. Yes, he has had a lot of stress lately, but there is no way he would ever leave us. Never." She finished firmly. "We have to ask these questions Mrs Reid." said DCI Fields sympathetically. "The forensic team are on the scene at the moment checking for fingerprints on the car. Yours and the children's bags are in our car outside. I'm sorry we had to open them, we have to check every available avenue. My colleagues will be here shortly to take you the rest of the way to Blackville Meadows." He concluded "I'll be in touch first thing tomorrow morning to let you know the results of our initial enquiries".

At that moment, Gladys brought Jake and Emily back inside, "They want their mum" she said kindly. "Oh, I nearly forgot" said DCI Fields, turning to Emily, "I believe this little guy might be yours" he said, pulling Milky from his pocket. Emily reached up and took him, smiling shyly. "Thank you" she whispered. Lucy clutched the children to her, she still couldn't believe what was happening. It was just like her worst nightmare.

"Mrs Reid…Mrs Reid…" Lucy was vaguely aware of someone gently shaking her shoulder, and looked up to see a blonde woman smiling down at her sympathetically. "Er yes, oh sorry, I was in a world of my own" Lucy replied weakly. "My name's Cathy and this is Jill," said the woman, gesturing to her colleague. "DCI Fields has asked us to take you all home". "Come on Lucy" said Nick, taking her arm lightly.

Lucy thanked Gladys and her husband for all their help and kindness. The old lady hugged Lucy telling her it was a pleasure, but although her eyes were smiling, Lucy couldn't miss the pity in them. Cathy and Jill lead them all outside to the waiting blue people carrier. For a second, Lucy thought it was Ben's car and that he had come back to tell her it was all a big mistake, but it wasn't. There was a man in the driving seat, he didn't say a word, just smiled as they got in. They drove for about 20 minutes, leaving one town behind and entering another. As the car rounded a bend, Lucy noticed a sign saying 'Welcome to Blackville Meadows' on the grass verge. 'Some welcome' Lucy thought sadly, she should have been making this journey with Ben beside her.

As the car started to climb the hill on its way out of town again, there didn't appear to be much in the way of scenery…in fact, there didn't seem to be anything around at all, apart from a huge house at the end of a long, sweeping driveway. Lucy thought it looked more like a mansion, far bigger than anywhere she had ever lived before, she couldn't take her eyes off of it and had been admiring it all the way up the hill. Suddenly, the driver turned right toward the large black gated entrance. 'Maybe we're lost?' Lucy thought, but to her surprise the gates opened and they began to drive towards the house. "Where are we?" She asked, puzzled. "Home" Cathy replied. "Who's home?" Lucy asked, growing more confused. "Your home, Mrs Reid", said Cathy. Lucy gasped in amazement, "This place is mine?". She knew Ben had said it was bigger, but he hadn't told her it was this big! "You have a lovely house Mrs Reid, the children will love it here," said Jill. "Thank you" was all Lucy could mutter, unable to believe what was happening.

As they got out of the car, Lucy stared in awe at the beautiful dwelling. Suddenly, the huge oak door opened and a tall, well-dressed man with neat dark hair, came hurrying down the marble steps to meet them. "Hello Mrs Reid, I'm Tom Baker" he said, shaking her hand. "Your father in law has told me so much about you" "Hello" Lucy replied. "I've made sure you have all the essentials you should need for the next few days" Tom continued. "Thank you, you're very kind." Lucy said. "This is Jeff, your handyman and gardener," he said, introducing the dark haired man to his left, "I have taken the liberty of employing a nanny as well," Tom went on, "when I spoke to Ben the other day he said you would be needing one, as you would be spending a lot of time at the store initially. I have of course looked through all of her references, but they are available for you to double check. Ahh, here she is now" he said, turning to greet a pretty young woman with dark hair that fell loosely round her shoulders.

The woman took a step forward and approached the family, "This is Amira Bentley" Tom said. "Hello" Amira said, smiling broadly at Lucy.

"Oh! And you must be Jake and Emily" she said, bending down to the children who immediately hid behind Lucy's legs. "So you're Jake and you're three, and this is your big sister Emily?" Amira continued to Jake. "No I'm not!" Said Jake indignantly, "I'm five and she's three!" He said, pointing to Emily. "Silly me, of course you are! I can see what a big boy you are now" said Amira, offering Jake a high five. "You must be hungry, would you both like to come into the kitchen with me and see what we can find? That is if it's okay with you of course, Mrs Reid?" She asked, looking at Lucy questioningly. "That's fine, and please call me Lucy" she replied.

Once Amira and the children were gone, Tom turned to Lucy with a much more serious look on his face. "I didn't want to say anything in front of the children Mrs Reid - sorry, Lucy," he said, remembering her request, "the police called before you arrived and explained what happened. I am very sorry to hear about your husband, but I am sure he will be home before you know it." "I really hope so Tom, I really hope so" said Lucy, biting back her tears.

CHAPTER 2

HILLTOP MANOR

"Shall we go inside?" Asked Tom, in an attempt to break the awkward silence. Lucy and Nick followed him up the stairs to the front door, while Cathy, Jill and the driver brought the bags in. As Lucy entered the house, she gasped in amazement. They were standing in a large oak-panelled entrance hall, high ceilings festooned with sparkling crystal chandeliers hanging like frozen raindrops way above their heads. A striking staircase swept upwards to her left, with an equally striking display of artwork adorning the highly polished walls in every direction. "Welcome to Hilltop Manor Mrs Reid" said a voice from the top of the stairs. A small, extremely well kept woman came briskly towards them. "I'm Margaret Armstrong, your housekeeper." she said, offering Lucy her outstretched hand, "Please come and take a seat in the living room and I'll bring tea and sandwiches through, I thought you might be hungry" said Mrs Armstrong, smiling. Lucy and Nick followed her down the hallway to a door, somewhat concealed by the grand stairway. Inside, Lucy inhaled at the plush sofas and shiny floors that resembled something from an expensive country magazine. When Mrs Armstrong returned, she was carrying a large tray, heavily ladened with sandwiches, biscuits and a pot of tea. "Thank you Mrs Armstrong, but I'm really not very hungry" said Lucy. "Nonsense Mrs Reid, you have the little ones to worry about, so you need to keep your strength up" Mrs Armstrong replied. Lucy smiled weakly as she nibbled on a biscuit.

"So how long have you been the housekeeper here, Mrs Armstrong?" Nick asked. "Thirty five years" She replied proudly. "A few months ago, your grandfather came here to tell me in person about the sad death of Mrs Reid. She was a great lady and I was very lucky to work for her. I didn't only see her as my employer, we were firm friends." "I know you were, I could see how close you both were" Tom said with a sad smile.

"I need to discuss something with you when you are ready please Lucy." He continued. "Of course" said Lucy. "I'll leave you to it, I have some things to finish in the kitchen" Mrs Armstrong said. "Thank you, but before you go, please call me Lucy. Mrs Reid is far too formal" Lucy said. "If you're sure, that would be wonderful Lucy, but please, call me Margaret." Mrs Armstrong replied. Both women looked at each other and laughed. "Stay a moment Margaret, as this concerns you too" Tom said.

"It's really rather awkward, but I did speak to Ben about this little problem last week, and er..now with him not being here..." he tailed off. "What is it Tom?" Lucy asked. "Margaret's sister is just getting over an operation and is due to come home from hospital tomorrow, but her husband isn't very well, so there is no one to look after her. Ben agreed that Margaret could take some time off and I would get someone in from the agency to cover while she is unavailable." "I do understand that it is inconvenient now, Lucy" said Mrs Armstrong, worriedly. "Margaret," said Lucy softly, taking the older woman's hand, "of course you must go, I wouldn't hear any different of it" "There are three applicants due here tomorrow at half hour intervals from 10am Lucy, I hope that is okay" said Tom. "That's fine" Lucy nodded. "Please give your sister and her husband my love and wish them both a speedy recovery" said Lucy, turning to Mrs Armstrong. "Thank you for being so understanding Mrs Reid, I mean Lucy" said Margaret with a laugh.

"Mummy, mummy!" Cried Jake, hurtling through the door and throwing himself at his mother. "Come and see our room! It's got tanks and lorries and a big car bed, and a desk, and...and..." said Jake, not stopping for breath. "Okay" laughed Lucy "Let's go and see. Where's Emily?" "She's in bed" said Jake, dragging his mother impatiently by the hand. "Amira is reading her a story". Once the children were finally asleep, Lucy wandered quietly around the house opening door after door, marvelling at the beauty of the things inside each room. When Lucy finally settled for the night, she slept in fits and starts. As much as her body desperately craved sleep, her mind would not settle. So many questions, and so many still unanswered…

The next morning Lucy dressed the children and went downstairs to a breakfast of succulent bacon, juicy sausages, light fluffy eggs, crispy toast with jam and marmalade, cereal and orange juice. Jake and Emily tucked in hungrily. Lucy knew Mrs Armstrong was right, with two energetic small children, she did need to keep her energy levels up, so she managed a modest breakfast. At that moment Amira entered the room. "Lucy, I'm sorry to bother you, but the police are here. They're waiting for you in the living room" she said. "Oh thank you Amira," said Lucy jumping up, "would you mind sitting with the children while they finish their breakfast please? I must go and speak to them straight away" "Of course I will" said Amira, sitting down at the table. Lucy hurried off, pausing for a second at the living room door. She was very eager for news of Ben, but was equally as scared of what she may be about to be told. Taking a deep breath, she turned the door handle and went in.

"Mrs Reid" said the officer getting up. "DCI Fields," greeted Lucy smiling apprehensively, "please tell me you've found my husband". "I really wish I could Mrs Reid, I really wish I could" said DCI Fields in that same soothing tone Lucy recognised from the previous day. "We do have some news though, is this your husband Lucy?" The officer asked, showing her a photograph he had taken from a brown envelope he was holding. The sudden change to the less formal addressing of her for some reason put Lucy on edge. It was as if DCI Fields was trying to soften the blow for something, to prepare her for a shock…and it was a shock when Lucy looked down into the smiling face of her husband in the photograph. "Yes..yes it is," stammered Lucy "where did you get this? Where is he?" "This man was seen boarding a plane today with three other men fitting the description of the ones seen leaving the Pineapple Diner with your husband yesterday Mrs Reid" said DCI Fields. "A plane? Where?" Said Lucy in confusion. "At Redwell Airstrip" said the DCI solemnly. "Oh my god" said Lucy, sitting down in the armchair heavily, recognising the name of the airstrip near her old home. The same airstrip Ben had waved his parents off from months earlier. "What's going on DCI Fields?" Said Lucy "Where were they taking Ben?" "Mrs Reid, the cleaner at the airstrip reports all four men as laughing and joking together. Your husband didn't seem to be under any duress" DCI Fields said quietly.

"No you have it wrong, Ben would never leave us willingly" Lucy insisted. By the look on his face, she could see that DCI Fields clearly had his doubts on that score. "We're trying to trace where the plane was heading Mrs Reid, but the airstrip was closed and no one was due to fly from there today. I'll be in touch as soon as my enquiries are complete" DCI Fields said, putting the photograph back in the envelope and heading for the door. "Please try to take comfort in the fact that this sighting is a good one Lucy" he said, turning to face her. "It means your husband is alive and well" he added as he closed the door behind him.

"Does Jeff have any children?" Lucy asked Tom later, as they stood together on the patio, watching him chase around the garden after a football with Jake and Emily. "The winner!" Screamed Jeff, punching his fist in the air and doing a funny little victory dance that made the children laugh. "No," said Tom, "Jeff lives alone in a cottage in the grounds. I'm sure he will have though in future years, he's a natural". "Yeah he is" agreed Lucy, instantly remembering back to how she had often watched Ben having fun with Jake and Emily in their own back garden. "Lucy, it's almost 10, we should go back inside. Your first applicant should be here soon" said Tom. "Oh yes of course, and I wondered if you would mind sitting in on the interviews with me? You have a far better knowledge of the house than I do, and I would welcome your opinion" said Lucy. "I'd be delighted" Tom replied smiling. Lucy and Tom had only just taken a seat in the living room when the door burst open and a rather robust woman with an equally robust voice pushed past Amira into the room.

"I'm so sorry Lucy, I asked Mrs Barton-Giles to wait in the hallway for a moment while I told you she was here, but as you can see she wouldn't" said Amira, glaring at the unannounced visitor disapprovingly. "Told her I was here? What utter nonsense!" Said Mrs Barton-Giles with a sniff. "Now she can see I'm here for herself, can't she?" She continued. "Now be a good girl and don't just stand there, tea with two sugars for me. Now run along, chop chop" she said, hustling Amira out of the room and shutting the door. "Now here's my references" she continued, striding across the room unperturbed. "Come along madam, please don't waste any more of my time. I had an appointment for 10am and it is already 4 minutes past."

She said to Lucy. "Oh and before I start, I don't cook, I don't clean, I want every Sunday off and children should be upstairs by 6pm. Those are my rules" she barked, before Lucy had time to answer.

"Well they aren't mine" said a stern voice from the doorway. "Margaret?" Lucy gasped, "But I thought you had already gone…" "Yes to cook dinner, that is right madam." Mrs Armstrong finished for her. Before Mrs Barton-Giles knew what was happening, Mrs Armstrong had taken her arm and was frog marching her to the door. "Your services won't be required after all. Mrs Reid took me on this morning with immediate effect" she said as she firmly placed the protesting Mrs Barton-Giles outside and closed the front door, calling "Thank you for coming!" as she did so. She turned to face a still stunned Lucy and Tom who were standing in the hallway behind her, and all three burst out laughing. "That woman!" Said Lucy. "How rude! I'm not often lost for words, but I just couldn't believe what I was hearing. I felt bad enough leaving you as it was, there was no way I was leaving you with her that's for sure." Said Mrs Armstrong solemnly. "Thank you again for taking charge, I thought you'd already gone" said Lucy. "No, I had a flat tyre and Jeff was changing it for me" Mrs Armstrong replied. "All done" said Jeff, coming through from the kitchen. "Oh thank you Jeff, you are a treasure" said Mrs Armstrong, taking her keys from him. "If it is okay with you, Lucy, I'll be off now" "Of course it is, you have a safe journey and please let me know how everyone is".

"Let's go and see Margaret off Lucy, shall we?" Said Tom, opening the door. "Jake, Emily, Margaret's going now!" Called Lucy, following him out. Five minutes later, they all trouped back inside after Mrs Armstrong had disappeared from view. At that moment, there was a knock at the door. "Ah! Must be your second applicant", said Tom opening it. "Hello and welcome to Hilltop…" said Tom, his voice stopping mid-sentence. Lucy stepped around the door to see what the object of Tom's shocked gaze was, and her eyes fixed on the young woman standing there. Her hair was bright blue and back-combed off to one side, her face was exceptionally pale, adorned with thick black eyeliner, bright red lipstick and a large purple stud through her nose. The girl's top had tatty looking tears at regular intervals, with a short denim skirt, black leather jacket and extremely high electric blue heels.

"Yo dudes!" Said the girl. "My name's Storm and I'm here for the job". "Err…the housekeeper's position?" Inquired Tom, regaining some composure. "Oh I dunno," said Storm, blowing a large bubble with the gum she was chewing. "can't remember what the old bird at the agency said" "I'm sorry, I was just about to phone the agency, the position has been filled" said Tom, quickly. "Oh what? No sweat geezer, I didn't wanna work anyway…much easier signing on then I get a lay in. I only came cos she said I had to. Catch you later" said Storm, as she turned and tottered away. "Oh deary me," Tom declared, "surely applicant three must be an improvement?" At 11am the doorbell rang, then again twice more in quick succession. Lucy opened the door to find a tall, prim woman standing there in a long floaty skirt, long jacket and a neat hat. Lucy's first thought was she looked like Mary Poppins and had to stifle a laugh when she realised the lady had a large brown carpet bag draped on her arm. The woman introduced herself as Alice Blythe and Lucy invited her in really hoping that she would turn out to be practically perfect in every way.

Tom, Lucy and Alice chatted contentedly over tea in the living room, discussing Alice's references and places she had previously been employed. Mrs Blythe had certainly worked at some pretty impressive establishments. While Alice poured another cup of tea for everyone, Lucy and Tom chatted quietly on the sofa. "She seems perfect" said Lucy. "She certainly does" whispered Tom. Alice settled herself back in the arm chair, just as the door flew open and Jake and Emily raced in. "Urgh!" Squealed Mrs Blythe, running to hide behind the armchair. "Children! No one said anything about children!" She declared, horrified. "Come and say hello to Alice" said Lucy, trying to ignore the rather unannounced outburst. "Oh no please keep them away from me! Children carry germs and diseases! Eww no! I can't work anywhere where there are children!" Blurted Mrs Blythe. "No Mrs Blythe, you're right. You certainly won't be" said Lucy, coldly, annoyed at this totally unprovoked attack on her children. "Tom, would you show Mrs Blythe the door please?" "With pleasure" said Tom, as Mrs Blythe scurried from the room. By the time Tom returned, Lucy was sitting at the patio table, staring wistfully across the lawn. "I've just rang the agency to complain about the three totally unacceptable people they've sent. They apologised and said the agency manager will call you when she is back in the office later today." Lucy didn't have chance to reply as Jeff appeared through the patio doors. "Lucy, there is a lady at the door wanting to know if the housekeeper's position is still available. She said she heard Margaret telling Mr Brown, the butcher, about it in his shop the other day. Do you want to see her?" Jeff asked. "Oh why not? Send her through please Jeff" Lucy said.

A few seconds later, a rather homely looking woman appeared in the doorway. The woman had a smart, but relaxed, appearance, grey hair swept into a loose bun and red rosy cheeks. "Mrs Reid, thank you so much for seeing me. I do hope you don't consider my arrival too much of a cheek" she said. "I'm Phyllis Snow by the way" "No, not at all. In a funny way we are rather glad you have come, aren't we Tom?" Said Lucy, smiling at Tom knowingly. "Here are my references" said Phyllis, handing them to Lucy. "They're certainly very impressive" said Lucy leafing through them. "You do realise this position is for a cook as well as a housekeeper, I presume?" Asked Tom. "Yes of course, I don't stand on ceremony. I'm not afraid of doing a day's work" replied Phyllis."It's a live-in position, with a small cottage next to the gardener's at the rear of the house. You get every other Sunday off and a day in the week on the week in between. How does that sound?" Lucy asked. "Just perfect" said Phyllis. "I don't have much luggage as I am waiting for it to be transferred from my previous employer"

Just at that moment, Amira arrived with Jake and Emily. "Oh what gorgeous children!" Gushed Phyllis. "What have you been up to this fine day?" Phyllis asked Jake. "Playing football with Jeff, but Emily keeps missing the ball. Girls aren't any good at football!" Jake declared. "Is that right?" Said Phyllis. "I'll have you know I'm rather a good footballer!" She laughed. "Bet you're not!" Said Jake. "I'll bet I am" said Phyllis, chuckling at the banter. "Okay then, boys against girls!" Challenged Jake. "You can even have Amira as girls need extra help" he added. "No Jake, Phyllis doesn't want to be playing football" said his mother. "Oh I don't mind at all if it is okay with you" said Phyllis. "Well no, please be my guest!" Said Lucy, unable to hide the surprise in her voice. Phyllis stayed for lunch and it certainly looked like Hilltop Manor had found its very own Mary Poppins after all. During a chat that afternoon, Lucy offered Phyllis the job.

That evening at Tom's suggestion, and in an attempt to take Lucy's mind off of things a little, it was decided they would all go out for dinner. "It can be a welcome to our family meal for Phyllis as well!" Emily suggested, smiling up at her as she placed her hand in hers. "Awh, thank you poppet" said Phyllis, giving her hand a little squeeze. Jeff said he'd stay behind so that the house wasn't left empty. Tom wouldn't hear of it, insisting that's what all of the alarms were for. They piled into Lucy and Jeff's cars, Lucy's had been returned earlier that morning after no prints were found matching any in the police's database. When they arrived at the restaurant, the car park was full, so Lucy and Jeff had to park on the verge opposite. As this trip had been so spur of the moment, no one had bothered to make a reservation, though Lucy was now fast regretting that decision. "Come on Nick, let's go and see if they can fit us in" said Tom.

Lucy watched as the two men started to cross the road, when out of nowhere a silver four wheel drive appeared, driving far too fast. "He's not going to stop! Oh my god he's not going to stop!" Screamed Lucy as she watched helplessly, the car heading straight for Nick and Tom. Tom had seen it and started to run, but Nick hadn't. He was too busy waving to Emily who was still strapped in the back seat. Lucy closed her eyes tightly, she couldn't bear to watch as another member of her family was taken from her. Lucy heard the car disappear into the distance. She opened her eyes and words couldn't describe her joy, seeing Tom helping Nick up from the verge on the other side of the road. Lucy leapt from the car, "Are you okay?" She cried, running over to where Tom and Nick were standing, brushing themselves off. "Yes I think so" said Nick, visibly shaking. "Tom pulled me out of the way. You saved my life and risked your own. I don't know what to say" said Nick, turning to thank Tom. "It was nothing. I only did what anyone else would have done" said Tom modestly. Lucy threw her arms around Tom's neck in gratitude, then hugged Nick to her and promptly burst into tears.

"I'm calling the police" said Nick. "No let me do it, you take your mother back to the car." Tom insisted. When Tom came back, he said that they were all to return home and that the police would send somebody out. "Let me drive" he said to Lucy, seeing that she was still in no fit state to do so herself. Tom stopped on the way home to pick up fish and chips for those that had any appetite left to eat, and then sat with Lucy and Nick in the living room to wait for the police to arrive. About an hour later, Lucy's mobile rang. "Hello...Yes it is...No that's not a problem, we realise DCI Fields needs to rest." She said into the receiver. Lucy listened intently to whoever was on the phone. "Oh...okay...if you really think so" she said in a puzzled voice. "Yes of course…I'll see him then" she said, ending the call. "That was the police, they said DCI Fields will be here in fifteen minutes and for some reason he has asked to see Nick and I alone. He wants everyone else to be in the kitchen at the back of the house and remain there until he leaves" Lucy said. "How strange!" Exclaimed Nick. "Never mind, I'm sure he has his reasons" said Tom. "I'll go and round everyone up now" he added, getting up to leave. "Thank you Tom" said Lucy.

There was a knock at the door ten minutes later and Nick went to answer it. "Hello again Mrs Reid" said DCI Fields entering the room. "I apologise for the delay, but I asked to be contacted at home immediately if there was any developments. How are you Nick?" He asked, turning to him. "Calming down now thank you. If it hadn't been for Tom, it could have been a very different story" said Nick. "So I heard. I'm glad you're both okay" nodded DCI Fields solemnly. "I've given this a lot of thought and have come up with an uncomfortable conclusion that something is very wrong here." DCI Fields continued. "First, Frank and Janet go missing, then Ben, and then a vehicle travelling at high speed tries to run Nick over on a relatively straight road." "Nick?" Questioned Lucy "But Tom was there as well" "Yes he was," said the DCI, "but with all the other disappearances, my hunch is that it was more likely to be Nick that they were after." "Oh my god. You think that someone tried to kill Nick don't you?" Said Lucy. "To be honest Mrs Reid, I don't know, but I certainly intend to find out." Said DCI Fields.

"This is DC Paul Henson" he added, introducing a good looking young man in a suit that had been standing quietly behind him. "There's a seven seater Ford Galaxy parked outside. It is fully equipped with all mod cons, most importantly, it has a fool proof tracking system on board." He continued "I want you to introduce DC Henson as your cousin who has come to stay when he returns in the morning. He will live as part of your household, but his sole mission will be to drive the children around. Of course, Miss Bentley will go along as well, we don't want to arouse any suspicion. But for now, anywhere the children go, DC Henson will go too, and it must be in that car. We will of course have to disable your car, Mrs Reid, to prevent Miss Bentley from going anywhere with them alone." DCI Fields finished.

"Are you saying Jake and Emily are in danger?" Asked Nick. "Nothing points to that at present, but I don't want to take any chances" replied DCI Fields firmly. "I must ask that you don't leave the house alone either Mrs Reid. That is also of the utmost importance" the DCI said. "Why do you want the staff kept in the dark though? I don't understand" said Lucy. "You have new staff members Mrs Reid, and even Tom and Jeff are new to you. We still have no idea what we could be dealing with here, so for now the fewer people that know what safeguards we have in place, the better." Said DCI Fields. "Okay, I'll do what you say. I don't want to put my children at any risk." Lucy agreed. "We shall bid you goodnight Mrs Reid, and Paul will be back at 9am sharp" said DCI Fields. "I'll say goodbye to the staff on the way out and let them know they are free to go about their business."

The next morning Lucy opened the front door, "Paul, it's so good to see you, it's been such a long time!" Said Lucy, giving him a welcoming hug. "Lucy, you're looking so…grown up!" Paul laughed. "I should think so as we haven't seen each other since we were seven" chuckled Lucy, linking her arm in Paul's and leading him through to the kitchen. "Tom, Phyllis, this is my cousin Paul. He is going to stay with us for a while." Lucy said. "Hello," said Tom, shaking Paul's hand. "Lucy has told me so much about you after you rang last night". "Oh dear, all bad I bet… but none of it true of course! You must tell me later what little secrets you have told everyone about me" Paul turned to Lucy and said with a wink. Lucy nodded in agreement, realising that she and Paul would need to get their stories straight if they were to pull this off. "Wow, I don't remember you having a good looking older sister" said Paul, turning his attention to Phyllis. "Sister? I could be her mother!" Phyllis laughed, blushing. "Never! There can't be more than a couple of years in it. With you of course being the better looking" Paul said to Phyllis cheekily. "Dear me, you are a charmer. Come and have a slice of my lemon sponge" twittered Phyllis. Lucy laughed at the way that Paul had expertly charmed Phyllis so quickly.

At that moment Jeff walked in through the back door and after the introductions were made, was soon sitting at the kitchen table chatting to Paul about motorbikes and fast cars, with a little bit of football thrown in for good measure. "Ah, here comes Amira and the children for their breakfast. They had a bit of an unexpected late night last night, so I let them lay in" said Lucy. "Mummy!" Emily and Jake chorused as they came in, and stopped abruptly at the sight of this stranger. "Amira, Jake, Emily, this is my cousin Paul" Lucy said. She wasn't happy lying to anyone about Paul, especially the children. Lucy decided if it might help to keep them safe, this lie was worth it, and it was only a little one after all. "Hiya guys" said Paul, smiling at them. "Do you play football?" Jake asked suspiciously. "Yes I do" laughed Paul. "Bet you aren't as good as Phyllis is" said Jake, taking a step closer. "Oh I'm sure I'm not, but maybe you and Emily could teach me?" Said Paul. "Okay" chirped Jake happily. "Can we play now?" Asked Emily, stepping forward to where her brother was standing. "Of course we can, but only until your breakfast is ready, if it's okay with your mum" said Paul, glancing at Lucy. "That's fine by me" Lucy laughed back. Jake grabbed Paul's hand and began to drag him towards the garden. "Hi," Paul said to Amira as he passed. "would you like to come and watch me teach these children how this game is played?" He invited. "Most definitely" chuckled Amira.

After lunch that afternoon, Amira was watching TV with Jake and Emily while Lucy looked through some paperwork with Tom at the dining table. "Oh Lucy, could I borrow the car please? I was thinking I might take Jake and Emily for a burger" said Amira. "Burger? Did someone mention burgers?" Asked Paul, walking into the room. "Yes, Amira wants to borrow the car to take the children out" Lucy replied. "That's what I was just coming to tell you, the car's head gasket has gone and the garage can't fit you in for at least a week" said Paul. "Oh no, that means no burger kids. I'm sorry" said Amira. "Hang on, why does it?" Said Paul. "Let's make this a special adventure and I will be Jake and Emily's personal chauffeur until the car is fixed. Where to, your royal highnesses?" Said Paul in a posh voice, turning to the children. "Yay!" Chorused Jake and Emily together. "Come on then, we won't be more than a couple of hours" said Amira to Lucy, as she took a child in each hand. "Your carriage awaits sir, madam" said Paul, offering a linked arm to Emily. "It's not a carriage, it's a car!" Laughed Jake as they all trooped out together.

"Lucy, I was thinking, while the children are busy, how about we call in at the shop? I appreciate you have a lot on, but maybe just to meet the staff? What do you think?" Asked Tom. "Why not? It's not fair to leave the staff to run it all the time, and Amira and Paul have both our mobiles incase they need us" Lucy replied. As Lucy and Tom left the dining room,

Phyllis was just coming down the stairs. "Nick said to tell you he has gone to Captain Marvo's Burger Palace as well" she laughed. "Oh okay, I was just going to see if he wanted to join us" Lucy said. "Are you off somewhere nice?" Phyllis asked. "Just to the store for a short while" Tom said. "So you'll be gone all evening will you?" Phyllis continued. "No more than an hour I shouldn't think" said Tom. "Is Jeff going with you?" Phyllis persisted. "No, why would he?" Said Tom, a little puzzled why Phyllis would think that their gardener would be coming to the shop with them. "Oh, er…erm.. er…no reason. I just thought that he may enjoy the break away from the house." Phyllis said, averting her eyes from Tom's gaze. "No no, he is far too busy working on the hedgerows in the top field. He will be up there until dark" Tom said. "So, it looks like you will have the house to yourself" smiled Lucy. "Ah, that's good" said Phyllis, seeming to regain some of her organised manner. "I wanted to bake Amira a surprise birthday cake, she is 27 tomorrow" "That's very kind of you" said Tom, now understanding a little more of Phyllis's interest in everyone's whereabouts. "See you soon Phyllis, and I promise I will keep Amira out of the kitchen when she gets back" said Lucy with a knowing wink.

CHAPTER 3

BARTONS

Lucy settled back into Tom's car, it was a lovely midnight blue colour and was always so shiny. 'But considering Tom spends every spare minute polishing it, that is hardly surprising', she thought, smiling to herself. She couldn't help noticing how very like Paul's it was, even down to the strange gold crest on the dashboard. It looked very much like a panther's head, but with a solitary amber light right in the centre. Paul told Jake that it was an eye and meant that mummy could always see if he and Emily were on their best behaviour in the car. Just as they neared the sign saying they were in Blackville, Lucy spotted some sort of commotion ahead. Traffic was starting to build and Tom drew to a halt at the back of the queue. There was a large dirty white scaffold lorry pulled over onto the double yellow lines in front of the cottages by the old cotton mill. Lucy only knew it was a scaffold lorry because there were three old rusty looking scaffold poles poking out from the rear. As if reading her mind, Tom voiced her thoughts on how it was quite odd there was no company name on the vehicle and there didn't appear to be anyone working at the lorry or any of the properties nearby. "Maybe they live there" Lucy offered helpfully. "Hmmm" frowned Tom. At that point an older man got out of the lorry, pulled down one of the sides and busied himself, appearing to sort whatever was on the back, out of sight.

The man had a shock of unruly grey hair that kept tumbling down over his eyes, that he kept pushing back irritably with the backs of his well worn hands. He was wearing dirty, well-faded jeans and a grubby black jacket pulled high around his neck. Lucy couldn't help but think how hot he must be as she glanced down at her t-shirt clad arms and over at Tom's short sleeve shirt. With the traffic still not moving, Lucy had nothing else to do but watch the man sorting his lorry. Without warning, the driver's door swung open and a much younger man climbed down from the cab and went round to join the first man on the pavement. This one was wearing baggy joggers and the most unusual trainers Lucy had ever seen. They were a deep purple with shooting yellow stars along the outer edge. Lucy figured he can't do much of the work, as where the first man's boots were filthy, these trainers looked like they had just been taken from the box. This man also had the seemingly customary high collared black jacket, but Lucy couldn't see the colour of his hair as he had a red woolly hat pulled snugly down over his ears. Lucy couldn't help but smile because at that moment, Tom reached for the car's climate control, turning it up another notch to cool the car's interior further.

As Lucy had been so busy intently studying the attire of the new workman, she hadn't noticed that the first one was on the phone and looked up just in time to see him ending his call. He said something to the other man, although she couldn't hear what. Suddenly, the older of the two men lurched into the road, stumbling as he crossed between Tom's car and the red Fiesta in front. Lucy started to get out of the car, sure that he was going to fall, but he seemed to regain his balance, steadying himself with his hands on Tom's car bonnet. As the man reached the other side of the road, the younger man got back in the driver's seat and turned right into the street opposite. "Thank heavens for that" said Tom as they finally started to move, now that the obstruction was no longer there.

Lucy gave the workmen no further thought as Tom's phone rang out and she reached over to put it on speakerphone for him. "Tom, it's Luke" said a deep male voice. "Err hello Luke, I've got company and I'm on speakerphone" said Tom, rather sharply. "Oh okay, I need you to call me asap please" said the voice. "Yeah no problem, an hour alright?" Tom asked. "Fine, I'll speak with you then" said Luke, and the line went dead. Tom didn't say who the caller was, and turned the radio back up staring at the road ahead. Was it her, or was Tom suddenly gripping the steering wheel a lot tighter than he had before? And who was that voice? Lucy was almost certain she knew it, but couldn't quite place where from. 'No you're being silly' Lucy thought, telling herself off mentally. All the antics of late were making her read more into situations than there clearly was.

"That's a nice store" Lucy said, admiring the large building illuminated in its forecourt lighting, on the other side of the dual carriageway. "Do you like it?" Asked Tom, raising an eyebrow. "Oh yes, very modern looking compared to the other properties nearby. Reminds me of where we used to live and shopped at in the city" Lucy replied. "Ah, I'm glad, because that's Bartons, your new business" said Tom, glancing sideways at Lucy with an amused grin. "Is it? Oh my god, it's so much bigger than I imagined and certainly way beyond anything I expected!" Lucy exclaimed. "Oh Tom, what is going on? The house is huge, the store's huge and all the other happenings of the last couple of days. Think, less than a week ago Ben and I were still at our old home with the children. We were together and happy... and now this." Lucy finished sadly. "I know" said Tom, quietly reaching over to pat at her hand reassuringly. "Come on, show me my empire" said Lucy, smiling brightly as she got out of the car. Tom could see through her guise she was sure, but decided to put on her best smile and try to make as good as she possibly could of a very difficult situation.

Tom had pulled into a space with staff written across it at the rear of the building, so they had to enter the code into the large keypad on the wall to get in. Lucy expected to walk into a corridor or a hallway that would lead to the main shop, but found herself in a large carpeted room, sofas on one side and lockers and tables on the other. "The staffroom" smiled Tom, seeing her surprise. The room was empty apart from an elderly man snoozing in the corner, his cap half over his face. Tom coughed and the eye that was visible snapped open. "Ah, young Thomas!" Said the face from beneath the cap. "Hello Bill" laughed Tom, shaking the old man's hand after he had struggled to his feet. "Ooh, the old bones get stiff when I'm sitting. You wouldn't believe I was only 21, would you?" Chuckled Bill, grinning broadly at Lucy. "You look 21 to me Bill, and I need you to be on your best behaviour, as this is your new boss, Lucy Reid" Tom said, introducing Lucy. "Charmed to meet you, I'm sure" said Bill, bowing to Lucy, cap in hand. "Hello Bill" laughed Lucy. "Bill is our trolley man and the reason why our carpark always looks spotless" said Tom. "Trolley man? Trolley man? I'll have you know I am the carpark manager!" Bill said grandly, in the poshest voice he could muster. "Oooo la-de-dah!" Chuckled

Tom, putting an arm around Bill's shoulder. "You're doing a fabulous job, I can see" said Lucy. "Thank you Mrs Reid" chirped Bill, clearly pleased that Lucy had noticed. "Please, call me Lucy" she replied, giving Bill a friendly smile. "Come on Lucy, come through to the storeroom and see the guys" Tom said.

Lucy followed Tom through a small gap at the far end of the room, along a brightly lit corridor and through a set of big white double doors. Inside, Lucy was met with rows and rows of boxes, every shape and size you could possibly imagine. Two men were in front of her, both wearing dark blue overalls. They turned on hearing them come in, both smiled and came over. "Hi guys, this is Lucy Reid. Lucy, this is Derek Jacobs, the warehouse manager and also Bill's son, and this is Tyler, Bill's grandson" said Tom. "Awh, how lovely, all one family" said Lucy, shaking both men by the hand. "Lucy will catch up with you both soon, we are just here for a quick visit today" Tom said to Derek and Tyler as he lead Lucy through another set of double doors, and out into the store itself. Lucy let out a gasp, she was seriously impressed. The shop was cool, with spacious aisles, but not overly large. "How many staff operate Bartons, Tom?" Lucy asked. "About 30 on a rota basis, and the majority are part time" Tom replied. "Lucy, I wonder if you'll excuse me for a short while please? I need to return a phone call" said Tom. "Of course, I'll have a wander round while I'm waiting" nodded Lucy, smiling. "If you're sure. I can always get someone to wait with you if you prefer?" Tom asked. "Honestly Tom, I'm fine. You go right ahead" Lucy insisted.

She happily ambled up and down the aisles, taking in what a vast array of products Bartons stocked, considering they weren't a city store. As Lucy rounded the corner into aisle 7, her nostrils were met with a heavenly aroma of freshly baked bread. Lucy inhaled deeply as she passed the succulent apple turnovers, crusty white bread and thick crust pies. At the end of the aisle was a sign with a large red arrow on it, saying 'Interviews this way'. Curiously, Lucy followed the arrow. Tom hadn't mentioned any interviews taking place, 'Mind you he's such a sweet, thoughtful guy he probably didn't want to worry me' she thought. At the end of the narrow corridor was a door marked 'Reception', inside two young women sat at their desks, totally oblivious to her presence. One of the women was in her late teens, Lucy thought. Her carefully manicured nails of one hand drummed absentmindedly on the desk, while she leafed through the pages of a magazine with the other. The blonde to her right appeared slightly older, her hair piled high into a tousled bun. Lucy watched as her jaws worked ten to the dozen chewing gum, whilst every so often blowing a huge bubble that popped with a loud crack. Lucy was amazed that during all this frenzied chewing, she still managed to chatter non-stop to her colleague.

"Erm, excuse me" Lucy said politely, approaching the blonde woman's desk. She barely glanced at Lucy, and turned her back on her and carried on chatting. "Excuse me" said Lucy, slightly louder this time. "What?" Snapped the woman. "Just take a seat over there, interviews aren't meant to start until four" said the other woman, shutting her magazine with a swipe of her hand. "I'm not actually here for..." Lucy started to say. "Look, if you must turn up early, just take a seat. Some of us have work to do" said the blonde woman haughtily. Lucy took a seat as she was told and watched bemused as the younger woman started to paint her nails. "You better not let the new boss catch you doing that, I've heard she's a right old witch" said the older woman, who Lucy now knew was called Lara Prince after spotting a name plaque on her desk. "Yeah I bet she is" said the younger woman, as they both collapsed into fits of giggles. At that moment Tom rushed into the reception, "Ah there you are Lucy, I'm so sorry I've been so long. Have Lara and Penny been keeping you entertained?" Tom said, turning towards them. "Lucy?" Croaked Lara, her face suddenly draining of its colour. "Oh yes, very entertained thank you Tom" said Lucy, smiling sweetly at the two women, whose mouths had fallen open as realisation dawned on them. "Lucy Reid?" Asked Penny, recovering her composure. "Yes the very same, but you can call me the old witch" said Lucy curtly, as she turned and left without a backward glance.

"Lucy, Lucy! What's the matter?" Said Tom, rushing after her. "I'll tell you in the car. Amira's just text to say Jake isn't feeling a hundred percent and she is taking him home. So I'd like to go back if that's okay with you please" Lucy said. "Yes, of course" said Tom. As they pulled out of the carpark, Tom's radio was interrupted with a traffic report. "Oh no" said Tom after it had finished. "What's up?" Said Lucy "We had better go back the scenic way, as it says Blackville Carnival is causing major tailbacks in the town" Tom said."Oh, okay, I didn't know there was a carnival in

Blackville today. The children would have loved that" said Lucy. "No problem, we'll catch up with it at Bartons tomorrow if you like. It's a weekend event and comes back into town to finish on the field behind the store where it joins the fairground there." "What a great idea. I hope Jake will be well enough" Lucy said. "Much better this way, no traffic at all" said Tom as they drove out of the town on the main country road. "It's very pretty out here" said Lucy, admiring the view. "I'll stop up here for a moment, the view is amazing from Blackville Ridge" said Tom, after Lucy had come off of the phone from Amira, who had rang to tell her that Jake seemed fine now. "Oh damn, that was close!" Exclaimed Tom, glancing in his rear view mirror at the rabbit that had just darted across the road, making him break harshly. "There's a lay-by coming up, we'll stop there" said Tom. "Okay" Lucy replied.

Tom signalled to pull into the lay-by, but swerved out again sharply. "What's wrong Tom?" Said Lucy, glancing at him with surprise. "We don't seem to have any breaks" said Tom, panic in his voice. "Oh my god!" Cried Lucy. "There's a field on this bend, I just hope the gate's open. I'm going to try and get the car in there. The grass is very long and the ground should be soft after all the rain" Tom explained quickly. Lucy didn't reply, just sat bolt upright, gripping the door handle. "Brace yourself Lucy!" Tom cried, as he steered the car through the open gate into the farmers field. The car bumped and bounced into the grass, eventually coming to a halt. "Are you okay Lucy?" Said Tom, concerned. "Yes, I think so" she replied shakily. Tom pulled the phone from his pocket and called the breakdown services. The mechanic arrived quicker than expected and after tinkering for a short while, walked towards Lucy and Tom, wiping his hands on an oily rag. "Do you know what caused it?" Lucy asked. "I'm afraid I do" the man replied "your break hoses have been cut" "Oh my god, are you sure?" Said Tom. "Definitely sir, no doubt about it" said the mechanic. "I'm calling the police" said Lucy, taking her phone out. "No, let me do it" insisted Tom. "You come and sit in the truck madam" said the mechanic.

"DCI Fields is coming out to the house to see you, he is going to arrange to have the car taken to the station to be examined and he is sending a car to collect us" said Tom, once he had put the phone down. Good as his word, a car arrived and took Lucy and Tom home. "Let me make you a cup of tea, you are still shaking" said Tom. "Thank you" said Lucy, following Tom up the stairs to the front door. "Lucy, the door is open. You wait here" said Tom urgently. "No, I don't want to be out here on my own, please let me come with you." Lucy replied. "Okay" said Tom, slowly pushing open the door. The flowers from the large crystal vase on the hall table were strewn across the hallway and the vase itself lay in pieces beyond the doormat. Tom and Lucy ventured slowly inside, and Lucy saw straight away a number of paintings from the wood panelled hallway were missing. "The paintings!" Lucy exclaimed "Oh my god, we've been robbed" said Tom. "Mrs Reid, are you okay?" Said a voice from behind them. Lucy and Tom turned to see the two officers that had just dropped them off standing in the open doorway. "No, we've been robbed!" Exclaimed Lucy. "We were told to wait until you were inside before we left, but we noticed you hadn't closed the door" said the male officer. "I'll call the station" said the female officer, stepping back outside. "I'll check the rest of the house" said the policeman. "Lucy!" Came Tom's rather panicked voice from the kitchen. Lucy hadn't noticed him go while she was talking to the officers, she hurried through to the kitchen and stopped in horror. There, tied to the kitchen chair and gagged, was Phyllis. "Oh my god, Phyllis!" Said Lucy, running to help Tom untie her. A sobbing Phyllis tried to get up and collapsed immediately back onto the chair. "Take it easy Phyllis, stay there and rest for a minute" warned Tom. DCI Fields rushed into the kitchen, followed by the policewoman. "What the hell?" He exclaimed. "Come on Phyllis, let's get you through to the living room" Tom said softly, helping her to her feet.

"Can you tell us what happened Phyllis?" Asked Lucy gently, when they were all seated on the sofas, and Amira and Paul had taken the children upstairs, as they had just returned home. "Err, yes" said a very tearful Phyllis, wincing as the policewoman was cleaning the graze to her cheek. "Go on Phyllis" encouraged Tom. "I was just putting the cake I had been making for Amira down to cool, when there was a buzz from the gate. They said they had parcels to deliver, and I knew that you had been waiting for the lovely outfits that you had ordered for Amira's birthday Lucy." She said, smiling weakly, as a tear trickled down her cheek. "Oh Phyllis" said Lucy, her voice full of emotion. "When I opened the door, a man was standing there with two boxes. I asked him if he would put them on the hallway table, as I was still covered in flour. As soon as he stepped inside, a second man appeared from behind him, and they both grabbed me. I knew there was no point in screaming, as I was alone, so no one would hear me. I struggled as much as I could, I wasn't going to make it easy for them!" Said Phyllis, a trace of her usual no nonsense attitude in her voice. "Phyllis, is that where you got the injury to your face? When I think how much more they could have hurt you…I'm so sorry you were left here alone" said Lucy earnestly. "Lucy dear, don't blame yourself, you weren't to know" said Phyllis, squeezing her hand. "What happened next Mrs Snow?" Coaxed DCI Fields "They pushed me into the chair and tied me up with the new washing line that was on the table waiting for Jeff to put it up tomorrow. Then they gagged me with the baking cloth that was laying over Amira's cake to keep the flies off. They didn't speak to me, or each other, the whole time. Once I was secure, they left the kitchen and shut the door, I haven't seen them since, I was so scared. I don't know how long I was sitting there before Tom found me" said Phyllis, dabbing her eyes with the tissue Lucy had given her.

"The doctor's here" said Jeff quietly from the living room doorway. "You go off and see the doctor Mrs Snow, I'll speak to you again afterwards. Thank you, you've been very helpful" said DCI Fields. "Could I have a word please sir?" Said the policewoman who had brought Lucy and Tom home. "Of course, please excuse me everyone" said DCI Fields, following the officer out of the room. "I just can't believe all of this. Are we ever going to wake up from this nightmare?" Said Lucy sadly. "Ben would know what to do if he was here." "I know, I know" said Nick, giving his stepmother a reassuring hug. "Lucy, I need you to listen to me please very carefully" said DCI Fields, taking a seat in the armchair opposite her. "We've had the car examined and the break hose was definitely cut. Tom said he had to break hard to miss a rabbit, just before he had to go off road into the field. The break fluid had probably been leaking since you left Barton's and that harsh breaking was likely to have been the last straw." He continued "We've checked the CCTV at the store and it shows a hooded figure approaching your car shortly after you left it. He takes what looks like a small torch from his pocket and shines it onto the bonnet, before going underneath with a pair of pliers he took from his other pocket. After a few moments he gets up and leaves. We've had the car bonnet examined and it appears that it has some sort of film on it, only visible under ultra violet light. The film is in the shape of hand prints, but there are no finger prints, so whoever put them there must have been wearing gloves" "Oh my god, the old man Tom! The one that fell in the road, he must have done it" "Tom rang the station with the number plate of the lorry as he thought it was suspicious, but the plate is registered to a white Fiat that was scrapped six months ago. The scrap yard was closed down shortly after and we have not been able to trace the owner" said DCI Fields.

"How was this allowed to happen at the store? The CCTV is manned at all times" said Tom. "We have spoken to Joe Hughes, who should have been in the CCTV room today. He had received a call on his mobile just after you arrived at Barton's, saying that his wife and child had been involved in an accident. He left straight away obviously, and Lara Prince was meant to be holding the fort until a replacement could be found. Unfortunately, she hadn't arrived by the time your car was sabotaged" said DCI Fields. "No, I'm sure she hadn't" said Lucy wryly, remembering her earlier altercation with Lara and Penny in reception. "We've also obtained Joe's phone records. The call was made from an unregistered pay-as-you-go phone" said DCI Fields. "I don't understand, why didn't they just give the person who damaged Tom's car the numberplate? Why go to all the hassle with the scaffold lorry?" Said Lucy. "The people they use for these sort of things are often people who are known to the police, often reliant on some kind of substance, and will do anything for the money to get their next fix. They may be so out of it they aren't thinking straight, but these people mean business, they clearly wanted to get it right" said DCI Fields gravely.

"What about the robbery here DCI Fields? Do you think that there is a connection?" Asked Lucy. "Well if there isn't it's one hell of a coincidence. We just don't know what the link is yet" replied DCI Fields. "Was anything else taken apart from the paintings?" Lucy asked Nick. "Not that I can see" he replied "Do you know what the paintings were of, that have been taken?" Asked DCI Fields. "Er, yes some of them" said Lucy. DCI Fields took out a notebook and pen, "Ready when you are" he said, pen poised. "Well, there was a large fruit basket, but not just apples and pears, it was overflowing with more exotic fruits, like mango and papaya. There was a rather strange looking one with multi-coloured intertwined lines on it. To be honest it looked more like something Jake or Emily would have drawn" said Lucy. "Oh and that really awful one that has the ghost and ghoul faces in vivid purple" said Nick. "Okay, I've got that, what about the other two?" Asked DCI Fields. "I'm sorry but I really can't seem to remember" said Lucy. "No, but I can. I clean them every day" said Phyllis, coming back into the room and sitting down on the sofa next to Lucy. "Mrs Snow, I'm glad to see you with a bit more colour in your cheeks. If you could remember that would be fantastic" said the DCI. "There was one of a lamb ambling through a meadow, with a sheepdog in the distance and the other was of a dinner party, with lots of diners dressed in all their finery sitting at the table" finished Phyllis. "We can't find any prints on the surrounds Mrs Snow, yet you say you clean them everyday, but not even your own fingerprints are apparent" said DCI Fields. "I do, but with a telescopic duster. Those paintings are valuable sir and some far too delicate to be tarnished by human hand" Phyllis said. "I see, now I understand, as we thought, the intruders would have been wearing gloves" said DCI Fields.

"What about the CCTV here?" Said Tom. "We've also looked at that and it was switched off" said the DCI. "Off?" Questioned Nick, shocked. "Yes, we were puzzled by that as well Nick. Someone has clearly turned the CCTV system off" said DCI Fields. "Oh dear" said Phyllis worriedly "What is it Phyllis?" Said Lucy. "I think I may be responsible for the CCTV being off" said Phyllis, clasping her hand to her mouth. "Why's that Mrs Snow?" Asked DCI Fields, raising an eyebrow expectantly. "I was making a cake earlier, and when I switched the mixer on, I think it must have tripped the fuse. I did go to switch all the switches back on at the fusebox, but I didn't realise that I had to go and switch the CCTV back on separately." Said Phyllis. DCI Fields sat back in his chair, his chin resting on his hand, and stared intently at Phyllis for a few moments. "Ah, that would explain it Mrs Snow" he said at last. "I'm so sorry Lucy, I'm such a silly old woman" Phyllis said, starting to cry again. "Please Phyllis, don't cry. You've had a terrible experience" said Lucy kindly. "Tom, I have arranged for your car to be repaired and returned to you in the morning" said DCI Fields. "Thank you, that is very kind of you" said Tom.

"DCI Fields, is there any news on my husband?" Lucy asked hopefully. "I'm afraid not Lucy, the trail seems to have gone completely cold. Please rest assured we will be reinvestigating all leads. No stone will be left unturned. I know it's hard, but please try not to worry. I'll call you again tomorrow" said DCI Fields, standing up to leave. "Thank you sir, I'll see you out" said Tom. "Mrs Reid, do you happen to know the value of any of the paintings by any chance?" Asked DCI Fields. "I'm sorry I don't, but Mrs Armstrong, our permanent housekeeper may know more than I do. Or Mr Benson, Great-Aunt Maud's solicitor." Lucy replied. "Do you know how to contact Mrs Armstrong?" DCI Fields said. "I'll get you her number from the book in the hall desk on the way out" said Tom. "Okay, I'd appreciate that Tom. Goodnight everyone" said DCI Fields as he left the room. "I'm going to say goodnight to the children and then go to bed. I need a clear head to think this all through tomorrow. Goodnight Nick, Phyllis" said Lucy.

As Lucy approached the children's bedroom door, she met Amira on the landing. "Oh, I'm sorry Lucy, they're both asleep, they were so tired" she smiled. "No, please don't apologise. Thank you for looking after them." Said Lucy. "You're very welcome. They're lovely children, an absolute pleasure" said Amira. Lucy went in to the children's bedroom and quietly closed the door behind her. She stared down at them, Jake with the covers kicked off, she could never get him to keep the bed clothes on, even as a baby, and Emily, her long hair splayed across the pillow and cuddling Milky tightly. Suddenly, Lucy was overcome with emotion, at the thought of the events of the last few days, and she sat weeping silently on the bedside chair. "Mummy, why are you sleeping in my chair?" Asked a voice. Lucy opened her eyes to see Jake standing by her, his little eyes fighting to stay open, but so heavy with sleep. "I sat down for a moment and fell asleep, aren't I silly?" Said Lucy, scooping him up in her arms and popping him back into bed. "I love you mummy" said Jake, sleepily. "I love you too, my darling" said Lucy, bending to place a kiss on his forehead. Lucy walked over to the other bed to kiss Emily and then softly shut the bedroom door behind her. When Lucy reached her own room, she collapsed onto her bed. She had so much on her mind, but she was oh so very tired.

CHAPTER 4

MORPH JOINS THE FAMILY

The next morning, she was woken by a gentle tapping on her bedroom door. "Come in" Lucy called. "I'm so sorry to disturb you, but I was wondering if you had any problem with the children starting at the village craft club as the new term starts soon? I bumped into the lady that runs it at Captain Marvo's yesterday, and she was telling me they have space. I just thought that they might enjoy mixing with the other children and the lady assured me that no one gets in or out as it is all on a security buzzer system. I was thinking it might be good for them as it is in the same building they will be going to school in." said Amira. Lucy mentally stopped herself from saying no, she wanted the children with her at all times, but she knew Amira was right, they did need to mix with other children. "Yes Amira, that's fine, I'm sure they'll have a lovely time. Maybe Paul could take you for lunch somewhere until it is time to collect them? You've worked so hard the last few days, I don't know what I would have done without you" smiled Lucy. "Are you off to the store again today, as yesterday's visit was cut short?" Asked Amira. "No, I think Tom will want to get his car shining and back to his standard, now that the mechanics have had their hands on it, so I am going to sort through the filing cabinets in the study" Lucy said with a laugh. "Okay, I'll send the children up to say goodbye" Amira said.

Once Amira and the children had left with Paul, Lucy had a shower, put on her favourite top and comfortable joggers, and went down to the kitchen to see Phyllis, in the hope it wasn't too late for breakfast. Lucy couldn't remember the last time she had slept after 8am, yet here she was strolling down to breakfast at gone 10. "Hello Lucy dear" beamed Phyllis, seeming much more like her old self. "Good morning Phyllis, how are you feeling?" Lucy asked. "Me? I'm fine poppet, it would take a lot more than those hoodlums to keep me down" Phyllis breezed. "I'm so glad to hear it" smiled Lucy. "Now, what can I get you for breakfast?" Phyllis said, raising an eyebrow at Lucy quizzically. "Oh, if you're sure, eggs on toast would be lovely" Lucy replied. "Of course I'm sure, you sit yourself down and I will be two ticks" Phyllis insisted, spraying the pan with a little oil. Lucy absentmindedly watched Phyllis at work, marvelling at just how lucky they were she had come into their lives, and quite by coincidence too. Phyllis was so capable, and always a clear head in any crisis. "Thank you Phyllis, that looks lovely" Lucy said as Phyllis placed a plate in front of her. "You're very welcome pet" she replied, patting Lucy's shoulder and then bustling off to load the dishwasher. As Lucy was finishing her last mouthful of breakfast, the back door burst open and Tom came in, followed by Jeff carrying a blanket bunched up in his arms. "Lucy will you come through to the utility room please?" Asked Tom. "We've got something to show you" "Yes of course" said Lucy, getting up and following them.

Tom gently moved the blanket in Jeff's arms to one side. "Oh my god, a puppy!" Exclaimed Lucy. "Jeff found it injured in the top field. No idea how it got there though, as I can't find any holes in the boundary fencing" Tom said. "Oh the poor thing, that leg looks quite nasty. Should I call the vet, or would it be better to take it there ourselves?" Asked Lucy. "I've got to drop some paperwork off in town, so I will take him on the way if you like" said Tom. "Okay, you go as well Jeff, as it seems quite happy nuzzled in your arms" laughed Lucy, giving the puppy's head a stroke. "Why don't you come along too, Lucy? Our little furry friend seems to have taken quite a shine to you" said Jeff, laughing at the way the puppy was licking her hand. "Do you know, I think I will. I'd like to make sure this little guy is okay" said Lucy grabbing her bag and following Tom and Jeff out to the car. Lucy smiled to herself, noticing the brilliant shine coming from the paintwork of Tom's car. The police had only returned it an hour ago.

When they got to the vet they weren't quite open yet, but the veterinary nurse told them to come in anyway. Mr Pinter, the vet, saw them straight away. "Oh dear, not you again Morph?" He said, stroking the dog's head. "Morph? You know him?" Asked Lucy, looking puzzled. "Oh yes, I know him. He's a right little monkey, he should be renamed Houdini as he has escaped 3 times in the last month from the animal shelter next door. Miss Wilcox is at the end of her tether with him" said Mr Pinter. "Oh dear, he certainly does sound like Houdini, don't you fella?" Said Tom, tickling Morph's ears. "Catherine, could you give Miss Wilcox a call please and let her know we have Morph here?" Said the vet. "Of course" said Catherine, hurrying off. "Ah this is going to need stitches my little friend" said Mr Pinter soothingly to a shaking Morph as he examined his leg.

Just then, the surgery door sprang open and a rather harassed looking woman rushed in. "There you are Morph, you are a menace! I just wish I knew how to stop you getting out." She said, giving him a stroke. "Hello Miss Wilcox, I'm Lucy Reid, and this is Tom and Jeff. We found Morph in our field" Lucy said. "Oh dear, I do hope he hasn't caused you any damage. Thank you so much for bringing him in here" Miss Wilcox said gratefully. "No, not at all he is lovely, and to be honest we can't see how he got into our field either. There's no damage to any of our perimeter fencing" said Lucy. "I think whoever ends up adopting Morph should enter him into talent contests, as he certainly seems to have a unique skill, doesn't he?" Said Mr Pinter, with a hearty laugh. "Adopting him? I thought when Mr Pinter said Morph was from the animal shelter, he was yours, not an actual resident" said Lucy. "No, no, Morph has been looking for a new home for a few weeks now, ever since his owner moved away and left him in the empty house" said Miss Wilcox grimly. "Oh no, the poor little thing, how could anyone be so cruel?" Said Lucy. "Well, I think that is you all done!" Declared Mr Pinter as he fixed on the lead that Miss Wilcox had brought with her, and placed Morph gently onto the floor. "Goodbye little guy" said Lucy, as she bent down to stroke his silky fur. "Goodbye Mrs Reid, gentlemen" said Miss Wilcox. "Bye Paula, please don't worry about the bill, Morph can have this one on me" said Mr Pinter kindly.

Lucy watched as Miss Wilcox lead Morph away, with him stopping every few feet and looking back at her. For a moment, she was sure she could see her own confusion mirrored in his big brown eyes. "Wait, Miss Wilcox" called Lucy "Yes Mrs Reid?" Said Miss Wilcox, turning to face her with a smile. "I was wondering if there was any chance that Morph could come home with us please? We have plenty of room and the children would love him." Said Lucy. Miss Wilcox beamed warmly "I'm sure you'd love that, wouldn't you Morph?" She said, bending down to stroke him. "Do you have time to come and fill out the adoption paperwork now? Or I can bring him to you tomorrow". Lucy glanced down at Morph, his big brown pleading eyes said it all, "No I'll fill it in now if that's okay" Lucy replied, following Miss Wilcox next door.

As Lucy filled in the paperwork with Miss Wilcox sitting by her side, seeing Lucy fill out her address, Miss Wilcox exclaimed "Oh, you live at Hilltop Manor? I knew the previous owner very well, she was such a lovely lady and did so much to help out all of our animals. I was only there two weeks ago, visiting Margaret!" Lucy grinned at Miss Wilcox's excitement, "She certainly was an amazing woman. She was my husband's great aunt" She replied. "I would usually do a home visit for a new adoption, but under the circumstances, that won't be necessary. I'll call you in a couple of days to make sure he is settling in okay, if that's alright?" Said Miss Wilcox, handing her the lead. "That's fine and thank you again" said Lucy. Morph stretched out in the rear of Tom's car and slept all the way to his new home. 'It's been quite a day for this little chap' Lucy thought, stroking his silky ears.

"Mummy!" Cried Jake and Emily running to meet her as she got out of the car. "Hello you two" Lucy laughed, bending to hug them both. "We have a surprise for you." Declared Tom "Shut your eyes" said Jeff. Both children stood with Amira, their eyes tightly closed, as Tom lifted Morph gently out of the car, took his lead off and placed him at Jake and Emily's feet. "Open your eyes quickly!" Said Lucy, wanting the children to see Morph before he darted off. "Ooh, a puppy!" Squealed Jake gleefully, bending down to stroke him. "Pretty colours!" Declared Emily, tickling Morph's belly, who had obligingly rolled over for her. "He's beautiful" laughed Amira, stroking Morph's ears. "Is he ours?" Asked Jake, staring hopefully at his mother. "Yes darling he is, this is Morph" said Lucy, smiling. "Can he sleep in my bed?" Jake asked. "No" laughed Lucy "In our room?" Asked Emily hopefully. "I don't think so" Lucy replied. She was just about to say she would put Morph's basket in the utility room downstairs, but suddenly thought better of it. With everything that had happened in the last few days, Lucy rather liked the idea of having Morph near her children overnight. "Okay, he can sleep in his basket in your room, but you must promise me you will go to sleep and not stay up all night" said Lucy in her best authoritative mummy voice she could muster. "We promise" said Jake "Yes, what Jake said" grinned Emily. "I think our new resident is a hit" laughed Tom, as he watched Morph scampering between the two children, frantically licking their hands and wagging his tail.

"Lucy, phone for you!" Phyllis called through the door. "Okay coming!" Said Lucy, running up the steps to the house. "Come and meet Morph Phyllis!" Cried Jake. "Oh, er, yes…I will do a bit later" said Phyllis, eyeing Morph warily. "Come on kids, time to have a wash ready for bed" said Amira. "Oh do we have to?" Said Jake and Emily together. "Yes, I'm afraid you do. The sooner you do it, the sooner you can show Morph around his new home" laughed Amira. "Oh okay, but I don't need to wash my face do I?" Asked Jake. "Yes of course you do" replied Amira puzzled. "But Morph's already washed it for me" said Jake indignantly, before racing off up the stairs with Emily and Morph hot on his heels. "Kids" Tom laughed.

Once Jake and Emily had washed and got ready for bed, they took Morph down to find Phyllis. They found her in the utility room sorting the washing. Phyllis turned as they came in, smiling warmly at Jake and Emily, her gaze fell on Morph "Err, hello Morph" she said, taking a step closer "Grrr..grr.." growled Morph softly, backing away. "Morph, don't growl at Phyllis, she's our friend" said Jake crossly. Phyllis took a step closer and tried again "Hello little fella" she said. By this time, Lucy had joined them and was surprised to hear Morph let out a bark at Phyllis. "Morph!" Said Emily in a chastising voice. "Oh dear, I don't think Morph likes it in here" laughed Phyllis nervously. "Jake, take Morph to look around the rest of the house and let Phyllis get on with her work" Lucy told him, trying to lighten the mood. Lucy went and sat at the kitchen table, pouring herself a cup of tea from the fresh pot Phyllis had just made. 'How very strange' she thought, Morph had a lovely temperament from what she had seen so far. He had greeted her, Tom, Jeff, Amira, Jake, Emily, all with full scale excitement, yet he didn't seem to like Phyllis at all.

"Mummy will you come and see our paintings" said Emily from the kitchen door. "Paintings?" Asked Lucy. "Yes, the ones we did at art club today" said Emily. "Oh of course I will" said Lucy, hurrying over to her. With the unexpected arrival of Morph, Lucy had totally forgot to ask about how Jake and Emily had got on at art club. Emily grabbed her mother's hand and lead her through to the living room, where an excited and impatient Jake was waiting for them with Amira and Tom. "Come and sit down mummy" said Jake "We loved art club mummy and we are going again tonight" declared Emily, climbing onto Lucy's lap. "I hope you mean tomorrow" Lucy laughed, hugging her. Emily looked up at Amira puzzled, then broke into a huge grin when she saw her nodding, "Yes tomorrow" Emily declared. "Miss Timms who runs it said they had a fabulous time, and the other children really took to them" Amira told Lucy. "Well these paintings are amazing! I think you better get yourself off to bed, so that you are bright eyed and bushy tailed enough to do me some more tomorrow" said Lucy to Jake and Emily. "Bushy tailed" giggled Emily. She always found that expression hilarious when Lucy used it. "Night night mummy, Amira has promised to read Morph a bedtime story" said Jake. "Okay, night" said Lucy, kissing them both. "Mummy?" Said Emily as she got to the door. "Yes sweetheart?" Lucy said. "Will daddy be back to take us to art club tomorrow?" Emily asked. "No, not tomorrow I don't think" said Lucy softly, trying her best to hide the sadness in her voice. "Hopefully he will be able to take you very soon".

Lucy sighed quietly to herself, her smile as the children left the room was a lot brighter than she felt. "I'm very surprised DCI Fields didn't call as he said he would" said Tom, once the door had closed. "He did, he rang earlier, but only to tell me that there was nothing to report" said Lucy. "Who on earth is that at this time of night?" Tom said, hearing the buzzer from the main gate. "Hello?" He said into the intercom. "Taxi" said a voice "I'm sorry, we didn't order a taxi" replied Tom. "Booked for 9pm from Hilltop Manor" said the voice. "I'm really sorry, but even though that is the right address, we haven't ordered a taxi" Tom insisted. "Okay" sighed the voice, and the buzzer went silent. No sooner had Tom stepped away from the intercom, it buzzed again. "Hello?" Said Tom "Pizza sir" replied a friendly voice "We haven't ordered a pizza, are you sure you have the right address?" Asked Tom. "Hang on, let me check the ticket" said the voice. "What on earth is going on here?" Said Lucy. "I've no idea" said Tom, puzzled. "Hello?" Said the voice on the buzzer "Hello" Tom replied. "Three meat feast pizzas, two garlic bread, and a large bottle of drink for Hilltop Manor" said the pizza man. "Oh dear, that's the right address, but we haven't ordered any food" said Tom. The delivery man didn't reply straight away, and Tom and Lucy could hear him talking to someone else. "Well I hope you did order the Indian takeaway, as there is a lady standing here trying to deliver one" said the delivery guy, much less chirpily now. "Dear me no, we have not ordered that either and we've just turned away a taxi no one asked for as well" said Tom apologetically. "It seems someone is pulling your leg and ours" said the voice. "I'm so sorry for the inconvenience" said Tom earnestly. "Not your fault sir, goodnight" said the voice and the intercom was once again silent.

As Tom sat back in the arm chair the intercom buzzed again. "Oh this is getting ridiculous" said Tom, as he went to answer it. "Hello?" He said. "Hiya, we're here for the party" said a young female voice. "Party? There's no party here" said Tom, struggling to hear over the chorus of high spirited voices clearly congregated at the gate. "Are you sure? The guy in the pub said there was a party here and everyone was invited" said the girl. "What guy at the pub?" Asked Tom, puzzled. "No idea who he was, I thought one of the others knew him" she replied. "No, I'm sorry, there isn't a party here" said Tom. "Should have realised really, I mean who comes to a party in joggers and purple trainers?" Laughed the girl. "Purple trainers with yellow stars?" Said Lucy, coming to join Tom. "Yeah that's him, do you know him?" Asked the girl. "No we don't, just someone we've seen about" answered Tom. "What pub was it?" Asked Lucy. "The Three Feathers on the green" said the girl. "Okay, thank you, goodnight" said Tom, replacing the buzzer. Tom turned to Lucy, "I'm going to call the police".

When he came off the phone, he told Lucy that the police said they were sending someone to the pub to see if the man with the purple trainers was still there and that they will call him back. "What on earth is going on? Who is this man? And why keep sending people here on a wild goose chase?" Lucy asked Tom, puzzled. "Hmm, I don't know for sure, but I would imagine the taxi and the food was just to unsettle us for some reason." Tom said frowning. Just then his mobile rang "Hello...yes it is... oh okay, thank you for trying...Yes I understand, I'll tell Mrs Reid" said Tom, before ending the call. "The police sent officers to the pub, the landlord doesn't know him. He kept his gloves on the whole time, ordered one drink, which he drank from the bottle and took it with him when he left, that way leaving no DNA whatsoever and the police lady said she would let DCI Fields know" he finished. "Oh Tom, I really don't like this,

I wish Ben was here" said Lucy. "I know you do, but I'll look after you until he is Lucy, please remember that" said Tom, giving her a hug. "Thank you Tom, I do appreciate everything you do for us, I really do" said Lucy

"Oh and remember Nick will be back the day after tomorrow, so that's something to look forward to" said Tom encouragingly. Nick had gone to stay with his mother for a couple of days. DCI Fields had arranged for a police family liaison officer to drive him there and collect him again to come home. Nick hadn't wanted to go, but his mother wanted him home for her birthday and Lucy was worried that she would turn up at Hilltop Manor if he didn't go, and start asking all sorts of questions as to where Ben was. Lucy had met Nick's mum Julie a few times and they always got on quite well, which made it easier for Nick. "I'm going to bed Tom, goodnight" said Lucy. "Goodnight Lucy, sleep well or at least try to" he replied, smiling sympathetically at her. Lucy quietly opened Jake and Emily's bedroom door and crept inside to give them a kiss. Jake and Emily were both sound asleep in the same bed with Morph curled snugly in between them. "What are you doing up there mister?" Lucy whispered, "That wasn't part of our agreement was it?" She said softly, stroking his head. Morph let out a huge sigh and settled his head across Jake's feet. "Oh okay then, just for tonight" Lucy said, chuckling to herself as she left the room, closing the door behind her.

"Lucy, have you seen Jake's hoody? He wants it for art club tomorrow" said Phyllis, appearing at the top of the stairs. "Oh I think it was on the chair in the bedroom" said Lucy "Never mind, I'll get it. I know he definitely said that he wanted it wear it" said Phyllis. Lucy was just going into her own room when she heard Morph barking and growling. She rushed back to the children's bedroom to see Phyllis rooted to the spot just inside the door, with Morph standing between her and the children, barking and growling for all he was worth. "Oh dear, I think I must have startled him" stuttered Phyllis "Yes, that must be it" said Lucy, staring puzzled at the usually docile Morph still barking and growling. "What's happened mummy? Why is Morph barking?" Said Jake, sitting up and rubbing his eyes. Emily, amazingly, was still sound asleep. "Phyllis startled Morph when she came into the room I think. You lay down, there is nothing for you to worry about. I'll get the hoody Phyllis, if you want to wait on the landing" said Lucy, turning to her. "Oh, er, yes of course, that might be best" stammered Phyllis. Once Phyllis had left the room, Morph immediately stopped barking and jumped back onto the bed to take up his original position back between Jake and Emily. Lucy picked up the hoody and left the room, what on earth was wrong with Morph? When Phyllis was in the room, it was almost as if he was stopping her going near Jake and Emily. Lucy gave Phyllis the hoody and went into her room, closing the door behind her. Maybe it was just going to take a while for Morph to take to Phyllis, but why is it only Phyllis that he seems to have a problem with? It was all very strange.

Lucy waved the children off to art club with Amira and Paul the next morning after breakfast and went straight to the study to busy herself with the long overdue sorting of the filing cabinet. There were all sorts of documents in there, house insurance, purchase receipts for household items, invoices for repair work that had been undertaken over the years and even a copy of the deeds to Hilltop Manor, but the original didn't seem to be there for some reason. 'Maybe Mr Benson the solicitor had those?' Lucy thought. At the back of the very bottom drawer was a scrapbook, Lucy settled into the chair to have a closer look. She loved old photographs, and there were a lot of people she didn't recognise, but lots she did. There was Great Aunt Maud, starting as a baby, through to what looked like not long before her death. Lucy marvelled at the photos of Great Aunt Maud winning contest after contest, she knew she had been quite an attractive woman in her day, but never realised she'd been a beauty queen. She had never said anything, but then it seemed that there was rather a lot that Great Aunt Maud never said, the existence of this house and the shop for starters. Lucy missed Great Aunt Maud a great deal, she just felt sad to find out now that she hadn't been able to confide in her and Ben, it was almost as if she had been living a double life.

Lucy turned the pages and found Frank as a boy, Frank and Janet's wedding and even the photograph Maud took of her and Ben, the first night he brought her home. On the final page was a photo of Frank and another man, the other man looked very similar to Frank, and when she looked she could actually see quite a likeness to Ben. Lucy ran her hand over the photograph absentmindedly. 'Wait what was that?' When Lucy looked more closely, she could see that the photo had been torn in two, and an attempt had been made to stick it back together again from the rear. 'What happened to the photograph?' Lucy wondered, 'Had it been torn by accident?' But somehow she doubted that, as the tear ran quite neatly between Frank and the other man, almost as if the perpetrator of the damage was trying to rip one of them from the picture. Was it Frank or the mystery man that they had been trying to remove? Suddenly, Lucy felt like she wasn't alone. A dark shadow appeared on the wall in front of her. Lucy span around in shock but there was no one there, just rows and rows of neatly stacked books on the bookcase. She jumped, 'what was that scratching noise?' Lucy followed the sound and ripped open the door of the study and there was Morph wagging his tail furiously.

"Oh hello Morph, are you lonely with Jake and Emily out?" She said softly, bending down to pick him up. She was secretly quite glad to see him, she was still feeling quite uneasy from when she saw the shadow a few minutes ago. Morph settled across Lucy's feet contentedly, as she put the photo album to one side and started to sort through the next pile of papers from the filing cabinet. The study was so dark and didn't have the large windows that all of the other rooms in the house had. These windows were much narrower, with wicker blinds, which made the place a lot darker than it should. There was no main ceiling lighting either, which struck Lucy as very strange. The light itself was there, but there didn't appear to be a switch on the wall anywhere, the only lighting in the room came from two matching brass wall lights and a large light on the desk itself. Lucy shuddered and immediately reprimanded herself for being so silly, what was the matter with her? She wasn't afraid of the dark. She glanced down to Morph who was curled up, sleeping happily at her feet and smiled.

As Lucy looked back up again, she froze in horror. There, on the wall was a shadow, and this time she could clearly see the outline of a head, a face. In that split second, Morph leapt up and began growling and barking at the bookcase behind her. Lucy quickly turned, but there was nothing there. Her heart hammering in her chest, she grabbed Morph and fled from the room, meeting Tom coming up the stairs as she was coming down. "Lucy whatever's the matter?" Cried Tom, seeing her distressed state. Morph was still growling and looking over Lucy's shoulder. "There was a shadow and a face in the study up there" Lucy gasped "Someone's up there?" Asked Tom, starting to go back up the stairs. "No, they're gone" garbled Lucy "Who's gone?" Asked Tom confused. "I don't know, I don't know" said Lucy. "I heard Morph barking, that's why I was coming to see what the matter was" said Tom gravely. Tom led Lucy into the living room and sat her down at the dining table. He listened patiently while she explained what had happened. "How very odd" said Tom "I don't scare easily Tom, but I am sure there was someone in that room with me, and you heard Morph barking" said Lucy. "I'm going to take a look" Tom insisted. "Take Morph with you, please Tom, I'd be happier if you did" Lucy stammered.

Tom left the room with Morph trotting obediently by his side and returned a few minutes later. "There's no one in there Lucy, and Morph rolled over to have his tummy tickled on the rug inside the door. There was no barking this time" Tom said. "I don't understand it, maybe it was Phyllis?" Lucy said hopefully. "I've just passed Phyllis in the hallway and Jeff has gone into town. Phyllis said she has not been up there this morning" Tom said. "Oh" said Lucy despondently. "Must have been a trick of the light, but I can report this if you think it is best Lucy" Tom said. "No, no, no, I don't want to bother DCI Fields with this. Like you said, it must have been a trick of the light" said Lucy, although deep down she still wasn't so sure. "Excuse me" said Tom, as his mobile began to ring in this pocket. "Hello...yes it is...yeah, she's right here with me...oh my god, is she okay?... We'll be right there" said Tom, in a horrified voice. "What is it Tom? What's happened?" Cried Lucy jumping up. "That was Miss Timms from the art club. She said a woman has turned up there, posing as you, and tried to abduct Emily. She said to assure you that Emily is fine and that she would explain when we get there" said Tom, rushing to the door. "Oh my god!" Exclaimed Lucy, chasing after him.

CHAPTER 5

THE PLOT THICKENS

When they arrived at the school where the art club was held during the holidays, there was a police car across the entrance. Paul was standing by the gate, he said something to the officer in the car and he moved forward whilst Paul waved them through. DCI Fields was waiting at the reception when Lucy, Tom and Paul rushed in. "What on earth happened?" Cried Lucy and Tom at once. "Please come and take a seat in here" said DCI Fields, opening the door to the room to his left. "No, I'm sorry, I need to see Jake and Emily first. I need to know they are okay" insisted Lucy. "Of course, they're just across here" said DCI Fields crossing the corridor and opening the door to another room. "Mummy!" Cried Jake and Emily running to her. Lucy fell to her knees, throwing her arms around them both and crying as if her heart would break. She was just so relieved to see them both safe. "Would you two like to keep playing in here with Amira while mummy and I have a little chat?" Asked DCI Fields brightly. Both children nodded eagerly, "Don't worry mummy, I'll look after Emily" said Jake solemnly. Lucy gave them both a reassuring smile, she didn't dare speak for fear of breaking down again.

Miss Timms was waiting for them back inside the first room. "Mrs Reid, I'm so sorry you have been put through this" she said when Lucy entered. "Hello Miss Timms, please tell me what on earth happened" said Lucy. "A lady turned up at reception, about an hour ago, saying she was you and that Emily had a toothache and she was taking her to the dentist. Emily had complained of a toothache when she arrived this morning, so staff didn't think anything of it. When this woman arrived

Miss Hargreaves got Emily from the classroom she was in, but she was crying as her tooth was starting to hurt more, so wasn't really taking any notice of what was going on" said Miss Timms. "Why didn't someone call us if Emily was upset?" Asked Lucy. "We tried to but there was no answer, the woman arrived before we had chance to try any of the other mobiles you had provided us with" replied Miss Timms. "My mobile! I must have left it in the study" said Lucy, clasping her hand over her mouth. "Carry on Miss Timms" DCI Fields said gently. "Just as Miss Hargreaves and Emily reached the woman, Jake came out of the classroom wanting to go to the toilet, and seeing Emily, he wanted to know where she was going. Miss Hargreaves told him that Emily was going to the dentist with mummy and Jake started shouting "That's not my mummy!" and pulled Emily away from Miss Hargreaves and the woman. Emily had calmed down a little by now, and realising it wasn't you started screaming and clung to Jake for all she was worth. The woman turned and ran, we did go after her, but she must have got into a waiting car" finished Miss Timms.

Lucy could not believe what she was hearing, all these things that had been happening, she felt sick, realising that if Jake hadn't chosen then to go to the toilet, she could have lost Emily too. "Lucy, I want you to see the CCTV footage of this woman" said DCI Fields, pressing the control in his hand. "Well I never" said Tom in shock. "She looks just like me, in fact, looking at her, if you didn't know any better you would think it was me." Said Lucy, unable to mask the horror in her voice. "The woman has clearly gone to a lot of trouble to make herself look like you" said DCI Fields. "She certainly has" said Tom, still unable to believe his eyes. "Miss Hargreaves said the woman didn't speak much, I'm assuming that this was in the hope that with Emily being so young, she wouldn't look any further than her initial appearance" said DCI Fields. "How can someone plan to do this and take a child from their family?" Said Lucy hopelessly. "I've no idea, but they do" said Tom. "What we did notice though," said the DCI, enlarging the image of the woman on the screen. "A butterfly" gasped Lucy, seeing what looked like a tiny tattoo behind the woman's right earlobe. "That's a very distinctive mark, and in my opinion, very silly to leave it visible" said DCI Fields. "How will that help though?" Asked Lucy. "It may not unless we catch her, but the station are running it through our computer to see if we have anyone listed with that sort of distinguishing mark on our database." Said DCI Fields, "What puzzles me is how this woman knew that Emily had a toothache" said Tom. "I think I may be able to help there" said Miss Timms. "How's that?" Asked Lucy, raising an eyebrow. "When Miss Bentley brought Jake and Emily in this morning, she told Emily's teacher and unfortunately a little boy in her class overheard and went running around the playground shouting out that Emily had a toothache in a bid to try and tease her. There were lots of people about at that time, anyone could have overheard" said Miss Timms. "I'd like to view this morning's CCTV footage as well if I may please Miss Timms" said DCI Fields. "Of course" she replied, nodding.

"I don't know if I should be asking this now Mrs Reid, but the children have settled in so well over the last couple of days. Will you be letting them come back tomorrow?" Asked Miss Timms apprehensively. "Oh no, I don't think so" said Lucy shaking her head. "If I may be as bold as to suggest you may reconsider and let the children return tomorrow" said DCI Fields. "What?!" Gasped Lucy incredulously "If, and this is still if, anyone is watching your movements, it may be best to carry on as normal to not arouse any suspicion" said DCI Fields. "I can't put the children at risk" said Lucy firmly. "No, of course not, and I wouldn't expect you to" said DCI Fields. "So what is it you're proposing?" Asked Tom. "I'm suggesting that with Miss Timms' agreement, Amira joins the class as an assistant and that Paul remains on the premises, maybe in this room, the entire time the children are here" said DCI Fields. "I'd be happy with that" said Miss Timms. "Thank you" said the DCI. "We would, of course, require both Amira and Mr Henson to have the required DBS disclosures" said Miss Timms. "Miss Bentley has that anyway" said Lucy "Mr Henson was telling me he works with children, so I imagine he may have that already" said DCI Fields. "How do you feel about this Lucy?" Asked Tom. "I can't say I'm happy, but I want these people caught, and as long as my children are safe I will agree" said Lucy with a frown. "If you are finished with us for now, I would like to get Lucy and the children home, if that's okay" said Tom. "Of course, I shall be in touch soon Mrs Reid" said the DCI. "Thank you" said Lucy, getting up to go and get her children. Jake, Emily, Amira and Paul were all engrossed in drawing pictures when Lucy and Tom walked in, princesses for Emily and Amira, and of course footballers for Jake and Paul. "Look at our drawings mummy!" Said Jake proudly.

"Woah they're fantastic! Let's take them home to show Morph" said Lucy as brightly as she could.

As Tom opened the front door when they got home, Jake and Emily ran past him calling "Morph! Morph!" "Hello Phyllis" said Lucy, as she walked into the kitchen. Phyllis was sitting at the table with her head in her hands and jumped up upon seeing Lucy. "Oh I've been so worried! How's Emily?" She cried. "Emily's fine thankfully" said Lucy. "Sit down Phyllis, while I make a cup of tea, and Lucy can tell you everything" said Tom, coming into the kitchen. As Lucy started to explain, Jake and Emily ran in still calling for Morph. "Mummy, Morph's not here!" Said Jake in a very upset voice. "Of course he is, he must be hiding. I'll help you look" said Tom with a laugh. "Have you seen Morph, Phyllis?" Said Lucy. "No I haven't seen him at all, I thought you must have taken him with you" said Phyllis. Tom returned with Jake and Emily ten minutes later, "They're right Lucy, I don't think he's in the house" said Tom worriedly. Emily started to cry, "I want Morph!" "I know darling, we'll find him" said Lucy reassuringly. "Maybe he is in the garden" said Tom. "Yes maybe, I've not been out there today" added Phyllis. Tom, Jake and Emily checked the garden, but still nothing until Tom heard a faint muffled barking as they passed the edge of the vegetable patch. Tom listened for a second, it seemed to be coming from the old rundown shed on the other side of the tomato plants. "You two wait here for a minute" Tom said, as he carefully made his way around the vegetables. He opened the shed door, and out scampered Morph.

"Morph!" Cried Jake and Emily. "How did you get in there little fella?" Said Tom picking him up. 'Morph's paws are slightly grazed from where he had been scratching at the door, and he could probably do with a drink, but other than that he doesn't seem too much the worse for wear' Tom thought, relieved. "Oh thank heavens, where was he?" Said Jeff, who had been helping to look for Morph. Jeff had heard them all calling for him and had been checking the fields. "He was in the old shed by the veg patch" said Tom. "Oh no, Phyllis must have shut him in there earlier by mistake" said Jeff. "No, I don't think so. She said she hasn't seen Morph today, and hasn't been out in the garden" said Tom. Jeff grabbed Tom's arm to stop him walking for a moment, and Tom looked at him in surprise. "Tom, Phyllis was out here, not long after I got back from town earlier, and I saw her coming out of that shed" said Jeff quietly. "Was she?" Said Tom, raising an eyebrow. "Yes, I saw her coming down the stairs when I came through the door, and Morph was asleep under the hall table at that point. Then at the shed, about 20 minutes later" said Jeff. "Okay, thank you for telling me Jeff, and thank you for helping us look for Morph" said Tom. "Oh you've found him!" Clapped Phyllis, as they came through the back door. "Where on earth was he?" Said Lucy, taking Morph to give him a cuddle. "He was in the shed by the vegetable patch" said Tom "The shed? How on earth did he get in there? Isn't that only used for storing the machinery we don't use anymore?" said Lucy. "Yes it is" said Tom, sneaking a fleeting glance at Phyllis. "No, that's right Lucy, no one ever goes near there apart from Jeff. He must have locked poor Morph in when he went in there for something" said Phyllis. "Yes, that must have been what happened" said Tom, looking directly at Phyllis. "Well at least he's safe, that's all that matters" said Lucy. "Let's take him to find Amira, she'll be so relieved to see him" said Tom.

Lucy, Tom, Amira and Paul all sat together on the patio, laughing at the antics of Jake, Emily and Morph, racing around together on the lawn. "Jeff, come and take a seat" said Lucy, seeing him standing in the doorway. "I'll go and get us some cold drinks, what's everyone having?" Said Tom. "No, you stay there, I'll get them. Is everyone okay with lemonade?" Asked Jeff. "Yes please" they all chorused. As Jeff walked into the kitchen, he could hear Phyllis talking in a hushed voice. "No, I told you not the children, do you never listen? We've come this far and you could have spoilt it with your stupidity" she hissed. Jeff followed her voice across the kitchen to the utility room, where Phyllis was stood just inside the door with her back to him on a mobile phone. She clearly hadn't heard him come in. "Now don't give me reason to ring you again, understand?" Said Phyllis, snapping the mobile phone shut. Jeff darted back across the kitchen and took the lemonade from the fridge, making a decided effort to be heard. "Oh hello Jeff, let me do that for you dear" said Phyllis. "No no, I've got it. You do enough for us already" smiled Jeff. "Okay, if you're sure" said Phyllis. Jeff poured everyone a glass of cool lemonade and sat back in his chair watching Jake and Emily play. No matter how much he tried, he couldn't come up with a feasible explanation for what he had heard. He didn't want to worry Lucy, so decided to speak to Tom the first chance he got. That chance came later that evening when Tom was polishing his car, whilst Lucy, Amira and Paul watched a DVD with Jake and Emily.

"Tom, can I speak to you?" Said Jeff. "Yes of course you can mate" Tom replied. Just at that moment, Phyllis walked round the side of the house and came over to join them. "What are you two boys doing on this lovely evening?" She said, smiling across the car bonnet at Tom, then turning to Jeff and giving him a cold stare. "Nothing apart from giving this old car a clean" laughed Tom, not looking up from his polishing. "Clean Tom? You could eat your dinner off of it" said Phyllis with a chuckle. "Tom, I'm going to take a walk to the off-licence as it is a nice night, to get the kids some sweets. I wondered if you wanted to join me and maybe have a chat?" Said Jeff. "Yes of course, just give me a second to put this away" replied Tom, gesturing to the cleaning materials. "I'll do that for you" said Phyllis. "Oh Phyllis, you are a star" said Tom, giving her a kiss on the cheek. Tom and Jeff chatted about football as they walked down the drive together. Jeff turned back towards the house just as he pressed the code to get out of the electronic gate, Phyllis was standing on the steps on a mobile phone, watching them intently.

As Jeff walked further from the house, he started to feel relaxed enough to talk. "Tom, what do you really think happened with Morph getting locked in the shed today? Lucy told me that Phyllis said I must have done it, but I've not used that shed for months" Jeff said. "Yeah I know mate, that one's been puzzling me too" Tom replied. "I don't understand why Phyllis lied about seeing Morph and about being in the garden, either" said Jeff. "Hmm, I suppose she just forgot and maybe Morph ran in the shed when she wasn't looking and she shut him in by mistake" Tom offered. "Oh I don't know, Morph doesn't seem to like her, so I can't see that he would be walking around the garden with her willingly" said Jeff, his voice full of doubt. "Willingly? What are you trying to say Jeff?" Tom asked. "To be honest I really don't know" said Jeff. "I do agree something doesn't quite add up" said Tom thoughtfully. "Then earlier, when I went to get the lemonade, Phyllis was on her mobile phone in the utility room. She hadn't heard me come in" said Jeff. "Right..." said Tom, eyeing Jeff's anxious face. "Well, she sounded very cross at having to ring the person, angry in fact" said Jeff, pausing for a moment to check the road behind them, to walk around a black Land Rover that was parked with two wheels on the pavement. "No consideration" grumbled Tom.

As Tom and Jeff stepped back onto the pavement, the car started up behind them. Jeff hadn't even realised there was anyone in it. The car sat there for a few seconds before moving off, suddenly there was screech of tyres and Tom and Jeff turned to see the car speeding towards them. "Oh my god!" Shouted Tom as he was tossed into the air, landing heavily in the ditch where the pavement ran out. Tom struggled to his feet, he ached, but seemed to be in one piece. "Jeff!" He said aloud, catching sight of him laying face down in the road. "Oh my god Jeff!" Tom cried, scrambling out of the ditch to reach him. Jeff didn't seem to be moving, but still had a faint pulse. "Thank god!" Said Tom. Jeff's right leg appeared to be trapped underneath him, and there was blood coming from a very large cut on his head. Tom fished around in his pocket for his mobile and punched in 999. "Operator, which service do you require?" Said a female voice. "Ambulance and the police, my friend has been run over" said Tom frantically. The operator took the necessary details and promised help would be on its way. "Urghh…" groaned Jeff. "I'm here Jeff, stay still mate, help's on it's way" said Tom, bending down by Jeff's side. "Phyllis…keep away…kids" Jeff said in a strained voice, before he lapsed back into unconsciousness. "Hang on in there" Tom said to Jeff's still figure. He didn't know if he could hear him, but decided to carry on chatting away anyway. Tom chattered on about just about anything, football, gardening, TV, Jake, Emily, he just hoped that Jeff could hear.

"Thank god for that, help's here Jeff" he said. The ambulance screeched to a halt and the paramedics leapt out and ran over. "What's his name?" Said the older of the two men. "This is Jeff, he's 32, he was hit by a Land Rover in a hit and run" said Tom. "Was he alone?" Asked the other paramedic. "No, we were walking to the shop. There was a car parked on the pavement, we had to walk round it, we didn't even realise there was anyone in it, but once we passed it, it just came at us" said Tom, starting to shake. A police officer had now joined them, whilst another blocked the road. "Did you get a look at the driver, or the number plate?" Asked the policeman. "No, we just thought it was a parked car, we had no reason to look at the number plate, and by the time we realised it was going to hit us it was too late" said Tom. "We're going to get your friend off to hospital, and I think you should let us take a look at you too" said the first paramedic. "Honestly, I'm okay, but I will come after I have gone home to let everyone else know what is happening, and I'll bring Jeff a few things" said Tom. "You're in no fit state to be walking sir, especially alone" said the policeman. At that moment a car pulled up and DCI Fields got out. "Tom, I've just heard. Are you okay? How's Jeff?" He asked. "I'm okay thank you, but as for Jeff he looks in a pretty bad way" said Tom, running a hand distractedly through his hair. "Let me have a word with the paramedics and I'll be back with you. Please take a seat in my car with DS Lowe" he said, gesturing to the blonde police sergeant with him, to come and get Tom.

A few seconds later, the ambulance pulled away, although there was no sirens this time, it was still travelling fairly rapidly up the lane. DCI Fields spoke briefly with the police officer who had been speaking to Tom and then got back in the car. "Tom I'm going to take you home to do the things you need to do, then I will run you to Blackville General, where they have taken Jeff. Does he have any family do you know?" Said DCI Fields. "He's never spoken of any" said Tom. "When you're feeling up to it I would like you to tell me exactly what you remember please" said the DCI. "Yes of course, but I'd like to let Lucy know what is happening please, and I'd like to get to the hospital, so Jeff has a familiar face there when he comes round" said Tom. "You take your time" said DCI Fields with a sympathetic smile. "If it's all the same to you, would you mind if I go in alone please. This will be a big enough shock to everyone as it is without me walking in with the police." Said Tom. "That's fine, we understand and we will wait in the car" the DCI replied. When Tom walked in, Phyllis had joined Lucy and the others in the living room, all watching a DVD. "Hello, you've been a while. Where's Jeff?" Said Phyllis chirpily. Ignoring her question, Tom turned to Jake and Emily. "Do you two think you could do me a very big favour?" He said. "What's that?" Asked Jake. "Oh I don't know, maybe I shouldn't ask you, as this is normally only a job for big boys and girls" said Tom. "I'm a big girl!" Said Emily, sitting up straight."Oh I know you are" said Tom, ruffling her hair. "What is it we have to do Tom?" Asked Jake excitedly. "Do you think you could take Morph into the kitchen and feed him please? Just one scoop. But here's the very important bit, could you stay there with him until he's eaten it?" Said Tom. "We can do that" said

Jake. "We can do that" said Emily, echoing her brother. "Morph's been fed" said Phyllis. "He can have some more" said Tom forcefully.

"Come on Morph" said Jake, and taking Emily's hand, off they went. "What's wrong Tom? And where's Jeff?" Said Lucy. "There's been an accident. Jeff and I were hit by a car on purpose. It started up and drove right at us, hitting us from behind." Blurted Tom. "Oh my god! Sit down Tom, are you okay?" Said Lucy. "Do you need me to get you anything?" Asked Amira, rushing over to him. "No thank you, I'm fine…Jeff looked rough though, he was unconscious. They've taken him to hospital" said Tom. "He isn't dead is he?" Asked Phyllis, her eyes wide. "No Phyllis, thankfully he isn't dead" said Tom, looking her straight in the eyes. "We must get to the hospital, I'll drive you" said Paul. "If you and Amira want to go I'll gladly watch the children" offered Phyllis. "No, no thank you" said Tom a little sharply, he couldn't get what Jeff had been trying to say out of his head. "I really don't mind" said Phyllis. "No honestly, it is very kind of you all, but DCI Fields is waiting outside to take us to the hospital. Will you come though Lucy?" Asked Tom, regaining his composure. "Yes of course. Will you put the children to bed Amira, please?" Asked Lucy "You know I will, and please give Jeff our love" said Amira. "I need to pack Jeff a few things" said Tom. "I'll go and do that now" said Paul. "The police are asking about any family, but I've told them I don't know of any" Tom said. "All the more reason we should be there for him" said Lucy. "I may just give Mrs Armstrong a ring, incase Jeff does have any relatives anywhere that we don't know about. I was just thinking, she may know more than we do" said Tom. "Yeah, that's a good idea" said Lucy. "I'll go and sort the children out" said Amira.

Tom took the diary from the desk drawer and found Mrs Armstrong's contact number at her sister's. "Hello?" He heard her voice. "Hello Mrs Armstrong, it's Tom" he said. "Oh hi Tom, is everything okay?" She said, obviously surprised to hear from him. "No, I'm afraid it's not. There's been an accident, Jeff is in a bad way, he's in hospital." Said Tom as gently as he could, he knew Mrs Armstrong had a soft spot for Jeff, always saying he was like a son to her. "Oh no! What happened? How is he?" Cried Mrs Armstrong. "We don't know" said Tom, filling her in briefly on what had occurred. "Oh Tom, you were involved as well? How are you feeling? Shouldn't you be in hospital as well?" She asked, concerned. "No

I'm fine, honestly. We are just off to see Jeff now, but wondered if you knew if he had any family that we should contact, as I've never heard him speak of any" Tom said. "Yes he does, Jeff's father lives in Canada. He took early retirement there a few years ago. Bruce Fisher is an ex-military serviceman and a real gentleman. Jeff's been saving all he can to get the money together to go and see his dad, as I know he misses him terribly" finished Mrs Armstrong. "Oh, he's never mentioned him" said Tom. "I have his number, would you like me to call him?" Asked Mrs Armstrong. "If you could I'd appreciate it, and give him my number" said Tom. "I feel awful not being able to come and see Jeff, my sister still needs me and her husband isn't allowed back on his feet again yet, but please give him my love" said Mrs Armstrong. "He will understand, and of course I will" Tom reassured her. "Okay, I'll let you go. But will you promise me something?" Said Mrs Armstrong. "Yes?" Said Tom. "Keep me informed on how Jeff is please" she said. "Of course," Tom replied, "that goes without saying". Tom said goodbye to Mrs Armstrong and took the small holdall that Paul had packed for Jeff, and went outside to the car where DCI Fields was waiting for them.

"Hello Lucy" said DCI Fields. "Hello" she replied quietly. DCI Fields introduced Lucy to DS Lowe and they were soon on their way. "My colleague at the hospital said they have taken Jeff into surgery and the doctors won't tell him anymore." Said DCI Fields. "Oh god, poor Jeff" said Lucy worriedly. Tom told DCI Fields what had happened earlier that evening, right up to what Jeff had said to him after the accident. "Why would Jeff want you to keep the children away from Phyllis?" Said Lucy, puzzled. "I really don't know" Tom replied. DCI Fields was silent for a moment looking deep in thought, "What do you know about Mrs Snow?" He asked. "Well nothing really apart from she turned up at our house unexpectedly for the housekeeper's position" said Lucy. "Unexpectedly?" Asked the DCI, "Yeah, she said she had heard Mrs Armstrong discussing we would be needing a temporary housekeeper when she was in the village butcher's shop" said Lucy "We had been sent three rather disastrous applicants from the agency, and Phyllis was like a breath of fresh air after those" said Tom. "Yeah, I'm sure she was. Did she have any references?" Asked DCI Fields. "Yes, they were exemplary" said Lucy. "Lucy did check them all out and all were full of praise for her, apart from her last employer, who had apparently moved overseas." Said Tom. "I see. Did Mrs Snow have much luggage? As I am assuming she would have had everything transferred to Hilltop Manor if her employer had moved abroad." DCI Fields asked. "Well, no she didn't, very little in fact" said Lucy. "She said she was waiting for it to arrive" said Tom.

"What about the agency you used for the housekeeper post? What did they say about sending you so many unsuitable applicants?" Asked DCI Fields. "When I rang to complain the young girl didn't seem to know much about it. She said she couldn't seem to find any record and would get her manager to call later that day" said Tom. "Which she didn't" added Lucy. "Which agency did you use?" Asked DS Lowe. "Err, Poppyfields Employment Agency, I believe they were called" said Tom. "Poppyfields have provided cover at the station a few times I think, and their representatives have always seemed very competent" said DS Lowe. "That's just what I was thinking, and it has been established years" added DCI Fields. "Lucy would you be so good as to get together all of the details you have on Phyllis please? Name, date of birth, employment record, just about anything you have" said DCI Fields. "Yes of course, I'll do that for you first thing tomorrow" Lucy said. "Thank you. Now this is Blackville General, let's go and see how Jeff is" said DCI Fields, as DS Lowe eased the car into a parking space. As Tom took his mobile from his pocket to switch it off, it rang. "Hello Tom, it's Margaret Armstrong" said the caller. "Hello" said Tom. "I just wanted to let you know I have spoken to Jeff's father. He is understandably very upset. He is booked on a flight first thing tomorrow, he's also on standby for any cancellations tonight. I've given him the number at Hilltop Manor and also your mobile. I do hope that was alright" said Mrs Armstrong. "Of course it was and thank you so much for all of your help. We've just got to the hospital and will let you know as soon as there is any news. We know that Jeff's in surgery, but that's all for now" said Tom. "Thank you, I'd appreciate that. Goodbye" said Mrs Armstrong, and the line went dead.

Tom switched his phone off and put it back in his pocket, he told Lucy and DCI Fields that Jeff's dad was on his way. DS Lowe had stayed in the car to make some phone calls. Just as they reached the hospital doors, she came running after them, calling DCI Fields' name. "I've just heard a black Land Rover was found abandoned a mile from the accident site. It's being finger printed as we speak" she said. "Have they run a PNC Check on the owner?" Asked the DCI. "Yes sir, it's registered to a local address, to a Pearl White who reported it missing about 10 days ago" said DS Lowe. "Have they been to see Mrs White yet as she's local?" Asked DCI Fields. "Yes sir, Mrs White is housebound at the moment with a broken leg and she declared the car SORN three weeks ago" said DS Lowe. "Any news on Poppyfields?" asked the DCI. "Not yet, we have a number for Donna Josephs, the owner, on the station files from when we have used the agency before, but the phone's on answer phone. A message has been left and we are waiting for a reply" said DS Lowe. "Okay, keep me informed please" said DCI Fields. Jeff was still in theatre when they arrived at his ward. The nurse at the desk showed them to a side room and said she would let them know when there is any news. Tom went to get some coffees from the machine in the main waiting area, whilst DCI Fields went to find the officer that came in with Jeff. Lucy sat back in the huge armchair, shut her eyes and sighed heavily. How can people's lives change so much in a few short days? Hours even? She thought of poor Frank and Janet, their bodies still hadn't been found, Ben saw that as good news, something positive to hang on to. Ben, oh where was he? There had been no more sightings of him since the airfield. She knew that Ben would never leave her and the children, not willingly. She could see the doubt in others' eyes, but she and Ben were happy together. She wished Ben was here so much, he would know what to do, because she didn't, she was so confused. Lucy thought of the house, the shop, she knew she was so lucky to be so well provided for, but she certainly didn't feel very lucky right now.

Her mind darted back to when someone had tried to run Nick and Tom down, she knew the police thought that they were after Nick, but she wasn't so sure, after someone had actually hit Tom this time when he was out with Jeff. 'Oh my god Jeff, he is such a lovely guy, so sweet natured and here he is fighting for his life'. Then there was Phyllis, why had she lied about seeing Morph and being out in the garden, and what had Jeff been trying to tell Tom? There was the incident with the scaffold lorry and someone cutting the break hoses on Tom's car, were they trying to hurt her, or was it really someone out to get Tom and she just got in the way? Then Lucy thought about Jake and Emily, and her eyes filled with tears. Poor innocent Emily, why would someone try to take her? Then there was Jake, her brave little boy who would do anything for the little sister he adored. "Lucy, Lucy, Jeff's out of theatre. The nurse said the doctor will see us soon" said Tom, softly. "Oh I'm sorry, what time is it?" Stammered Lucy. "Just after 10, you fell asleep" Tom said smiling. "Oh did I? I didn't realise. I've not been sleeping well recently" Lucy said. "Please don't apologise" said Tom.

Lucy hadn't noticed DCI Fields and DS Lowe sitting quietly in the corner of the room, seeing she was awake DCI Fields came and sat next to her. "Lucy, the station have received a call back from Donna Josephs, the owner of Poppyfields and she didn't send the housekeepers to you…" said the DCI. "Didn't send them? I don't understand" said Lucy puzzled. "Miss Josephs said she received a call from a Mrs Reid just before she closed the previous evening, and that's why she thought it was an old message to call you when she found it on her desk the afternoon Phyllis arrived" finished DCI Fields. "Oh my god, so you're saying Phyllis' arrival was a set up?" Said Tom shocked. "Yes it certainly seems so, what we have to work out is why Mrs Snow wanted into Hilltop Manor so badly." Said the DCI.

"We've also had a report back from the officers at the accident scene and there is no evidence of any braking, so whoever was driving appears to have made no effort to stop" said DS Lowe. "I assume there was no joy with any prints?" Asked Tom. "No, nothing" said the DS, shaking her head. "This is terrible" said Lucy, putting her head in her hands. "Lucy, in light of this new evidence it is even more vital that I have all the details you may have on Phyllis Snow please" said DCI Fields. "Yes of course, but I'm not too sure I like that woman being in my home with my children still. Are you not even going to speak to her?" Said Lucy, looking at DCI Fields questioningly. "No not at the minute, not until I have had chance to check everything out. I'd rather you tried to carry on as normal where Mrs Snow is concerned please, so she doesn't become suspicious. I will arrange for everyone coming in or out of Hilltop Manor to be kept an eye on" said DCI Fields. "Kept an eye on?" Asked Lucy raising an eyebrow. "Yes, I'll have officers watching, but from a distance. We don't want Mrs Snow, or anyone else for that matter knowing we are onto them" said the DCI.

CHAPTER 6

THE BUTTERFLY TATTOO

Suddenly the door opened and a tall, slim man came in. "Hello, I am Jeff's doctor, Mr Satoomi" he said, shaking each of their hands in turn. "How is he, doctor?" Asked Lucy. "Jeff is very lucky to be here" said Mr Satoomi. "He took the brunt of the impact" said Tom. "Jeff has a broken leg, four broken ribs, a fractured collarbone and there was evidence of bleeding on his brain. Jeff's brain was swelling and that is why we needed to operate to relieve some of the pressure. We've induced a comatose state to allow Jeff's brain time to heal. The next 12 hours are of paramount importance, if all vital signs after that are good and the swelling is reducing, we will gradually bring Jeff round, we won't know the full extent though of any damage until he regains consciousness" said Mr Satoomi. "Dear god that poor bloke" sighed Tom. "I'm sorry I can not give you any better news, but my advice for now would be to go home and get some rest as there's nothing you can do for Jeff at the moment" said the doctor kindly. "Thank you" said Tom. "Please try to get some rest, Jeff will need you to be strong when he wakes" said Mr Satoomi before he left the room. "This is PC Regan" said DCI Fields, as a uniformed police officer came in. "Hello" said Lucy and Tom together. "PC Regan will be staying with Jeff overnight so he won't be alone" said the DCI. "A police guard?" Said Lucy. "For the moment I'd rather Jeff had someone with him" said DCI Fields. "Come on Lucy, let's get you home" said Tom, gently taking her arm. "Wait, can we see Jeff for a moment before we go?" Said Lucy. "Hang on, let me see if I can catch up with the doctor" said DS Lowe hurrying off.

She returned with the nurse that had showed them in originally. "Mr

Satoomi said just a moment with Jeff please" she said. "Yes of course" said Lucy, following her to where Jeff lay in the room down the corridor. PC Regan had already taken up his post, sat on a chair just outside the door. When Lucy went in, Jeff looked like he was sleeping, the only evidence of any problems were the scratches on the right-hand side of his face and the crisp white bandage that curled itself around his head. Lucy walked over to Jeff's bed and took his hand, a lone tear escaping down her cheek. "Be strong Jeff, we will find out who did this to you. Get better soon, we want you home with us where you belong" she whispered. Lucy laid Jeff's hand gently back down on the bed and left the room, silently closing the door behind her. As they all walked back to the car, Tom turned his mobile phone back on and immediately received an alert telling him he had a voicemail. Tom dialled the number and then listened to the message. "Hello Tom, this is Bruce Fisher, Jeff's father. I just wanted to let you know I have a cancellation flight tonight, I should be with you, all going well, by lunch time tomorrow" said a well spoken male voice. "Jeff's father has managed to get a flight tonight, he should be with us by lunchtime tomorrow" he told everyone. "That's good, Jeff will need his dad" said Lucy. Nothing was said on the way home, it seemed all of the cars occupants realised that no words were good enough.

As they pulled up at the front steps of Hilltop Manor, DCI Fields turned round to Lucy in the back seat, as Tom got out. "Remember Lucy, try to act normally to Phyllis. We don't want her getting even the slightest inclination that anything is wrong. Get the documents to Paul please, and he'll see that the information on them reaches me" said DCI Fields. "Okay," said Lucy, "Goodnight" When Lucy and Tom opened the door, Phyllis came rushing out of the living room. "How's poor Jeff?" She cried. "Jeff is in a coma" said Tom, looking Phyllis straight in the eye once more. "Oh the poor love, I can't believe this has happened. How can someone run someone over and then drive off without stopping? It's so cold and callous" said Phyllis. "Isn't it" said Tom drily. Phyllis wittered on, seemingly oblivious to Tom's somewhat curt answers. "I've made you some sandwiches, they're in the fridge, and the kettle's not long boiled. I'm going to get off to bed if that's okay with you Lucy?" Said Phyllis. "Yes of course, goodnight Phyllis" said Lucy. "Goodnight dears, I'll say a prayer for Jeff" smiled Phyllis sympathetically. Tom walked off into the living room, not trusting himself to say a word. "Tom, you really must be careful how you are with Phyllis, we don't know how she is involved yet" said Lucy. "Hmm, we know she is involved Lucy and that's enough for me. But you're right, I will watch what I say" said Tom. Lucy and Tom decided they were quite peckish after all and that they would have the sandwiches and tea that Phyllis left.

After they had eaten, Lucy looked in on the children to kiss them both goodnight. As she opened Jake and Emily's bedroom door, a small furry canine figure jumped from the bed and darted into his dog bed. Lucy couldn't help but laugh, "Haha, too slow Morph, I saw you" she whispered. Lucy went over to take a look at Morph's leg, it clearly didn't seem to be bothering him. She picked him up and cuddled him to her whilst he frantically licked her face, he really was a sweet little thing. She gently placed him on the bed between Jake and Emily. "Go on little fella" she said, giving his soft head a stroke. Morph gazed up at her through big chocolate brown eyes before snuggling down with a sigh. Lucy smiled as she closed the door gently. It took her a long while that night to get to sleep, she had a lot of things on her mind, all the happenings of the last few days, there was so much to take in. Eventually, she lapsed into a troubled and unsettled sleep.

The next morning she was woken by three little bundles hurling themselves on her bed. 'Three?' She thought confused. 'Jake, Emily, oh and of course Morph' she chuckled. "Come on then you two, let's get you some breakfast" Lucy said. "Two? There's three of us mummy" said Jake with a giggle. "Of course there is, silly me" Lucy laughed. "You mustn't forget Morph" said Jake. "No you're absolutely right. Come on then my three little musketeers" exclaimed Lucy pretending to salute and then march from the room. "What are muskats mummy?" Asked Emily. "Not muskats silly, musketeers are like soldiers. I read about them at the school library" said Jake knowledgeably. "Good morning lovies" said Phyllis. Tom raised an eyebrow to Lucy, he clearly thought that Phyllis was acting like nothing had happened. Once breakfast was finished, Lucy fixed Jake and Emily into Paul's car, she kissed them both goodbye and had to bite back the tears as she waved them off down the drive, she really hadn't wanted to let them go, but she remembered what DCI Fields had said about keeping everything normal and Amira had promised she wouldn't let either of them out of her sight. Lucy reassured herself that Paul would be nearby the whole time too, and it was only for a few hours. As Lucy stood and watched the big drive gates close behind Paul's car, she was blissfully unaware that she was also being watched. Behind the shadows of the wicker blinds of the study, a face looked down at her, taking in everything that was going on. As Lucy went back inside, Tom was just coming off of the phone. "All the hospital would say is that there is no change in Jeff, but I suppose that's a good thing" he said. "Of course it is" Lucy replied, rubbing his arm sympathetically. "Do you want a hand going through the paperwork in the study?" Asked Tom. "Yes please" said Lucy gratefully. She had her suspicions Tom wasn't just offering to be helpful, she also thought he had guessed she didn't want to be up there alone after yesterday.

As Lucy and Tom reached the study door they heard a thud from inside. They stopped and stared at each other, rooted to the spot. "Let me go in first" said Tom. He slowly opened the door and peered inside, then began to laugh. "Just a book Lucy" he said, picking it up. "That's a very large book to just fall Tom. I didn't go near the bookcase the other day and no one should have been in here since" said Lucy nervously. "It's probably been like that for ages and finally fell" Tom reassured her. "Can we sort the paperwork at the kitchen table please?" Said Lucy. "Yes of course if that's what you want" said Tom. Lucy picked up the huge pile of papers and as she turned to walk away her eyes fell on the photo album. She picked that up as well, she wanted to show Tom and the children some of the old photographs. Tom opened the door for Lucy, then closed it behind them. A solitary figure rose from behind the large filing cabinet in the study, breathing a sigh of relief that they hadn't been discovered. That was close, very close indeed. They decided that they would need to be much more careful in future. Lucy spread the papers she had been carrying on the kitchen table and began to sort them into piles, a pile for household repairs, a pile of purchase receipts, a pile for bills. "We may need a miscellaneous pile" said Tom laughing, holding up a supermarket receipt for cat food. "Oh dear, and we don't even have a cat" laughed Lucy. Tom picked up the photo album, "Do you mind if I have a look?" He asked turning to Lucy. "No, of course not" she replied. Tom and Lucy leafed through the old photographs with her telling him about the people she knew in them. As they were about to turn the last page, Lucy and Tom heard a raised female voice coming from the hallway.

Lucy opened the door to find Phyllis ushering a slim brunette woman out of it, but she clearly didn't want to go. "Is there a problem Phyllis?" Lucy asked. Phyllis span round "Oh no, not at all Mrs Reid, Avril was just going" she said. "Avril? Is this your daughter Phyllis?" Asked Tom, who had been watching from the doorway. "Yes, the very same" said Avril, side stepping her mother and striding confidently over to Lucy holding out her hand. "Hello, I'm very pleased to meet you" said Lucy. "I'm very sorry Mrs Reid, Avril has a plane to catch and I did tell her I was working" said Phyllis uncomfortably. "Lots of time yet ma. I told you that" Avril breezed. "Would you like a cup of tea before you go?" Lucy asked, suddenly remembering her manners. "Yeah, sweet" said Avril, squeezing past Tom and taking a seat on the nearest chair at the table. "I'm so sorry Lucy" said Phyllis quietly, reverting back to Lucy rather than Mrs Reid when Avril was out of earshot. Tom poured the tea while they all sat round the table in an uncomfortable silence. "Oooh photos" said Avril, spinning the open photo album across the table towards her. "Avril, they're Lucy's!" Phyllis exclaimed. "She don't mind do ya chick?" Said Avril, barely glancing in Lucy's direction. "No" said Lucy quietly. Just then the phone rang out in the hall and Tom almost ran to answer it, clearly relieved to escape their unexpected guest for a short while. "Lucy, Lucy!" He cried after he had finished the call. "What is it?" She said, rushing out to meet him. "That was the hospital, they said Jeff's vital signs are good and if it's still the same at tea time they're going to start bringing him out of the coma" Tom said happily. "Oh that's wonderful news!" Said Lucy, hugging him. "Err, I've got to go" said Avril, coming hurriedly out of the kitchen clutching her bag. "Oh I thought you had lots of time before you had to be at the airport?" Said Lucy, puzzled. "No no I've made a mistake" said Avril, running towards the front door. Suddenly Morph appeared and bolted across the hallway, straight under Avril's feet, sending her headlong onto the rug. "Oh my god, let me help!" Said Lucy, rushing to her aid. "It's okay" said Avril, struggling to her feet. Lucy picked up Avril's scrunchie that had fallen out of her hair as she fell and stifled a horrified gasp as Avril pulled her hair back up into a ponytail. There, behind her right earlobe was a tiny butterfly. Avril, regaining her composure, kissed her mother on the cheek and left slamming the door behind her.

"Oh I'm so sorry about her" said Phyllis. "Er..it's, it's okay" said Lucy quietly. "Can I get you anything Lucy? You don't look very well" said Phyllis. "No, I'm fine thank you" Lucy insisted. "I'm just going to hoover the living room if that's okay" said Phyllis. "Yes that's fine, we're busy in the kitchen anyway" Tom replied. When Lucy was seated back in the kitchen, Tom closed the door and turned to her, "What's wrong Lucy?" He asked, his voice full of concern. "It was her Tom, it was her. Avril tried to take Emily from the school." Said Lucy. "Avril? But how?" Said Tom shocked. "The butterfly, Avril has a butterfly behind her right ear. I saw it when she put the scrunchie back in her hair just now" said Lucy. "Oh my god, are you sure?" Asked Tom, his eyes wide with alarm. "Yes, positive" nodded Lucy, her face was as white as a sheet. "I'm calling the police, they may be able to pick her up" said Tom, grabbing his mobile from his pocket. Tom put down his phone looking relieved. "They're going to pick her up, they have a unit in the road. I just hope she didn't get a lift outside our main gate" said Tom. There was a buzz from the intercom on the main gate. "Hello?" Said Tom, answering it. "Hi is that Tom?" Said a voice. "Yes it is" he replied. "Tom, it's Bruce Fisher, Jeff's father" said the male voice again. "Hi, Mr Fisher, please come in" said Tom, buzzing to open the gate. Moments later, a taxi drew up at the front steps and a tall, powerfully built man got out. Tom went to help him with his luggage. Bruce Fisher was in his late 50s, his hair greying slightly and ruggedly good looking. "Welcome to Hilltop Manor, I just wish it could have been under happier circumstances" said Lucy. She took an instant liking to Jeff's father, he had the same mischievous twinkling eyes as Jeff and his broad grin actually reached his eyes, which was always a good sign according to what Great Aunt Maud used to say. "Thank you" said Bruce. Tom carried Bruce's cases through to the hallway and placed them beside the stairs. "They aren't in your way there are they? I'll move them just as soon as I find somewhere to stay if that's okay" said Bruce. "Nonsense, you must stay with us. There's Jeff's cottage or you're more than welcome to a room in the house if you'd prefer" Lucy said. "Oh my, that's very kind of you. I think I'd rather stay at Jeff's place please. If it's all the same to you I can keep it clean for him for when he comes home" said Bruce smiling gratefully. "Of course, I'll help you take your cases out there as soon as you've had chance to sit down for five minutes" said Tom.

At that moment Phyllis came out of the living room. "Oh hello" she said, eyeing the stranger curiously. "Phyllis, this is Bruce Fisher, Jeff's father" said Lucy. "Oh you poor poor man, I'm so sorry" said Phyllis, running forward to hug Jeff's father. "Er, thank you" said Bruce, unable to hide his surprise from such an emotional greeting from a woman he had only just set eyes on. "Phyllis I wonder if you'd be good enough to make Bruce some tea and maybe something to eat please?" Asked Lucy. "Yes of course, where are my manners? What would you like?" She asked, letting him go and smoothing down her usually pristine apron. "Tea, white with two sugars would be lovely please and if you have a sandwich that would be very welcome. I don't mind what's in it, I haven't found anything yet that I don't eat" said Bruce with a chuckle. Phyllis scurried off to the kitchen while Lucy and Tom took Bruce into the lounge. "I'd like to ring the hospital if I may. I've heard what happened from the police, they telephoned me just as I got off of the plane." Said Bruce. "Of course you can, but I've spoken to the hospital not long ago and they said Jeff's body is responding well and if all vital signs are still good later today, they will be looking to bring him out of the coma" said Tom. "Oh that's wonderful news, my boy's made of strong stuff" said Bruce proudly. The living room door sprang open and Jake and Emily thundered in. "Mummy!" They cried, leaping onto the sofa next to her. Lucy laughed, hugging them both. "Jake, Emily, this is Mr Fisher, Jeff's dad" she told them. "Hello" they both chorused in unison. "Hi kids" said Bruce with a huge grin. "Mummy said you were going on a big plane" said Jake. "Yes I did, a very big one" Bruce told them. "Wow!" Said Jake "Wow!" Repeated Emily, grinning shyly. "I have some photos on my camera I can show you" said Bruce, taking it from his pocket. "Wow!" Said Jake "Wow!" Repeated Emily grinning.

"I took them at the airport as I was waiting to board. I thought Jeff might like to see them as he's liked planes since he was a small child" said Bruce, turning to Lucy and Tom. He sat Jake and Emily on the sofa next to him and showed Jake which button to push to move to the next photograph. Jake and Emily sat totally transfixed with just the odd appreciative comment on the airplanes size and colours here and there. Lucy smiled, they really were such lovely children. "There we are" said

Phyllis, coming into the room and placing a tray on the coffee table. There was a pot of freshly made tea and a large jug of orange juice. "I brought glasses for the children as well incase they were thirsty" said Phyllis. "Thank you" said Lucy.

"I'll move the tray onto the dining table shall I? As it might be safer when Morph appears" said Phyllis. "Morph?" Said Bruce, looking more than a little puzzled. "Yes, Morph is our dog" said Jake, handing the camera back to Bruce. "Erm, thank you for showing you the pictures" reminded their mother. "Thank you" said Jake and Emily both at the same time. Suddenly there was a clatter of little claws scampering down the hallway and Morph came hurtling through the door. "Morph!" Jake and Emily cried with joy, throwing themselves on the floor to greet him. "This is Morph" said Tom with a laugh. "Lively little fella isn't he?" Grinned Bruce as Morph turned his attention to him, jumping around and licking his hands excitedly. "Shall we take Morph out into the garden?" Said Amira as she entered the room. Amira was introduced to Bruce and then ushered the children, and a still very excitable Morph, out onto the patio. "What lovely kids and a cute dog" drawled Bruce. Lucy hadn't noticed until now that Bruce had that America drawl on some of his words. She hadn't realised that Jeff's father was actually American, until she had been chatting with Mrs Armstrong on the phone earlier, when she had rang to ask how Jeff was. Phyllis had returned with a large tray of sandwiches, pork pies, sausage rolls and fruit cake. "I made enough for everyone" Phyllis said. "Thank you, that was very thoughtful" said Tom, with a smile that Lucy couldn't help but notice barely left his lips.

She called the children and Amira in to eat. As everyone took their seats at the table, Paul appeared at the living room door. "Just in time, come and join us" Lucy invited. Once every scrap was eaten, Tom and Paul carried the trays back to the kitchen. Phyllis was getting all of her baking things ready. "I thought I'd make a nice meat pie for later" she informed them. "What a great idea, I shall look forward to it" said Paul, kissing her on the cheek. As Paul walked back into the hall, the intercom system at the gate buzzed. "Hello?" Said Paul. "Hello" said a female voice. "It's DS Lowe, I'd like to see Mrs Reid if I can please" "Yes of course, come in" said Paul, pressing the button to open the drive gates. Paul went in to the living room to tell Lucy that DS Lowe was here. "Thank you Paul, I wonder if you'd be good enough to show Bruce out to Jeff's place please? His cases are in the hall and he would like to freshen up a bit before we set off for the hospital" said Lucy. "No problem" said Paul. Lucy went to open the front door but found DS Lowe already standing in the hallway, as Tom had beaten her to it. "Mrs Reid, is there somewhere we can speak in private please?" Said DS Lowe. "Yes, come this way" said Lucy, leading her back into the now empty living room. "DCI Fields asked me to call as we both came back on duty early. Uniformed officers have picked up Mrs Snow's daughter and she's down at the station now. DCI Fields is going to speak to her soon, but he wanted me to let you know she's demanding to call her mother, and she is entitled to a phone call. He's worried that this could prove a problem, as if Avril speaks to her mother, then Mrs Snow will know that we're on to her. He told me to tell you she will be granted her phone call at 6pm" said DS Lowe. "Oh no, it's quarter to now" said Lucy worriedly. Tom looked thoughtful for a moment "Please excuse me ladies, I have an idea" he said. "I won't keep you anymore Mrs Reid, it's just DCI Fields wanted me to let you know in person." Said DS Lowe. "No, thank you for coming. I'll see you out" said Lucy.

"Come and smell this amazing baking, I am trying to persuade Phyllis to do some smaller meat pies as well" said Tom. "Smell? There isn't any smell. I've not cooked anything yet" laughed Phyllis. "Okay then, if you won't make them, let me try" said Tom, making a clumsy grab for the rolling pin, and knocking the glass of water Phyllis had been drinking all down the front of her apron. "Oh no, my phone!" Cried Phyllis, desperately trying to rub the flour from her hands. "Don't worry I've got it" said Tom, deftly fishing her mobile from her apron pocket. "I'll dry my hands to make sure it's okay" said Phyllis anxiously. "It's fine" said Tom, examining it closely and placing it on the work top on the other side of the table to Phyllis. "Oh, er, okay" said Phyllis, rather unsurely. She began to rush to finish her baking, clearly unhappy with her phone not being directly on her person. Suddenly the soulful tones of Percy Sledge rang out from Phyllis's mobile. "Oh dear" said Phyllis, running to wash her hands. "No problem Phyllis, I've got it" said Tom grabbing the phone. "Er, no I'll…" started Phyllis. It was too late, Tom had pushed the answer button. "Hello?…Oh hi Avril…She's a little bit tied up at the minute, she's been baking and her hands are covered in flour…yes of course I will…Have a lovely time, bye!"

Said Tom, replacing the mobile on the side. "New phone Tom?" Said Paul, coming into the kitchen. "No that's Phyllis' mobile" said Lucy. "That was Avril for you Phyllis, she said to tell you she is boarding her plane now and her phone will be switched off, so she'll see you in two weeks" said Tom. "Oh okay" said Phyllis, drying her hands and grabbing her mobile phone.

"Are you okay Phyllis? You've gone very quiet" said Lucy. "Yes fine, I'm just going to change my apron" she replied, going out of the back door. "Hello" said Bruce, passing Phyllis on the path that linked the staff cottages to the house. "What? Oh, er, yes hello" said Phyllis rushing past. Just as Bruce got to the back door of the main house he realised he had forgotten his wallet, so turned round to go back for it. As Bruce put his key in the lock he heard Phyllis' voice sounding quite angry. He looked around and realised that she hadn't closed the front door to her cottage properly. "No, I told you I didn't speak to her. That interfering busy body Tom got to it first…I told that stupid girl to stay away and not to come here but she never listens!… Yeah his father's here now…Couldn't even trust you to do that properly could I…Now I've got to get back before I'm missed, and do me a favour, try not to mess anything else up, got it?" Said Phyllis snapping her phone shut. Bruce let himself in to Jeff's cottage and closed the door silently. What had Phyllis meant and who had she been talking to on the phone? He must be careful around her, there was something about Phyllis he just didn't trust. Bruce decided he would talk to Lucy on the way to the hospital. By the time he returned to the kitchen, Phyllis was in there alone. "Oh where were you? I passed you coming back from the cottage" she said laughing a nervous chuckle. "We shall have to stop meeting like this" smiled Bruce, sensing something in Phyllis' tone. "Were you at the cottage when I was?" Phyllis almost snarled. "Oh no I went for a walk" said Bruce, maintaining his smile. "That was a good idea, the grounds here are lovely" said Phyllis, the edge now gone from her voice. "They certainly are, anyway I must go as we are off to the hospital soon" "Of course, give Jeff my love" Phyllis smiled. Something wasn't quite right and Bruce couldn't work out what.

As he walked through to the hallway he bumped into Tom coming the other way. "Ah Bruce, I was just coming to find you, we're ready to go if you are" he said. Lucy was already waiting by the front door and once they were all safely in the car, Bruce told Lucy and Tom what he had heard at the cottage door, and how offhand Phyllis had been when he saw her in the kitchen a short while ago. "I don't know what I've done to upset her and whatever that phone conversation was about, it certainly didn't seem right" said Bruce puzzled. "No it didn't" agreed Tom drily. "I think we should speak to DCI Fields" said Lucy worriedly. "Is there something I should know here?" Asked Bruce. "Let's go and see Jeff now and we can chat later" said Tom, switching off the car in the parking space at the hospital. Lucy and Tom led Bruce to where his only child lay. "Oh my god" said Bruce, looking through the window, visibly shocked by the sight of his usually fit and healthy son. Lucy put a reassuring hand on his arm as Bruce took a deep breath and opened the door. He stared down at the motionless figure that lay before him. Bruce slowly sank into the chair next to the bed and took Jeff's hand in his and gently he began to talk. "Jeff it's your dad, how are you son? You never do things by half do you eh? Most people would have just invited me for a visit" he said with a soft chuckle. The door opened and a nurse walked in. "I'm sorry I won't be a minute" she said with a sympathetic smile. Bruce mustered a weak smile, watching as the nurse made her checks and then left again. "Bet you're loving this aren't you, having all of these pretty young women running around after you?" Said Bruce, taking Jeff's hand again. Bruce lay his head down, his cheek resting gently on Jeff's arm. He smiled to himself at the thought of six foot 2 inch Jeff's face having his dad hold his hand.

As manly as Jeff tried to behave, Bruce knew that they were still very close. They may spend their lives separated by thousands of miles, but they still loved each other very much. Bruce had no idea how long he had been sitting there when he felt a hand on his shoulder. He turned to see Lucy standing by him. "The doctor would like to speak to you" she said softly. Bruce got up and followed Lucy to the door, "I won't be long" he said, turning back to Jeff. Mr Satoomi was waiting for them in the little room they had all sat in the previous night. "Mr Fisher, I am Mr Satoomi, the doctor in charge of Jeff's care." He said shaking Bruce's hand. "Thank you for looking after my son" said Bruce warmly. "You are most welcome. Jeff is doing very well, his progress is a lot faster than we expected and all the signs are encouraging. We'd like to start bringing him round. This will be a gradual process and the time is different from patient to patient" said Mr Satoomi. "What does that involve?" Asked Bruce. "We have decided that if all still remains well tomorrow, we'll gradually reduce his medication. Jeff was taken for a MRI this morning and there is no evident lasting damage. The swelling has reduced drastically, which again is a good sign" said Mr Satoomi. "Will he be okay?" Asked Lucy. "It's still very early days but please take comfort in that the signs are all very positive" Mr Satoomi replied. "Will he come out of the coma okay?" Asked Tom hesitantly. "Okay? What do you mean?" Asked Bruce, his eyes full of worry. "The gentleman is correct, we don't know the full extent of the damage, if any, until the patient is fully awake and sometimes a patient can behave out of character as they come round" said Mr Satoomi. "Out of character?" Asked Lucy. "Yes, upset, disorientated, frightened, sometimes even violent. It's a very confusing time for them, everyone is different, please remember that. Jeff may have no adverse reactions at all" said Mr Satoomi. "What time will you decide if you're going to wake him?" Bruce asked. "Jeff will be monitored constantly, but if all is still as it is now after lunch tomorrow, we will start then" said Mr Satoomi. "Okay, can I be with him?" Asked Bruce. "Of course, please go and get some rest now though" said Mr Satoomi.

"I'd like to stay with him for a short while if I may and then I will go home and get some rest, as I know I will be no good worn out tomorrow when Jeff wakes up will I?" Said Bruce, smiling hopefully. "Of course, of course, keep talking to him when you're with him. I'm a firm believer this helps" said Mr Satoomi warmly. "Do you think so?" Asked Bruce, his face breaking out into a grin. "Most definitely" said Mr Satoomi, patting Bruce's shoulder reassuringly. "Thank you again" said Bruce. "We shall speak again tomorrow, I must be going now" said Mr Satoomi, checking his pager as it started to sound. "Would you like me to get a taxi back to save you waiting?" Bruce asked Lucy and Tom. "Not at all, you take as long as you like" Lucy replied. "Thank you, I won't be too long and I do appreciate your help, both of you" he said with a wry smile. The door closed behind him and opened again a few seconds later. "What did you forget?" Lucy asked with a laugh, looking up from the magazine she was flicking through. "DCI Fields" said Tom in surprise. "Hello Lucy, Tom, I called Paul and he said you were here. How's Jeff?" Asked DCI Fields. "The doctor said he is looking good and they may start to wake him tomorrow" said Lucy. "That's excellent news. I have one very disgruntled Avril down at the station is what I came to tell you" said the DCI. "Oh really? Not half as disgruntled as we were when we heard she tried to abduct Emily" said Tom, failing to hide the disdain from his voice. "Exactly" said DCI Fields, sitting down in the armchair next to Lucy. "How did she take not being able to talk to her mother earlier?" Asked Tom. "I'm afraid I can't discuss Miss Snow's phone call with you, but she didn't seem at all happy and is still demanding to make another call" said the DCI with a glint in his eye. "Oh no. Will she be allowed?" Asked Lucy fearfully. "From a police point of view she's been granted her rights" said DCI Fields with a grin. "Will you be charging her now? Why did she try to take Emily?" Asked Lucy. "We won't be charging Miss Snow for the time being" said the DCI. "What?" Asked Tom incredulously. "At present Miss Snow is refusing legal representation, and my gut feeling is she is holding off for the opportunity to speak to her mother first. So, for now, we will let her stew." The DCI replied. "Surely you have enough to charge her" said Tom. "Oh yes, most definitely. If the CCTV footage from the school wasn't enough, we've searched her flat and found the clothes and the wig she was wearing." He answered. "Oh my god!" Said Lucy gasping, her hand to her mouth in shock. "We will be applying for extra time to hold Miss Snow, as we need to speak to her about other things" said the DCI. "You will keep us informed though won't you?" Said Lucy. "Of course" DCI Fields nodded.

"We wanted to speak to you about something that happened at home today between Phyllis and Jeff's dad" said Tom. "Mr Fisher? But hasn't he only just arrived?" Said the DCI, looking bemused. "Yes, that's just it" said Tom solemnly. "When Phyllis was first introduced to Bruce she threw her arms around him and hugged him for all she was worth, saying how sorry she was" said Lucy. The DCI raised an eyebrow in mock surprise "She couldn't do enough for Bruce, making him sandwiches and tea, which was all very nice until the phone call and then her sudden turn on him afterwards" said Tom. "Phone call?" Enquired DCI Fields, sitting up straight in his chair. "Yes, Bruce had passed Phyllis when he was leaving Jeff's cottage. Having realised he had forgotten his wallet he returned and overheard Phyllis in a rather heated discussion with someone on her mobile phone. Bruce said that she was complaining about not being able to speak to someone, which we assume was Avril, and that she told her not to come here. She called me interfering, which is what confirmed to me she was talking about Avril" said Tom. "Did she now?" Said the DCI with interest.

"What's even more worrying is she told whoever's on the phone that Bruce was here and she couldn't even trust them to do that properly" said Lucy. "Did she indeed?" Said DCI Fields, scribbling some notes on a pad he had taken from his pocket. "When Bruce came back into the house later, he said Phyllis was very hostile to him, cross examining him on where he had been and if he had been at the cottage when she had. She only reverted back to being friendly once Bruce told her he hadn't been" said Tom, failing again to hide the distaste that crept into his voice lately whenever he spoke about Phyllis. "Bruce understandably is asking questions, which is why we wanted to ask you if you thought we should tell him what's been happening" asked Lucy. "Hmm, ideally no, the less people that know the better, but we don't want to risk Bruce falling out with Phyllis at this delicate stage in our investigations" said the DCI. "That's what we were worried about" replied Tom, nodding. "I'll speak to Bruce once he's seen Jeff" agreed DCI Fields. Lucy, Tom and DCI Fields settled back to wait for Bruce, making small talk every now and again, but most of the time was spent in silence, mulling over the latest events.

CHAPTER 7

LUCY BRINGS EVERYONE UP TO SPEED

Things were starting to quieten down for the night back at Hilltop Manor, Amira had put the children to bed and she and Paul were watching a film in the living room. Phyllis had bid them goodnight as she had a headache, but unknown to them had slipped back into the house. She crept slowly and quietly up the stairs, her fingers paused on the door handle, she must make sure that no one heard. Phyllis turned the handle and slipped inside, she reached out and switched on the wall lights in the study. Phyllis had already managed to sift through the pile of paperwork that sat on the desk earlier when she had brought it up from the kitchen after Avril had left. She tiptoed over to the filing cabinet and reached inside, her fingers nimbly searching the contents. "It must be here somewhere" she whispered aloud. Suddenly the study door sprang open and Phyllis slammed the filing cabinet shut with a start. "Phyllis, I thought you'd gone home for an early night" said Paul. "Oh er I had, but I wanted a drink and thought I'd bring some paperwork up for Lucy. I didn't want it getting ruined" she said, clearly flustered. "Ah okay, I'd come up to check on Jake and Emily and needed something from my room. I noticed the light on in here as I passed" said Paul. "How are the little poppets?" Said Phyllis, anxious to change the subject. "Sleeping soundly" said Paul with a laugh. "That's good, I'll bid you goodnight anyway" she said, clearly wanting to make a hasty exit. "Goodnight Phyllis" Paul replied, turning off the study lights and closing the door behind him. After the footsteps had died away, a face appeared from the shadows, silent footsteps made their way over to the study desk, barely illuminated in the moonlight squeezing through the cracks in the blind. Fingers reached out and came to a rest on the photo album. Taking a folded sheet of paper from their pocket, they opened the back page and slipped it securely inside. There came the sound of car doors slamming, steel blue eyes gazed out of the window to the driveway below, Nick was back. The big black car turned and drove slowly down the drive and Nick was lost from sight as he climbed the steps to the front door.

Back at the hospital, Bruce had rejoined Lucy and Tom in the waiting room. He had read the newspaper to Jeff and told him all about his job and his life in Canada. He promised Jeff he'd be back tomorrow. Lucy and Tom slipped in to see Jeff to say goodnight. "DCI Fields was here" they told Bruce when they returned. "We would like to speak to you when we get back to the house if that's okay, there's some things we think you should know" said Tom. "Yes of course, I'd like to be brought up to speed, I'd really appreciate it" said Bruce. Lucy got a coffee and a sandwich from the machine for PC Regan, who had just come back on duty to sit with Jeff through the night. He really was a nice guy and told her he had been hit by a car in the line of duty the previous year. The way Lucy saw it, Scott Regan was living proof that Jeff could make a full recovery. Only a year ago Scott had been in intensive care, and since then he was back at work, had got married and had his first child on the way. "Thank you Mrs Reid, you're very kind" said PC Regan. "You're very welcome" Lucy replied with a smile. "See you tomorrow, oh and Mr Fisher" said PC Regan. "Yes?" Said Bruce, turning back to face him. "I'll look after him for you, don't you worry" he said earnestly. "Thank you son, I appreciate that" said Bruce gratefully. "Shall we pick up something to eat on the way home?" Asked Tom. "That's a good idea, let's take back a couple of pizzas and some garlic bread as I'm sure Paul will be hungry" said Lucy laughing. Tom couldn't help but feel very uneasy waiting in the lay-by outside the pizza shop for Lucy, it was literally feet from where he and Jeff had been run down. By the time Lucy and Bruce returned with the food, he was very pale and had broken out into a nervous sweat. "Oh Tom I'm so sorry, I'd never have suggested pizza if I had thought. How selfish of me" said Lucy, realising where they were parked. "Not your fault. This is a spot I'll probably end up passing every day while I live at Hilltop Manor. I'll need to get used to it" said Tom quietly. He drove the short distance home, pushed the button on the key fob attached to his car keys and the large drive gates creaked open.

Lucy opened the door and Bruce carried the food through to the kitchen while Tom went to see if Paul and Amira were still up. He found them in the living room and invited them both to come and eat. As they all trooped into the kitchen, Lucy was putting the take away out onto plates. "Have you got any spare for me?" Said the last person to enter. "Nick!" She cried, running to hug him. "Hi Lucy" laughed Nick, giving his step mum a kiss on the cheek. "When did you get back?" She asked. "Not long ago" Nick said. "I thought the police couldn't collect you until tomorrow" Said Lucy. "They couldn't and then DCI Fields rang and said he'd sort something out as he thought you might need me here" Nick replied. "I'm so glad you're home" she said, still hugging him tightly. "I've only been gone a few days, but with this sort of welcome I think I may go away more often" said Nick with a chuckle. "Can I get anyone a drink?" Asked Tom. Everyone settled on cold orange juice, cool and refreshing, straight from the fridge. "While I have everyone together I need to talk to you" said Lucy, casting a glance around the table at everyone. "Phyllis is missing" said Amira. "I know" said Lucy solemnly, pushing the bolt across the back door. "Are you okay?" Asked Amira worriedly. "I just don't want to be disturbed" said Lucy sitting back at the table. "Tom and I spoke with DCI Fields tonight at the hospital, and he was going to speak to you himself, but he was called away. What I'm going to tell you is very important, but it's essential no one speaks to Phyllis about it, no one must tell her we had this conversation, and above all, no one must treat her any differently. It's so hard to believe I've been here for such a short time and so much has happened. My husband Ben and I were so happy in our home in Primrose Hill where we lived with Jake and Emily and Great Aunt Maud. In such a short space of time, that wonderful lady passed away, and then Ben's parents went missing, presumed dead. Frank and Janet Reid went on a last minute holiday, but never returned. Their bodies still haven't been found and the only explanation the police can offer is that the accident site was so near a river it washed their bodies out to the sea it's linked to." Said Lucy, taking a large gulp of orange juice.

Amira put her hand on Lucy's and squeezed it tightly. "Go on Lucy" Tom encouraged. "Frank and Janet took on the houses and the shop, as there was a delay in the will reading, and with them unable to run the business, here we are. Well… here I am" said Lucy sadly, tears springing to her eyes. "Oh Lucy, you've been through so much" said Amira quietly. "On the way here we stopped at the Pineapple Diner and Emily left her favourite toy in the toilet there. We didn't realise until we stopped at the store further up the road to get a few things. Ben returned to the diner alone but he never collected the toy and was seen leaving there with three men in suits. No one has seen or heard from Ben since, apart from one sighting at a local air field" sobbed Lucy, clearly overcome. "You don't have to carry on" said Bruce, his eyes full of sympathy. "Yes I do" said Lucy determinedly.

There was a knock at the door and Tom went to open it, Phyllis was standing there. "Oh er, Tom, the door was locked" said Phyllis, gazing past him to the packed table. "Was it?" Said Tom casually. "Is there something wrong?" Phyllis said, gesturing at everyone with her head. "No, not at all, we were all hungry" said Tom. "Yeah, we didn't want to disturb you as you went off to bed with a headache, we assumed you'd be asleep" said Paul. "Oh er yes, my headache" stammered Phyllis. "That's what I came for, headache tablets." She was holding her head dramatically and leaning against the door frame. With Tom still blocking the door way, Phyllis had no choice but to remain on the back step. "There you go Phyllis" said Paul, appearing at Tom's side with a carton of orange juice and a packet of paracetamol. "Let me walk you back, you should be in bed if you're feeling under the weather" said Tom, stepping out the back door and steering Phyllis back down the path by her arm, before she had chance to answer. "Oh, er, erm, err, thank you Tom" said Phyllis when they reached her cottage. "Not a problem, always happy to help. You sleep well Phyllis" said Tom. Without another word he was back off down the pathway to the main house. Once inside, he pushed the bolt back across the door. "Shall we move to the living room, away from the kitchen door?" Asked Lucy. "I think that might be a good idea" Tom replied.

Once everyone was settled at the dining table Lucy took a deep breath and began to speak again. "Then so many things have happened since we came here. Someone drove straight at Tom and Nick when we went for a meal, then the brake hoses were cut on Tom's car at Bartons, that's the store we took on with house" said Lucy looking at Bruce. "So this has happened before then? Two attempts to run someone over and Tom was involved in both and the break pipes?" Asked Bruce. "I can see where you're coming from Bruce, but DCI Fields thinks its attempts at the family in general and I just happen to be the common denominator" said Tom. "Then someone tried to abduct Emily from craft club dressed as me" said Lucy. "What the hell's going on here?" Said Bruce in shock. "We conducted housekeeper interviews when we first came, Tom had arranged them with a reputable employment agency. The interviewees were awful and then Phyllis arrived unexpectedly after hearing of the vacancy in a local shop" said Lucy. "Oh that was very lucky, what were the odds of that happening?" Said Bruce. "Yes, what were the odds?" Said Tom darkly. "The police have since discovered some disturbing facts surrounding Phyllis, and so have we come to that. Someone cancelled the housekeepers the night before they were due saying they were me" said Lucy. "But I thought you said the applicants arrived?" Said Bruce puzzled. "They did, the question is who did send them if the agency didn't? And wasn't Phyllis a breath of fresh air after meeting them?" said Tom. "So you're saying Phyllis coming here was much more than just coincidence" said Bruce, his eyes wide. "Certainly looks that way" added Paul, who had been listening intently.

"Morph took an instant dislike to Phyllis and won't have her within a few feet of the children" said Lucy. "Morph? But he seems so friendly" said Bruce in surprise. "He is" said Tom. "Morph disappeared when we were out one day and we eventually found him in a disused shed in the garden" said Tom. "Do you think he got in there somehow?" Asked Bruce. "No I'm certain he had a bit of help" replied Tom grimly. "Jeff saw Morph with Phyllis and then Phyllis coming away from the shed, despite her insisting she hadn't seen him and hadn't been in the garden that day. She tried to blame Jeff for locking him in there accidentally." "But why did she lie?" Asked Bruce, looking even more puzzled than ever. "That's what we'd all like to know" replied Tom. "The police have picked up a woman for the attempt at abducting Emily from the school and it's Phyllis' daughter Avril." Said Lucy gravely. "Her daughter? Oh my god no! Surely there must be some mistake" cried Bruce. "No I only wish there was" said Tom. "Avril has been identified from a distinguishing looking mark on the CCTV footage" "That's horrendous" said Bruce indignantly. "I know" Lucy agreed. "Here's the important part guys, Phyllis doesn't know we are on to her, and I managed to intercept a phone call so she doesn't know Avril has been arrested, she thinks she's on holiday for two weeks. DCI Fields said to stress it is of vital importance that everyone treats Phyllis exactly the same, however you may be feeling inside. Phyllis must not suspect" Tom finished looking seriously at everyone around the table in turn.

They all nodded, but remained silent, clearly struggling to take in everything they just learned. "Well there's absolutely no way I will ever be leaving that woman alone in the room with Jake and Emily, or Morph come to that" declared Amira with a shudder. "I'd appreciate that" said Lucy with a grateful smile. "Bruce overheard Phyllis on the phone to someone complaining of him being here and calling me an interfering busybody for stopping something. We don't quite know what that something is and Jeff was trying to tell me about another call that he had overheard that was troubling him just before the accident" said Tom, giving Bruce a sympathetic smile. Lucy glanced warily at Bruce, not wanting to upset him. "Just before Jeff lost consciousness he was insistent that Tom kept Phyllis away from the children" she said. "Phyllis is always asking how Jeff is to the point of being over the top in my opinion, if I'm being honest" added Tom. "What the hell has this woman done that Jeff was trying so hard to tell you about?" Said Bruce thoughtfully. "I never really thought anything of it at the time, I just thought she was worried about Jeff, but Phyllis keeps asking me if I think he'll die" said Amira quietly. "Me too" said Paul. "Nick, you okay?" Said Lucy, looking at her step son, he hadn't said a word. "I just can't believe that someone who appears so wonderful is actually involved in all this in some way or another" he said, shaking his head in disbelief. "We don't know if she is involved in all of it" said Lucy. "Nothing would surprise me now after what I've just heard" Nick declared. Everyone once again nodded in agreement.

"Look it's getting late, please everyone just promise me you'll be very careful around Phyllis" begged Lucy. "We will" they all chorused. Bruce got up to leave and Tom unlocked the back door to let him out. "Goodnight mate, chin up eh, Jeff's a good guy he will be fine, you wait and see." "I really hope you're right, goodnight Tom" replied Bruce, and walked off down the path with a wave over his shoulder. As he passed Phyllis' cottage something caught his eye. He glanced sideways and there was Phyllis scowling at him for all she was worth. Remembering Lucy's request he smiled cheerily and gave her a little wave. Phyllis dropped her curtain back into place in disgust.

The next morning as Bruce entered the kitchen, Tom and Paul were seated at the breakfast table reading the newspaper and Phyllis was busy with a large pan of bacon and eggs. "Good morning Bruce, I trust you slept well!" She trilled, shooting him a beaming smile. "Oh er yes thank you" said Bruce, struggling to come to terms with this being the same woman who had been glaring at him just a few hours earlier. "Take a seat, this will be ready in a tick. Full English okay?" Said Phyllis. "Yes that's great, thank you" said Bruce, eyeing Phyllis warily. "Orange juice is back in the fridge to keep it cool and that's a fresh pot of tea on the table" said Phyllis, flashing him another beaming grin. "Thank you" said Bruce again. "Here would you like the paper? I've got to get Jake and Emily to their club" Paul said. "Yes please" said Bruce, opening the paper to read. "I rang the hospital a little while ago, I thought you might be a bit jet lagged" said Tom. "Please tell me the news was good" said Bruce, his face anxious. "Yes it was very good. The nurse said Jeff is responding well and it's all systems go for today. The doctor has asked if you can come in for around 2pm" said Tom smiling. "Oh thank heavens, I may have my boy back very soon" said Bruce, relief washing over him. Tom noticed how Phyllis had gone very quiet, clearly listening intently to what was being said. "Could I come and visit Jeff today please?" She asked. "Er yes, if you want to" said Bruce. "Do you mind if I go now?" Said Phyllis. "We aren't going until 2pm" said Tom. "Yeah I know, but I have some jobs that need doing, so I'll go now and get a cab there" said Phyllis quickly. "Oh okay, but visiting doesn't start for the afternoon until 1pm" said Tom. "That's okay, I have a few errands to run first anyway" said Phyllis, placing the breakfast plates on the table, removing her apron and hurrying out of the back door.

"Why all the hurry?" Asked Tom thoughtfully. "I think I'd better ring DCI Fields and warn him that Phyllis is coming. She wouldn't normally be allowed to see Jeff, but with him being in a private area with all that's gone on, DCI Fields will arrange it." He continued. "I've no idea what she's up to" said Bruce. The more he saw of Phyllis, the more concerned he was that something wasn't quite right with her. At that moment Tom's mobile rung. "Hello...oh hello DCI Fields...funnily enough I was just about to call you...Phyllis has asked out of the blue to visit Jeff...yes we thought that was strange too...No, she's gone on her own, insisted on getting a taxi there for visiting hours at 1pm...No I didn't think the hospital would let her in on her own, considering Jeff's condition but decided to let her go and let you know, as you said you thought she may ask…okay yes, that should be fine, we'll be at the hospital by 2pm, I'll let Lucy know you called… goodbye" he said, replacing the receiver frowning. "Is everything okay?" Asked Bruce. "DCI Fields wants to speak to us at the hospital today. He said he's going to make sure that Phyllis is allowed access to Jeff, but told you not to worry, he's perfectly safe" said Tom.

Lucy hadn't heard her phone ringing, she was back warily seated in the study, leafing through the next pile of paperwork and documents in the overflowing filing cabinet, Morph was curled contentedly at her feet. Lucy moved the pile with the large photo album on top, that she had already sorted, to one side. She eyed the album thoughtfully, she still couldn't work out why Avril had taken the old photograph of Frank and the mystery man, what had she wanted with it? She hadn't even realised until DCI Fields had told her it had been found on her when the police picked her up. Lucy pulled the album to her, an overwhelming urge to look at the picture of Ben. She felt sure he would have known what to do. She opened the book's cover and as she did, noticed a piece of crumpled paper. 'What's this?' She thought. That hadn't been there before, she was sure. "Oh my god" said Lucy out loud. It was a sheet listing the values of some paintings from the hallway at Hilltop Manor. Each valuation had a tiny image alongside it. Lucy looked closer, it was the five paintings that had been stolen in the robbery. Her eyes widened as she realised that 4 of the paintings had a value of nearly half a million pounds between them. Lucy read the description of each painting in turn, they were definitely the ones that had been taken. Lucy's eyes rested on the final value, the painting that Nick disliked so much, the one of all the ghosts and ghouls was worth a massive £14.4 million pounds. Lucy almost choked on the coffee she had been drinking, so whoever took those paintings knew exactly what they were looking for.

The study door opened and Tom appeared. "Ah here you are, I was wondering where you had got to. Are you okay Lucy?" Asked Tom, seeing her expression. "Yes, come and look at this" said Lucy, holding out the piece of paper. His eyes scanned the document and he let out a low whistle. "Well I never expected them to be worth this much" said Tom, his eyes wide with shock. "No, neither did I" said Lucy quietly. "DCI Fields is meeting us at the hospital today, bring this and show it to him then" Tom said. "What I don't understand Tom is that this was inside the photo album, and it wasn't there the other day, I checked. Then we checked." Lucy said. "Oh we must have missed it" said Tom. "Yeah maybe" said Lucy unconvinced. "Come on Lucy, I want to collect the photos we sent for developing, and I thought maybe we could grab a coffee before going to the hospital" said Tom. She got up and followed him from the room. As she turned to close the door, she took a last uneasy glance around the study. That paper hadn't been there, she knew it hadn't. Bruce was already waiting for them in the hallway, and as the front door slammed, fingers were turning the pages to the photo album on the study desk. Finding the document gone, a slow satisfied smile spread across a tired, worried face.

A short while later, Lucy and Bruce were sitting in Dee's Coffee Lounge enjoying a cappuccino and a large Danish pastry each, waiting for Tom to return with the photographs. The door opened and he appeared, leafing through them as he came towards them. "There's some fabulous ones of Jake and Emily" he said to Lucy, handing them to her. 'Ben would love to see these' thought Lucy with a sad smile, their family albums were bursting at the seams as Ben was an avid photographer. Lucy had to stifle a chuckle when she came across six photos of Tom's newly polished car from all angles. There was some lovely ones of Jeff mending the fence, Jeff fixing the washing line, Jeff playing football with Jake and Emily. Lucy passed them to Bruce who gazed at them and swallowed hard. 'Poor Bruce, it must be so hard for him' she thought. Lucy continued to flick through the photos, Morph with Jake and Emily, Morph with his squeaky bone and then one of Phyllis smiling broadly into the camera. She stared at Phyllis' happy face, how could she have been so wrong about her? She wondered. "So what's this store of yours like then, Lucy?" Asked Bruce, breaking the silence. "So much has gone on since I came here, I've only seen it once" said Lucy with a wistful smile."That's a real shame, I'd love to see it sometime" said Bruce. "Lucy, we have a bit of time before the hospital and it is on the way. How about we give Bruce a very quick guided tour now?" Suggested Tom. "What a great idea" she replied.

As they drove into Barton's carpark, Bill was busy rounding up stray trolleys. Lucy watched as he stopped to help an elderly lady lift the bag she was struggling with into her boot. 'What a lovely guy' she thought.

Bill hadn't noticed them pull up. "Err excuse me, I wondered if you could help me with my bag" she called. "Yes of course" Bill replied, quick as a flash spinning round. "Hello Bill" Lucy smiled at him. "Ah it's you! Hello Mrs Reid" said Bill laughing. Tom introduced Bill to Bruce and they shook hands warmly. "So is the kettle on Bill? I came for that cup of tea we didn't get chance to have last time" said Lucy. "Kettle's always on here Mrs Reid" said Bill with a chuckle. Lucy, Tom and Bruce followed Bill inside and took a seat at one of the tables. "Do you want me to do that for you Bill?" Asked Lucy. "Never let a pretty lady make her own tea. It's just an unfortunate setback I'm having to make it for the two henchmen as well" Bill laughed, gesturing to Tom and Bruce, and treating Lucy to a devilish smile and a wink. "I hear you have two little ones Mrs Reid? You'll have to bring them in to see me one day, I'm sure I'll be able to find a nice cake or biscuit that they would enjoy" said Bill. "That would be lovely" she replied, "I'm sure they'd like that very much. Would you like to see a photo of Jake and Emily?" Lucy asked, taking the pack from her bag. Bill took a seat next to her "What lovely children, such a fine looking young man and a gorgeous little girl" he said. "Oh thank you" said Lucy, unable to contain the pride in her voice.

"Well I'll be blowed. If it ain't Phyllis Kramer, not seen her for years!" Exclaimed Bill, looking at the photo of Phyllis baking with the children. "Phyllis? You know her?" Asked Lucy in surprise. "Oh yes, we all used to knock around together many moons ago, but not seen her since she ran off and married that rough looking bloke Fred. Oh, must be ten years ago now" said Bill. "Ah, so Snow must be her married name then" said Tom. "No, no, no, that wasn't his name, Snow was Phyllis' stepfather's name" declared Bill. "Oh maybe they're divorced" said Lucy. "I don't think so, my wife saw them together in town a couple of months back" Bill said. "Oh how very strange, Phyllis never mentioned having a husband" said Lucy. "Very strange indeed" agreed Tom. "Do you know Avril, Phyllis' daughter, Bill?" Asked Lucy. "Oh yeah I know her, not all the ticket that one. Would sell her own mother out for a chocolate bar she would" Bill grimaced. "So they aren't close then?" Asked Tom. "Well, like I say, I've not set eyes on them for years, but they never were. Avril was adopted and turned out to be all bad from what I know" Bill said.

At that moment the door opened and Lara and Penny walked in.

They both stopped in their tracks, their mouths opening and closing like goldfish. "Hello ladies" said Lucy with a wry smile. "Erm hello Mrs Reid" stammered Lara. "How are you?" Trilled Penny, with a nervous laugh. "Can I get you a cup of tea?" Asked Lara. "She's got one" hissed Penny, nodding towards Lucy's already full mug. "Oh yes of course you have" said Lara, blushing profusely. "Er, Mrs Reid, we, er, just wanted to say sorry for the other day. We didn't mean anything by it" said Lara, sheepishly. "Yes we are sorry" added Penny. Lucy looked at both women long and hard, "On this occasion I'm willing to overlook this ladies, I suggest that next time you show all staff and visitors the respect they deserve, and I think it might be a very good idea to keep your pre-conceived opinions to yourself" said Lucy in as stern a voice as she could muster. She was trying very hard not to laugh at their shocked faces. She was pretty sure they wouldn't be making the same mistake again in a hurry. Lara and Penny scuttled out and Bill burst out laughing. "That told that pair of flighty little madams" he said. "So it seems. Anyway Bill, we'll have to catch up with you soon" said Lucy finishing her tea. "We want to let Bruce take a look at the store very quickly, and then get off to visit Jeff" Tom said. "Yeah I heard about that awful business, I hope your boy gets better really soon" said Bill shaking Bruce's hand again. Tom gave Bruce a guided tour of the store room, then wandered along the top of the aisles pointing out various bargains and offers they were promoting that week. "Very impressive" said Bill appreciatively. Lucy glanced down the corridor that lead to reception and noticed Penny sitting on Lara's desk chatting. "Yes this way to reception" she said in a loud voice. Penny scurried back to her desk and began to type, whilst Lara buried her head in some paperwork as she walked in. "That's what I like to see ladies, hard at work" she said, smiling sweetly, biting her lip to stop the laughter escaping as she turned and walked back up the corridor. Lucy, Tom and Bruce said their goodbyes and set off to the hospital.

Lucy didn't say anything, but she could feel the car jolting slightly every so often when they first left. Tom was clearly testing his brakes, their last visit to Barton's obviously playing on his mind. When they arrived at the hospital, they bumped into Phyllis coming out of the front entrance. "Oh that poor boy" she said when she saw them, dabbing her eyes with a tissue she had hurriedly taken from her pocket. "Has something happened?" Asked Bruce anxiously. "He's so still and so pale" wailed Phyllis. "Phyllis for goodness sake! Has Jeff taken a turn for the worst?" Tom almost shouted. "No, I'm just so upset!" Sobbed Phyllis, hurrying away. "I'll catch you both up" Tom said to Lucy and Bruce. Tom turned his attention back to Phyllis who was now at the taxi rank, tissue nowhere in sight and laughing and joking with the lady standing there. Tom shook his head, 'Seems Avril wasn't the only one made of bad stuff' he thought sadly. He caught up with Lucy and Bruce at the entrance to the ward, where DCI Fields was waiting for them with a tall, slim, blonde woman in a smart navy suit. "Could I speak to you all before you see Jeff please, there's nothing wrong with him, I want to talk to you about Phyllis" he said seriously. The DCI lead them to the waiting room that was fast becoming their second home over the last few days.

"This is Marella Novak" he said, finally introducing the woman he was with. "Hello" they all said, "Marella is a psychologist friend of mine, we were at university together. I want you to take a look at some camera footage from today that she would like to discuss with you." Said DCI Fields. "Please be seated" she said in a heavy Polish accent. She pushed the button on the remote control and an image of Jeff laying in his bed filled her laptop screen. All eyes were on the door as it opened and they saw Phyllis walk in. They could see the police officer still standing outside the room. "Oh Jeff, my poor boy!" exclaimed Phyllis. Obviously her concern had been for the benefit of the policeman as it took on a much more menacing tone once the door was closed. Phyllis took a seat at the side of the bed and took Jeff's hand, she would look the picture of concern to anyone looking in as they passed.

Marella increased the volume "You need to hear this" she said. They watched intently as Phyllis leant forward and said in what could only be described as a loud whisper, "Do you know, I really liked you? But you got in the way, asking too many questions and overhearing things you shouldn't have. Why couldn't you have kept your nose out? I'm sorry it's come to this, but I've come too far to let you stand in my way. I want what's rightfully mine and I intend to get it." With that she stood up, rummaged in her bag for a tissue and then left the room dabbing her eyes. "Oh my god" said Lucy, horrified. "So she did have something to do with Jeff being run over" said Tom angrily. "That must have been what Jeff was trying to warn you about, he must have found something out and Phyllis got someone to stop Jeff before he blew the whistle on her" said Bruce, his voice full of anguish, disbelief and shock all rolled into one. "We have enough to pick Phyllis up, but if we do, we still don't have a motive for all this" said DCI Fields. "Phyllis is showing all the signs of someone still very aware that what she is doing is wrong. She is still struggling with the fact that she actually liked her potential victims, but she also shows she has a dangerous edge and will stop anyone who gets in the way of her getting whatever it is she has set her sights on." Said Marella gravely. "I've asked for further background checks on Phyllis under the name of Kramer that Tom rang me about. They should come through in the morning and I'm proposing we leave things as they are until then" said DCI Fields. "Against my better judgement I think I agree with you, as if you arrest Phyllis now, we don't know if any of us will be safe from any accomplices she may have" said Lucy. "I'm glad you can see it that way Lucy" said the DCI. "I want my boy safe and those children. With that woman and her connections on the loose, they wouldn't be. So you nail her as soon as possible Sir" said Bruce determinedly.

CHAPTER 8

LUCY BREAKS IN

There was a knock at the door and Mr Satoomi walked in, smiling broadly. "The news is very good, we are going to start to bring Jeff round" he said. "That's fantastic news!" Cried Bruce. "How long will that take?" Asked Lucy. "It depends on the individual, but not too long I hope" said Mr Satoomi. "Can I see him please?" Asked Bruce. "Of course, come with me" he replied, nodding. Once they had gone, Tom turned to Lucy. "I was thinking, I want you to see if you can take Bruce home" he said. "Home?" Said Lucy surprised. "Yes, I'm a bit worried how Jeff will wake up from this. It could be upsetting for Bruce. I just thought it might be better if he comes back when Jeff's already conscious" said Tom softly. "I'll try" said Lucy nodding. "You go and see Jeff and I'll wait here. We can speak to Bruce later" Tom smiled.

As she walked across to Jeff's room and looked at Bruce through the window, she knew that Tom was right, he really didn't need anymore worry. "Hello" she said softly as she stepped inside Jeff's room. Bruce's tired, tear-stained face looked towards her. "Hello" he smiled wearily. "Not long now and he'll be awake and telling us all off for not keeping the garden weeded" said Lucy jokily. "Oh no, I didn't do that for him" said Bruce, looking alarmed. She laid a hand on his shoulder, "I was just kidding Bruce, I didn't mean you should have done it. You have enough to think about and you're a guest" Lucy said. "I know…but I should have done it…for Jeff" he replied quietly. "Speaking of Jeff" said Lucy, deciding to take this opportunity, "You look very tired, you've come a long way and you've hardly slept since you got here. It could be hours and hours

86

before Jeff comes round and we were thinking, why don't you go home and get some rest? You'll be far more use to Jeff bright eyed and bushy tailed when he regains consciousness, than having him worry about you making yourself ill, and you know how Jeff worries about everyone else so much" said Lucy gently. "Yes he does worry" said Bruce, smiling over at his son. "Then come home and get some rest shortly" Lucy persisted. "I couldn't, he'll be on his own if he wakes up" insisted Bruce. "No he won't be, we can come back first thing in the morning, and he probably won't wake up until then anyway" Lucy said. "Yes but he will be alone" Bruce continued. "I know the police are here, but Jeff needs a familiar face to open his eyes to" he persevered. "Yes I know, and that's why Tom will stay with him, and he can ring you if there's any change" Lucy said. "Oh I don't know, I should be here" said Bruce doubtfully. "Please Bruce, it would just be for a few hours" Lucy pleaded. Bruce looked at his son, then at Lucy's concerned face, then back at his son again. "Okay, maybe just for a few hours" he conceded. "Thank you. I'm going to leave you to spend some time alone with Jeff, I'll be in the waiting room. You take as long as you like" Lucy reassured.

She closed the door of Jeff's room and breathed a sigh of relief. She didn't like having to pressure Bruce to leave, but she really did agree with Tom, it was probably for the best and she hoped now that Bruce knew his son was on the road to recovery, he may actually be able to rest. When she went back into the waiting room, Tom was sitting in the armchair, his eyes closed. She tip toed over to him, his bottom lip was slightly open and his breathing heavy. Poor Tom, she hadn't actually thought how tired and worried he must be as well. He and Jeff had become good friends though, she knew that. Lucy sat quietly in a nearby armchair, deciding it was best to let him sleep. She got herself some water from the machine that sat in the corner and settled herself back into the armchair next to Tom. She took a sip, the cool liquid soothing to her dry mouth, she was so tired, but didn't want to fall asleep again, she would need to drive Bruce home soon. Lucy took her mobile from her bag to let Amira know the news about Jeff and that Tom would be staying with him while she brought Bruce home. She asked her to kiss Jake and Emily goodnight for her, she pressed send and seconds later a message from Amira appeared. 'That's wonderful news about Jeff, and the children send you kisses back. Oh and Jake said what about Morph?' With a laughing smiley icon. Lucy smiled to herself and quickly typed back 'hugs and kisses to Morph too'. She placed her mobile back in her bag and picked up one of the magazines from the table and began to flick through it to pass the time.

Tom stirred beside her about an hour later, and opened his eyes. "Hi" said Lucy with a smile. "Hi" said a bleary eyed Tom. "Do you feel any better now?" Lucy asked. "A bit" he nodded. Just then Bruce came in, looking a bit glum. "Still no change" he said sadly. "It's going to take time mate" said Tom, struggling to his feet. "I know" nodded Bruce. "I'm going to get myself a coffee to wake myself up a bit, does anyone else want anything?" Tom asked. "No thank you" said Lucy. "I could do with one please, no sugar" said Bruce gratefully. Once Bruce had finished his coffee, he and Lucy said their goodbyes to Jeff, took Tom's car and set off for home.

This was the first time Lucy had driven it, she felt quite honoured in fact, that he had trusted her with his treasured possession. She settled down behind the wheel quickly, it was a lovely car to drive. She and Bruce soon left the city lights behind and chatted to pass the time as they ambled along the country lanes that lead to Hilltop Manor. As Lucy passed the country park, a van pulled out behind her. Suddenly, she was blinded by his headlights as they filled her rearview mirror, lighting up Tom's car. "Jeez! He's a bit close isn't he?" Said Bruce, turning round to look. "Yes he is" said Lucy nervously. The van roared nearer and nearer, Lucy sped up slightly, but the van just increased its speed behind her. "He's trying to force me to go faster!" cried Lucy. "Don't stop, you never know what could happen out on these deserted roads" said Bruce. "Do you have a phone on you? Mine went flat at the hospital" Lucy asked in desperation. "No, I didn't bring mine" replied Bruce. "Oh no, the one time I didn't charge my phone I really need it, and I'm usually so careful about that" Lucy said. "Is there anywhere to turn off up here?" Asked Bruce. "No, this next couple of miles are open farmland with deep ditches either side" cried Lucy, glancing fearfully at Bruce for a second. "Try to ignore them, just keep driving, you're doing great" encouraged Bruce. As Lucy rounded the bend, the van drew up alongside her, gradually moving over towards her, then dropping back and doing it again, each time inching closer and closer to Tom's car. "He's trying to force us off the road!" Screamed Lucy. "I know" said Bruce in an anxious tone. Lucy sped up again at the next bend, trying to put some distance between them. Suddenly there was a flash of yellow jackets and the van seemed to be dropping away. There was a wail of sirens and police cars appeared behind them surrounding the slowing van. Lucy had pulled over and was watching the scene unfold behind her. A police car sped towards them, lights flashing and blocked the road between her and the van. "Oh my god, he's not going to stop!" Cried Lucy in terror. At the last moment, the van veered off and into the ditch.

Police swarmed from all directions, grabbing the driver as he tried to make a run for it. A police officer went up to Lucy's window, "Are you okay?" He asked. "Yes, shaken but okay" she replied unsteadily, getting out of the car. As the handcuffed driver was bundled into a nearby police car, she saw them, Lucy's blood run cold. The man was wearing purple trainers with yellow stars. "It's him, the guy with the scaffold lorry!" Said Lucy. "Are you sure?" Bruce asked, remembering her telling him all about the incident. "It is, I'm positive" Lucy insisted. "How did you know we were being followed?" Bruce asked the police officer. "DCI Fields is having all movements of people in and out of Hilltop Manor monitored. I'm sorry we had to let it go on as long, but we needed to get him onto this stretch of road, to try to ensure the operation of our stinger was a success" said the policeman. "So that was why the van dropped back so suddenly" said Lucy, she had seen the police stop a vehicle they were chasing before on a police programme, by throwing the stinger into its path and puncturing its tyres. "Are you okay to get home Mrs Reid? I'm sure DCI Fields will be in touch when he hears about all of this" said the officer. "Yes, we're fine, thank you for your help" replied Lucy gratefully. They drove the last few miles in silence, neither quite able to believe what had just happened.

"Are you okay Lucy?" Asked Amira, seeing her pale shocked face as she came through the door. Paul came out of the living room at that point and could see something was wrong immediately. "Come and take a seat" he said to Lucy and Bruce, opening the door to the kitchen. Lucy sat down heavily on the chair and attempted to explain what had happened since they left the hospital. "Oh my god!" Exclaimed Amira in shock "Are you sure you're both okay?" "Yes but what I don't understand is how the guy with the purple trainers knew I would be leaving the hospital when I did" Lucy said puzzled. "Oh no, I think I might know" wailed Amira. "How?"

Said Lucy in surprise. "Paul had gone to get Jake and Emily a burger when your text came through earlier and I rang to tell him the good news about Jeff" said Amira sheepishly. "So you told him about me leaving Tom at the hospital? I don't understand" said Lucy puzzled. "I hadn't realised that Phyllis was standing behind me, and when I came off the phone, she couldn't get back to her cottage fast enough" said Amira. "Ah, now I see" nodded Lucy. "I'm so sorry" Amira said sadly. "It's not your fault, that woman is obviously pure evil" said Bruce in disgust. "Most definitely" declared Lucy in agreement.

Bruce decided to go and get some rest, he wanted to be up early to visit Jeff. As Lucy locked the back door, she heard the phone ringing in the hall. 'It's very late for someone to be ringing' she thought, glancing at her watch. "Hello?" She said, picking up the receiver. "Lucy, it's Tom" came Tom's voice. "Tom, what's the matter? Is it Jeff?" Lucy asked in panic. "No, there's no change with Jeff. I just wanted to ring to make sure you were okay, PC Regan just told me what happened. I'm so sorry" said Tom emotionally. "I'm fine, and sorry for what?" Lucy asked. "I should never have let you go home alone, I'm truly sorry" said Tom. "You have nothing to be sorry about" she reassured him. "What happened would have happened anyway". "PC Regan said they've got Mr Purple Trainers down at the station. They're going to interview him tonight briefly, and then resume in the morning" Tom said. "I'm glad they have him" replied Lucy. "Listen to me Lucy, this is very important. You need to get that mobile off of Phyllis before Mr Purple Trainers tries to ring her, as he may well when he is granted his phone call" Tom said worriedly. "I agree, but how? She never lets the phone out of her sight" said Lucy. "You'll have to steal it Lucy. If she hasn't got that phone it may stop her contacting her accomplices as well" Tom finished. "Yes but Phyllis always has the phone on her Tom" Lucy repeated. "Except at night time, when she's charging it. I know she charges it in the kitchen, as she asked me to call the electrician out as the plug in her bedroom isn't working. She said the sockets in the living room are taken up by the TV, a DVD player and a lamp, and the lead doesn't reach anywhere else, so she charges it on the work surface in the kitchen" said Tom. "Yes but I'm not in there while Phyllis is sleeping am I?" Said Lucy with a nervous laugh.

The line went silent for a moment "...no but you could be" said Tom quietly. "Break in Tom? Are you mad?" She cried. "Not at all, you can do this Lucy. There's a set of steps in the kitchen larder cupboard, Phyllis always leaves her small window open in the kitchen. You need to stretch your arm down and open the big one. Reach in and take the phone, but remember to lock the window again and push the small one to" said Tom. "Oh my, I can't burgle Phyllis' cottage" said Lucy in horror. "Yes you can, we need to get that phone. Once you have the phone, hide it, as you can bet Phyllis will rip that place apart looking for it when you're out. As soon as you get chance get the phone to DCI Fields" finished Tom.

Although Lucy knew what Tom was asking her to do was wrong, she knew he was right, she had to get that phone, so she had to at least try. "Okay" she replied hesitantly. "Good girl, I'll see you tomorrow. Good luck Lucy" said Tom, and the line went silent. Lucy looked down at her watch, it had just gone eleven, she hoped Phyllis would already be in bed, as she knew she rose early. She went back into the kitchen and made herself a hot chocolate, she needed something warm and milky to steady her nerves. Lucy didn't know how long she sat there thinking and worrying, but what she did know is that her hot chocolate went cold. She got to her feet, took the step ladders from the cupboard exactly where Tom said they would be, and let herself quietly out of the back door.

Lucy crept silently along the path in the dead of night, Phyllis' cottage was in darkness and she breathed a sigh of relief at that at least. She placed the steps by the edge of the kitchen and reached up to open the small window. The cold glass touched her finger tips, but Lucy was relieved at just how easily the window opened. She gently eased her hand inside, this was one time she was very grateful for the long arms that her tall frame gave her, her fingers gripped the lever to open the main window, but it wouldn't budge. 'Oh no it's locked!' Lucy thought in despair, she gave it one final pull and the latch clicked open. Adrenaline pulsed through Lucy's veins as she nimbly opened the window and peered into the room. Spotting the mobile on the side she stretched out her arm across the worktop towards it. She stretched as far as she could, but couldn't quite grasp it. There was nothing for it, Lucy was going to have to climb inside. She stood precariously on the top step of the ladder, placed her knee on the window ledge and her hand rested on the draining board. Lucy reached out for a second time, this time reaching the phone easily. Her fingers wrapped around it and she eagerly brought it towards her, but she hadn't noticed a spoon on the draining board as she did so. The spoon fell into the sink with a clatter. Lucy hurriedly locked the main window and pushed the small one closed, grabbed the step ladders and ran as fast as she could back towards the main house. She pushed the bolt across the back door and switched off the light. If Phyllis came looking, she needed her to think that they were all in bed.

Lucy sat at the table to get her breath back, her heart hammering in her chest. Absentmindedly she picked up the cold hot chocolate and took a large gulp. "Urgh!" She said grimacing as the cold congealed chocolate reached her throat. She looked down at Phyllis' mobile phone she was holding in her hand, she'd better turn it off incase Phyllis started to ring it when she noticed it was missing. Once she'd scanned quickly through it she'd turn it off. 'What was that noise?' Lucy watched in horror as the back door handle started to move up and down. 'Oh my god' she thought, she had woken Phyllis after all. "Is there anyone there?" Came Phyllis' agitated voice. Lucy quickly switched off the phone and slipped from the room, she didn't have time to look at it now after all, she needed to hide it…but where? She stood in the dark hallway wracking her brains, where could she hide it that Phyllis wouldn't look? The thing is, Phyllis was the housekeeper, she went everywhere to clean…except the study. Phyllis didn't like to go in there as the last couple of days she had reported hearing a wailing sound when she was cleaning the room. Tom brushed it aside though, telling her it would be the wind whistling down the chimney. In honesty though, there was something about the study that made her feel uncomfortable as well, it sounded so silly, even to her, but she always had the feeling she was being watched.

Lucy walked silently up the stairs, careful not to wake anyone, and slipped into the study. 'Wow this place is even more unwelcoming at this time of night' she thought, she had never been here this late before. Lucy looked around, where on earth was she going to hide the phone? Her eyes fell on the large array of books on the top shelf next to the filing cabinet. Carrying the chair from the other side of the desk, she carefully stood on it, removed a book and placed the phone behind it. She stepped down and stood back to admire her handy work. 'There' she thought, you couldn't see a thing. Happy that she had hidden Phyllis' mobile in the best place she could think of, she quickly turned off the wall lights, closed the door and tip toed to her own bedroom. Once inside, she breathed a sigh of relief, she could not believe what she had just done. Lucy changed for bed, she had to get some sleep, she felt sure she would have a visit from Phyllis in the morning very early indeed.

By the time she heard Phyllis coming up the garden path the next morning, she and Paul were enjoying a cup of tea at the kitchen table. Lucy had just finished telling Paul of the happenings of the previous evening, when Phyllis burst through the door, a face like thunder. "Morning" Lucy said sweetly. Phyllis glared at her, "My phone's gone" she snapped. "Gone?" Asked Lucy in mock surprise. "Yes, I put it on charge when I went to bed and it wasn't there when I got up this morning" snapped Phyllis. "Oh I do that all the time, put my phone down and forget where I left it" said Paul sympathetically. "I didn't forget where I left it, I put it on the worktop" said Phyllis shortly. "Oh maybe it's still there" said Paul, jumping up to look. "Not here, at my cottage" barked Phyllis, looking at Paul as if he had taken leave of his senses. "I'm sure it will turn up, maybe you put it somewhere else" said Lucy helpfully. "I didn't put it anywhere else, someone must have taken it" Phyllis replied, still glaring. "Taken it? But how? You didn't leave any doors open did you?" Asked Paul. "Of course I didn't" Phyllis rasped. "Then how could…" Lucy began. "I don't know do i?!" Spat Phyllis menacingly. "Well if you're saying you've been robbed I'll call the police" said Paul standing up. Alarm suddenly registered in Phyllis' eyes and her face softened. "No there's no need for that, like you say it will turn up. Now what would you like for breakfast?" Phyllis smiled. "Scrambled egg on toast would be lovely please" said Lucy. "Yeah that sounds great" agreed Paul. As Phyllis busied herself in the kitchen, Lucy breathed a sigh of relief. She smiled inwardly knowing that the missing phone was safe out of Phyllis' reach.

What Lucy didn't know was that the phone was safe at that moment, very safe indeed, for right at that point, in the confines of the study, long but nimble fingers were frantically pressing the keys, searching through the texts. There were some very interesting texts on Phyllis' mobile phone, some very interesting ones indeed. There were texts from Avril, texts from someone called Pete and Ray, all containing information implicating both them and Phyllis in what had been going on, and then there were texts from someone else that weren't very friendly towards Phyllis at all. Most seemed to be arguing and disagreeing with her, but the last was much more sinister. There were three texts over the last two days, but none of them were signed. The first said 'Answer the phone woman!', the second 'You're annoying me now woman! You're not answering my texts or phone calls, don't mess with me okay?' The last though, was a lot more worrying 'You just don't learn do you? I wanted to do it my way, but no, we had to try your way first, and look where that's got us. Nowhere, that's where! Stupid interfering woman, well you've blown your chance...You won't answer the phone, so now I'm going to pay you a little visit. I'm coming to claim what should be mine once and for all' Well well well, whoever would have thought Fred would finally have enough backbone to do his own dirty work? Seems Hilltop Manor will be receiving an unwelcome visitor soon enough. Those long fingers switched off the mobile phone and replaced it where Lucy had hidden it, whilst smiling a knowing smile that didn't reach those steel blue eyes.

When Bruce entered the kitchen, Phyllis greeted him like a long lost friend. "Oh such an exciting time for you today! I'm sure this will be the day that Jeff comes back to us" Gushed Phyllis. "I certainly hope so" said Bruce, smiling apprehensively at her. "Now what would you like for breakfast? You need to keep your strength up" said Phyllis. "I don't want to put you to any trouble" he replied. "No trouble at all, bacon and eggs coming up" she trilled. Later, with everyone eaten and the children off to their craft club, Lucy and Bruce set off for the hospital in Tom's car. Nick insisted on staying home to look after Morph, he really didn't trust what Phyllis might do to him. When they reached Jeff's ward, they met Tom walking down the corridor with a cup of coffee and a sandwich, "Hi" he smiled. "How's Jeff?" Asked Bruce "He's fine, but they've moved him to a room down here" said Tom, leading the way. "Moved him, why? How is he?" Asked Bruce worriedly. "Why don't you ask him for yourself?" Tom replied, suddenly stopping and opening the door to his left. Lucy and Bruce peered into the room and there, propped up on the pillows, lay Jeff. "Hi dad" he said quietly. "Jeff!" Cried Bruce, rushing to hug him. "Hey, what's with the hugging?" Said Jeff with a chuckle. "The amount of years you've made me age in the last few days, I deserve a hug" laughed Bruce. "Hello Jeff" said Lucy warmly, "I'm so glad you're awake, you'll be back home with us before you know it". "Do I know you?" Jeff asked, a confused frown appearing on his forehead. "Yes, this is Lucy, the lady you work for that I told you about" said Tom. "Oh right, hello" said Jeff, looking relieved. "The doctor said he wants to talk to you as soon as you get here Bruce" said Tom. "He said to have him paged at reception and he will see you in the waiting room.". "I'll go and do that now, are you coming Lucy?" Said Bruce. "Yes of course" she replied. "I won't be long" Bruce told his son, grinning broadly. "I'm not going anywhere" said Jeff with a cheeky wave.

Mr Satoomi entered the waiting room a few minutes later. "Please let's sit down" he said, gesturing to the armchairs with his hand. "Why does my boy not remember Lucy?" Asked Bruce, "He looks so alert otherwise". "This can happen, when Jeff came round he was very confused and disorientated, and although he seems fine in himself, he doesn't seem to have completely regained his short term memory. He recognised his father because his memory of him is long, but he didn't know who Lucy was. This is honestly quite normal and in many cases the memory can return very quickly. Tom and I spent an hour with Jeff today, explaining who everyone was" he continued. "He remembers Tom and Mrs Armstrong from your household, and surprisingly Jake and Emily. But no one else that is new to his life." "He remembers Jake and Emily?" Said Lucy in surprise. "Yes, but when the brain is traumatised it often blocks out events and times it doesn't want to remember, maybe subconsciously he sees no threat from the children" said Mr Satoomi. "But Lucy, Amira and Paul aren't a threat" said Bruce confused. "No, but maybe the events or happenings that Jeff is trying to eliminate are around the same time he met them" said Mr Satoomi. "Phyllis" Bruce said darkly. "Jeff will be with us for a little while yet to enable us to keep on eye on him and allow some of his other injuries to heal, but I wondered if you could arrange to bring in familiar objects from home, photos, that sort of thing. And arrange for some familiar faces to visit?" Mr Satoomi asked. "Yes of course" said Lucy. "Thank you, I must go, but we will speak again soon"

Lucy and Bruce went back to Jeff once Mr Satoomi had left. "I've got some photos if you'd like to see them" said Lucy. "Yes please, it's just so frustrating not being able to remember" said Jeff with a frown. Lucy slowly showed Jeff the photos she had taken from her bag, he smiled at the pictures of the house, and of him doing jobs there, he chuckled at the photos of Jake and Emily, and frowned hard at those of her, Amira and Paul. "I'm sorry, I just don't seem to know these people" he said apologetically. "Don't apologise son, it will come" said Bruce reassuringly. "Morph!" He said with a grin, running his finger across the photo of Morph and his squeaky bone. "You remember Morph?" Asked Tom surprised. "Yes, for some reason I do" he whispered. "Let's look at some more Jeff" said Lucy softly, but when she tried to show Jeff the smiling picture of Phyllis he pushed it away. "I don't want to look at any more, I'm tired" he said, turning his head away and gazing out of the window. "Okay of course" said Lucy, putting the photos away and frowning worriedly at Tom and Bruce.

"Did you recognise the lady in the photo?" Bruce asked softly. "No" said Jeff sharply. "Shall we let Jeff get some sleep and come back a bit later?" Asked Tom. "Yes please, I'll see you later" he said, closing his eyes. Lucy, Tom and Bruce decided they would go home and come back that afternoon. They stopped off for a few things they needed in town and decided to go and meet Jake and Emily from craft club as a surprise. Lucy leant against the tree by the gates, she was so glad Jeff was awake, but very worried about his reaction to Phyllis. "Mummy!" Cried a little voice. She looked up and saw Jake hurtling towards her with Paul not far behind. "Woah, hello Jakey!" She cried, picking him up and swinging him round. "Mummy I didn't know you were coming" said Jake excitedly. "I know, I wanted to surprise you" she said, hugging him to her. "Where's Emily?" Lucy asked with a smile. "Amira took her to the toilet" Paul replied. "Look Emily, it's mummy" said Amira, spotting her as they came out of the reception doors. "Mummy!" Squealed an excited Emily running over to her. "Hello poppet" beamed Lucy, bending down to give her a huge hug. "Hi, how's Jeff?" Asked Amira. "I'll explain in the car, let me just tell Tom and Bruce I'm going to travel back with you" said Lucy, crossing the road to where they had parked.

She settled in the back seat with Jake and Emily as Paul began the drive home. "Jeff was awake which is great news and a lovely surprise when we got to the hospital" Lucy started to explain. "He was talking fine, though tires easily. It does appear that his short term memory, mainly the last week or two doesn't appear to be up to speed yet" she continued. "So what does that mean exactly then?" Amira asked. "He remembers his father and Tom as he has known them longer, but not us, as he's met us more recently. The strange thing is though, he remembers Jake and Emily, and even Morph" she finished. "Oh how odd" said Amira. "The doctor suggested we show Jeff some photos to try to jog his memory, and he was looking through quite happily" said Lucy. "Oh that's good" said Amira smiling. "Until I showed him a photo of Phyllis. He looked totally alarmed, pushed the photographs away and said he was tired" Lucy continued. "Oh" said Amira in shock. "When his dad asked him if he recognised Phyllis he said no" added Lucy. "Obviously some sort of recognition there, even if he doesn't actually realise it" added Paul. "Poor guy" said Amira sympathetically. "I know" Lucy nodded.

"Can we go and see Jeff? I've got a football drawing in my bag for him" Jake piped up out of the blue. "Ooh yes, I want to see Jeff too" said Emily. Lucy gazed at both of her children, they'd missed Jeff these past few days. "Do you know, I think that would be a very good idea" she said. "Yay!" Chorused both the children together. Paul smiled at Lucy in the rearview mirror, he could tell what she was thinking. "Do you think that Paul and I could see Jeff tomorrow? We don't want to overwhelm him" asked Amira. "Yes, definitely" Lucy nodded. The post office van was just leaving Hilltop Manor as Paul deftly swung the car through the gates before they closed.

CHAPTER 9

THE TRUTH ABOUT PHYLLIS

When they went in, Tom and Bruce were already sitting at the kitchen table with Phyllis, telling her all about their visit to Jeff. "Oh I'm so glad he's on the mend, such a lovely boy" Phyllis cooed. "Yes he is" agreed Amira, and just for a second there it seemed like Phyllis actually meant it. "We're taking Jake and Emily to see him later today" said Lucy "Oh that will be nice" Phyllis replied. "In fact, why don't you come along? You haven't seen Jeff since his accident and I'm sure you're eager to visit him" said Tom. "Oh, er, no I don't want to intrude" stammered Phyllis, the panic clearly visible in her eyes. "You wouldn't be intruding, would she Bruce? And anyway, you're one of the family" Tom insisted. "No of course you should come and see him" Bruce agreed. "Oh I'd love to but I have some dry cleaning that is overdue for collecting, and I must get that today" stuttered Phyllis. "It's not a problem, we can collect it on the way. It will be much easier than you having to bring it back on the bus. There, that's settled then" finished Tom, before Phyllis got a chance to argue. "Oh, er, okay, that would be lovely" she said, seeing she was beaten. "Excellent" said Lucy. "It's my afternoon off, so if you'll excuse me I have some cleaning to do at the cottage" muttered Phyllis. "Yes of course, we'll be leaving at around five" said Tom, calling after her as she departed down the garden path. He leant against the back door and burst into laughter.

"I don't think someone was at all happy about visiting Jeff do you?" Laughed Paul. "Not at all, and I wonder why!" Said Tom sarcastically. Just after 4pm there was the sound of footsteps and the click of the latch on the rear gate, Tom quietly opened the back door and looked out. "Entirely as I thought" he tutted, "What is it Tom?" Asked Nick. "Look" he said, pointing towards the main gate. Everyone squeezed into the doorway, and there, hurrying down the drive, was Phyllis. "Well I'll be blowed, so much for visiting Jeff" said Bruce. "That woman never had any intentions of visiting Jeff mate" Tom said, shaking his head. "How awful" said Amira, turning her nose up in distaste. "That's okay, I know she's arranged to collect the dry cleaning today as I phoned to check a little while ago. How long does it take to get to town on the bus from here, does anyone know?" Tom asked. "Er, about 45 minutes I should think" said Amira. "Good, can you have Jake and Emily ready to leave in about 20 minutes?" Tom asked Lucy. "Are we going back to the hospital earlier than planned?" Lucy asked. "No, we're going to wait for Phyllis outside the dry cleaners, to save her the bus trip home of course" said Tom with a wicked grin.

Tom took the short cut, and he, Lucy, Bruce and the children were sitting outside Grey's Dry Cleaners with ten minutes to spare before Phyllis' bus was due to arrive. As it pulled in to it's stop, she got off, deep in conversation with an older man with grey hair, that kept flopping down over his eyes. As he and Phyllis chatted, he kept pushing it back as if it were annoying him. "Oh my, this really is our day. Isn't that Mr Purple Trainers' accomplice?" He said, turning to Lucy. "Good heavens, you're right it is. I'm calling the police" she said, grabbing her mobile. DCI Fields' phone at the police station was answered by DS Lowe, 'What luck it's someone I know', thought Lucy, explaining things to her. DS Lowe promised to get the man picked up as soon as he was out of sight of Phyllis. After about five minutes Mr Purple Trainers' friend kissed Phyllis on the cheek and walked off up the street with a cheery smile. She went straight into the dry cleaners, unaware she was being watched, and emerged a few minutes later with the clothes. Quick as a flash Tom was out of the car, "Phyllis!" He called. "Oh, er, hello" she said, clearly shocked at his sudden appearance. "Isn't that lucky bumping into you here? Let me take those for you to save you the bus ride home. We can call in to see Jeff on the way. There you go, mind your head" said Tom, grabbing Phyllis by the arm and steering her into the car, before she had chance to know what was happening. He jumped back behind the wheel and pulled out into the traffic before she could protest.

Minutes later they were parked in the hospital carpark. "Here you go

Phyllis, let me help you" said Tom, opening the door and helping her out, she hadn't uttered a word and continued to glare ahead and allow herself to be steered towards Jeff's ward. "You take Jake and Emily in to see Jeff, Phyllis and I will be just fine in the waiting room, won't we Phyllis?" Tom smiled to Lucy. Bruce opened the door and Jeff had his head turned looking out of the window. "You have two very special visitors son" he said. Jeff slowly turned his head, his whole face lighting up when he saw Jake and Emily. "Hi guys! Do I get a hug?" He grinned. Bruce lifted Jake and Emily up in turn, warning them to be very gentle. "I've got you a picture, it's a football one I made in art" said Jake, taking it from behind his back to show him. "Wow that's great, thank you so much" said Jeff, reaching out slowly to ruffle Jake's hair with his finger tips. "I drew the ball!" Added Emily. "A fine ball it is too! Thank you both very much" said Jeff. "High five" said Jake, raising his hand in the air. "Jeff hasn't got the energy for high fives Jake" Lucy said softly. "Nonsense, I've always got the energy for a high five, but you may have to come a little lower than that." Jeff told Jake with a chuckle. He chatted with Jake and Emily about all the things they were going to do when he was better. Watching him with the children, the old Jeff seemed to be fully back with them, thought Lucy. "I'm going to take Jake and Emily for a drink, I don't want them tiring you out" said Lucy with a smile. "You have another visitor Jeff" said Bruce. "Who?" He asked.

The door opened and Phyllis was ushered into the room by Tom. For a split second fear, panic, hatred, there was definitely something that appeared in Jeff's eyes momentarily, and then it was gone. "Hello Jeff, I'm sorry about what happened. I was so worried when I heard" blurted Phyllis "I'm sorry I don't mean to be rude, but do I know you?" He said. "I'm Phyllis, Lucy's housekeeper" she said warily. "Oh hello, I'm pleased to meet you" Jeff replied simply. "So...so you really don't remember me?" Asked Phyllis. "No, I'm afraid I don't" he replied. Realisation dawning at what Jeff's loss of memory might mean for her, a slow, satisfied grin spread across Phyllis's face. "Never mind, no point in living in the past I always say" she said brightly, patting Jeff's arm. "Amira and Paul will come and see you tomorrow, and Lucy's son Nick. Remember, I told you about them?" Said Tom, eager to change the subject. "Yes, I remember things that have happened since I woke up and things that happened before, it's just the last few weeks that have completely disappeared, as if that part of my life never happened" said Jeff, shaking his head sadly.

Lucy and the children were in the waiting room watching TV, a kindly nurse had managed to find them a cartoon channel. There was a knock on the door and PC Regan popped his head in, "Can I speak to you for a moment please Mrs Reid?" He said. "Yes, of course. Jake, Emily, I'll be just outside the door" she said. Jake and Emily were so engrossed watching the colourful characters bounding around on the TV screen, that they didn't even look up. Lucy followed PC Regan from the room and closed the door behind her. "Mrs Reid, I just wanted to let you know this is my last shift with Jeff tonight. DCI Fields feels that with Jeff having lost his short term memory, he's no longer under any threat from individuals that may have wanted to harm him" he said. "Oh…Thank you for letting me know, we shall miss your happy smiling face around here" Lucy said. "That's what I wanted to ask, do you think Mr Fisher would mind if I carried on visiting Jeff? We had a good chat earlier and being with him the last few days and seeing what he's been through, makes me feel like he's a mate I want to see get better." Said PC Regan. "I think that's a lovely idea Scott and I think Bruce would be delighted" said Lucy with a smile. "Thank you" he replied. Lucy went back into the waiting room, where Jake and Emily didn't seem to have moved an inch. Twenty minutes later, the door opened and Bruce came in. "Jeff's getting tired and says he needs a hug from his two best friends so that he can sleep well tonight" he smiled. "That's us!" Cried Jake and Emily, rushing to the door. As Bruce took them back across the corridor to say goodbye to Jeff, Lucy put her head back on the high armchair and sighed heavily. These last few months of her life had been such a whirlwind of emotions, she had spoken to DCI Fields this morning and still no news on Ben. He had disappeared without a trace it seemed. Lucy gave herself a mental shake…She knew she must be strong like Ben would be and tell herself it was a matter of when she saw him again…not if.

"Penny for them?" Said a male voice. Lucy looked up to see DCI Fields standing in the doorway, she hadn't heard him come in. "Hello" she said with a smile. "Fantastic news about Jeff. I called in this morning by chance and Tom told me he was back with us" said the DCI. "Yes it is great news, and even more so for Phyllis as it appears he can't remember her" Lucy said. "Yeah, I'm sure that does make things easier for her" said

DCI Fields thoughtfully. "So what brings you here?" Lucy asked. "Well to be honest I came to see Jeff, I just needed to ask him a few more questions. I also wanted a quick word with you" DCI Fields replied. "Oh?" Said Lucy, raising an eyebrow questioningly. "Yes, I managed to speak to Phyllis' last employer today. He's living in Kuwait" said the DCI. "That's good, and was she a good employee?" Asked Lucy. "Mr Harrison-Jones has never heard of Phyllis Snow, and Eastbourne Lodge is a stately home, which was closed to the public four years ago when he moved abroad. The lodge is now looked after by an on sight caretaker, Mr Rahman, who lives there with his family" said DCI Fields. "Oh my god!" Gasped Lucy. "I called out to see Mr Rahman a short while ago, he's an African man who speaks very little English, and his wife none at all" DCI Fields concluded. "So Phyllis lied" said Lucy. "Yes, I'm afraid she did" nodded DCI Fields. At that moment the door opened and Tom, Bruce, Phyllis, Jake and Emily walked in. Phyllis eyed DCI Fields suspiciously, "Is everything okay Lucy?" Asked Phyllis. "Yes fine, DCI Fields was very kindly keeping me company whilst you were all visiting Jeff" she smiled. "Very good of you to call here this late" said Phyllis, looking DCI Fields brazenly in the eye. "Not at all, I need a word with Jeff and chatting with Mrs Reid is a charming way to pass the time while I'm waiting" replied DCI Fields, eyeing Phyllis cooly. Lucy went to say goodbye to Jeff and reminded him that Amira and Paul would be in to see him the next day.

When they got home Nick told her that Bill had called. "Bill?" Asked Lucy blankly. "Yes, Bill from Bartons" said Nick. "Oh, of course, I wonder what he wanted?" Said Lucy in surprise. "He wants you to ring him back, he told me to tell you it doesn't matter what time, he'll be waiting." Nick replied. "Okay, I'll call him now" she said, taking the piece of paper with the number on from Nick. "I'll go and see Phyllis stays in the kitchen" said Nick. Lucy dialled the number and waited for Bill to answer. "Hello?" Said Bill's voice. "Hi Bill, it's Lucy Reid, I'm sorry I missed your call." She said. "Please don't worry about that Mrs Reid, I just thought I should call you" said Bill. "Oh, is everything okay?" She asked. "When you left Bartons it was playing on my mind what Phyllis Kramer's married name was, when my wife got in I asked her if she could remember. Lucy, that bloke she ran off to marry was called Fred Reid." Said Bill. "Reid? Are you sure?" Said Lucy, failing to hide the shock in her voice. "Yes, quite sure, my wife was adamant" declared Bill. Lucy felt like she'd been punched in the stomach and sat down on the sofa with a start. "Er, thank you Bill, I really appreciate you letting me know" she said, regaining her composure. "You're welcome Mrs Reid, I'll bid you goodnight then" said Bill, replacing the receiver. "Do you want a cup of tea Lucy? I've been told to tell you the kettle's on" said Amira, entering the room. Amira was going to get Jake and Emily ready for bed and had brought them in to say goodnight. Lucy opened her arms and cuddled her children to her. She kissed them both. When she went into the kitchen, Tom, Paul, Bruce and Nick were all sitting chatting. Phyllis was cooking bacon sandwiches. "Would you like a bacon sandwich Lucy?" Phyllis chirped. "No thank you" she replied. "Are you okay Lucy?" Nick asked, seeing something was wrong. "Yes, I'm fine" she smiled weakly. She couldn't tell them all about Eastbourne Lodge and Phyllis' real surname with Phyllis there.

"Jeff looked so well considering everything, didn't he?" Said Bruce. "Yes he certainly did" said Tom. Lucy glanced towards Phyllis, who had a big smile on her face. 'Urgh, that woman really is the limit' she shuddered. "I'm going to go and watch TV for a while before bed. Night everyone" said Lucy softly. Her news would have to wait until tomorrow. Lucy looked in on the children, they were asleep already, both squashed into Jake's racing car bed as usual, with Emily's princess bed laying empty. Morph opened a tired eye as she entered the room, and upon seeing it was her, let out a deep sigh and closed it again. She went into her own bedroom and took her mobile from her bag. She would ring DCI Fields and leave a message on his answerphone at the police station, asking him to call her tomorrow. She dialled the number and his extension began to ring, "Hello DCI Fields" said his voice. "Oh, er, hello, it's Lucy Reid, I was expecting your answer phone" she said. "I had to come back to the station for something, is everything okay?" Said the DCI. "I had a call from Bill, the guy who clears the carpark at Bartons" said Lucy. "Yeah I know Bill, lovely old guy" said DCI Fields. "When I was at Bartons he recognised the photo of Phyllis and told me her name was Kramer when he knew her. Well he couldn't remember the surname of that Fred guy that she ran off to marry, just that he was a bad lot" Lucy continued. "Yes I remember, he was going to ask his wife if she knew his name" said the DCI. "Well he asked her and Phyllis' married name is Reid" blurted Lucy. The line went silent, but Lucy could hear DCI Fields' breathing, so she knew he was still there. "Is it now? Well that's very interesting indeed" he said. "That's such a coincidence" said Lucy. "Or is it?" Said the DCI thoughtfully. "What do you mean?" Lucy asked in surprise. "Well didn't you say this Fred was disgraced from his family?" Said the DCI. "Oh my god, you don't think Phyllis could be part of the Reid family do you?" Asked Lucy, shocked. "I don't know, but I sure as hell intend to find out" said DCI Fields. "What a horrible thought" said Lucy. "Yes indeed, leave it with me, I'll call you tomorrow. Goodnight" said DCI Fields. Lucy put her mobile phone on the bedroom cabinet and pushed her charger lead into the end. She was never going to get caught out with a flat battery again. As she lay in bed her mind flitted from one happening to the next, 'What on earth is going on here?' She thought as she drifted off into a restless sleep.

When Lucy woke the next morning she text Nick, Tom, Amira and Paul, asking them if they would meet her on the garden patio at 9, but keep it a secret from Phyllis. "Oh someone's important, I feel quite left out" laughed Phyllis, as all their mobiles beeped together. "Remember to put my lottery tickets on" Nick chuckled, reading his message. "Anyway you two, who's up for football?" Cried Tom. "Can Phyllis play?" Asked Jake. "Not this time, she's very busy and we mustn't disturb her" said Nick, hustling them both out of the door. "You coming Bruce?" Asked Tom. "Oooh, too energetic for me, but I'll certainly come and watch" he said, trooping out of the door behind them. Lucy was sitting at the table on the patio waiting for them. "Jake, would you and Emily play with Morph for me? Just while I have a quick word with everyone else" said Lucy. "Yes mummy, let's play football!" Shouted Jake, kicking the ball onto the lawn. Lucy laughed as she watched the three of them race after it. She turned to face everyone, who were now sitting around the table expectantly. "When we were at the hospital last night I saw DCI Fields. He's looked into Phyllis' previous employer, he's living abroad, but has never heard of Phyllis. Eastbourne Lodge has been closed for about four years, and the resident caretaker there speaks little or no English" said Lucy. "So Phyllis has lied again" Bruce declared, shaking his head in disbelief. "But why?" Asked Amira puzzled. "I honestly don't know" replied Lucy. "She seems to have gone to a lot of trouble to get into this house" frowned Nick. "I know, but it gets worse. When I went to Bartons yesterday, Bill, who works there, recognised

Phyllis from a photo. He remembered her marrying some guy called Fred who was up to no good, but couldn't remember her married name. He rang last night to tell me his wife had remembered what it was. Phyllis' married name is Reid" Lucy declared solemnly. "What?!" Gasped Nick in amazement. "Are you telling us that you and Phyllis could be related?!" Asked Bruce in horror. "Good grief I hope not!" Spat Nick. "So do I. I'm waiting for DCI Fields to look into it and see what he comes up with" said Lucy earnestly.

"Paul and I were thinking, do you mind if the children come back with us again to see Jeff today?" Amira asked. "Not at all, but I was thinking we might take them to the fair on the field behind Bartons as well? They're doing a special event for under 10s between 11 and 1, Tom was telling me" said Lucy. "Oh okay, we can take them another time" said Amira. "No, I didn't mean that, I meant why don't we all pop into the fair first, and then visit Jeff when it's time?" Lucy said. "What a good idea, the fair has only extended its run here to mark the celebrations for the Mayor's birthday" said Tom. "That's settled then" Paul agreed. Just then the phone rang and Lucy got up to answer it. "Hello?" Said a gruff male voice. "Hello, can I help you?" Said Lucy. "Oh I'm sure you can, but we'll leave that pleasure for another time darling" said the voice lewdly, whilst laughing loudly at his own suggestive remark. "Did you want something? Who is this?" Lucy asked. "Don't matter who I am sweetheart, we can meet soon enough, but for now where's Phyllis?" The voice leered demandingly. "Nick, could you tell Phyllis there's someone on the phone for her please?" Said Lucy. "Phone for me?" Said Phyllis surprised, coming into the living room a few minutes later. "Yes it's a man, I didn't get his name" said Lucy, handing her the receiver.

At that moment Morph jumped up onto the coffee table, sending the phone crashing to the floor. "No!" Cried Nick, grabbing a growling Morph and taking him outside again. "Ere what's going on?" Came the distant voice on the end of the line. "Oh at least he's still there" Said Lucy, placing the base of the phone back on the table. Phyllis just stood there, rooted to the spot, staring at the receiver still in her hand. "Aren't you going to say anything Phyllis?" Asked Nick, who had just come back into the room. "Oh er, yes…hello?" Said Phyllis warily into the receiver. "Come on Nick, let's go back and join the others and let Phyllis have some privacy" said

Lucy. Tom was sitting facing the open patio doors and he watched Phyllis intently. Although he couldn't actually hear what was going on, there was something in Phyllis' demeanour that made him feel this phone call was not a pleasant one. When Phyllis had finished her call, she came out onto the patio. "Lucy I know it's an awful cheek, but Nick said you were going to the fair, would you mind if I came along too?" She asked. "Well no, I don't mind, but there's not enough seats in the car" said Lucy. "Oh okay, doesn't matter" said Phyllis, actually looking genuinely disappointed. "Unless Tom and Paul wouldn't mind taking both of their cars?" Lucy suggested. "Fine with me" said Tom. "Me too" Paul replied. "Oh thank you" said Phyllis, relieved. Tom stared at her, he couldn't make her out at all. Why was she so desperate to come to a fun fair? And then so relived when she was told she could, he wondered. No matter how hard he tried, he couldn't shake the uneasy feeling that Phyllis' sudden interest in fairs was something to do with that phone call. He just didn't know what.

About an hour later they were all settled in the cars on route to the fair, Lucy, Jake, Emily and Phyllis in Tom's car and Amira, Nick and Bruce travelled with Paul. Tom insisted Phyllis was in the same car as the children, as he thought that was safer. He knew the police had the guy that tried to run Lucy off the road, but just incase there was another of Phyllis' accomplices waiting to try a similar thing, Tom figured the car with Phyllis herself in was likely to be the safer place to be. "Can we go on the bumper cars please mummy?" Asked Jake excitedly. "I think we could arrange that" Laughed Lucy. "Can I go on them too mummy?" Asked Emily. She wasn't sure Emily even knew what bumper cars were, but she loved to do anything her big brother did. "Tell you what, we'll have a driving competition, Paul and Jake against you and me Emily" teased Tom. "Yay!" Squealed Emily happily. As they all walked across the field towards the fair, Phyllis was glancing furtively from side to side and kept sneaking glances over her shoulder. "Are you okay Phyllis?" Asked Bruce. When she didn't reply, he asked again "Phyllis is everything alright?" Lucy touched Phyllis' arm to get her attention "What?" Stammered Phyllis, jumping sky high. "Are you okay?" Lucy asked. "Oh, er, yeah fine thank you" she mumbled.

When they found the bumper cars, Paul and Jake climbed into a blue one and Tom lifted Emily into a green one. As the cars swept round the track, dodging and chasing each other, Jake and Emily roared with laughter. Lucy, Amira, Nick, Bruce and Phyllis cheered and smiled from the sidelines. When they were finished, Jake and Emily were both wearing beaming smiles. "What can we go on now mummy?" Asked Jake excitedly. "How about the Waltzer?" Suggested Nick. "What's that?" Asked Emily. "Come on I'll show you, who's going with us?" Said Nick, grabbing Jake and Emily's hands. "I will!" Shouted Amira, over the noise of the bumper cars beginning their next circuit. "This is fun, but I think I'll go and find myself a tea bar or something to take a breather" Phyllis laughed. "I'll come with you" said Bruce. "No" snapped Phyllis. Bruce looked taken aback at her abruptness. "Oh okay, I just thought you might have wanted some company" said Bruce. "Yes of course I would have, but I wouldn't want you missing out on all the fun" said Phyllis, softening her tone. With that, she walked off with a cheery wave. It seemed Phyllis had been right, there was a tea bar nearby, but she walked straight past it. She carried on along the small parade of shops on the opposite side of the field to Bartons. "Well I never, Phyllis Kramer" said a male voice. Phyllis spun round, straight into Bill. "Oh, er, hello Bill. Long time no see" said Phyllis. "Certainly is, so how's married life treating you?" Bill smiled cheerily. "Married? I'm not married" Phyllis said, with definite hostility in her voice. "The Mrs said you married that Fred Reid you went off with" Bill persisted. "Well she's wrong, I don't know anyone called Fred and I've never been married. Now I must go" Phyllis said coldly, and hurried off round the corner.

"Oh okay" said Bill, puzzled at Phyllis' offhand manner. He walked off back along the parade. 'Oh no, I've forgotten my paper, I'd forget my head if it weren't screwed on' he thought to himself. When Bill turned around to go back to the newsagents, he saw Phyllis going into the cafe on the end. 'I thought she was in a hurry' Bill thought, annoyed at her obvious rudeness to him a few minutes ago. He marched towards the cafe, he would ask her exactly what she was playing at. As Bill went to open the door, he glanced in the window and stopped dead in his tracks. There, at a table near the front, sat Phyllis and Fred Reid. Bill bristled with anger, there was two things he disliked, liars and rudeness. He decided that this wasn't the Phyllis Kramer that he used to know, being in with a bad crowd had obviously changed her. He would get his paper and then get off to work, he had more important things to think of than that woman.

Inside the cafe, Fred still hadn't said a word. He just sat eating his sandwich, not taking his eyes off of Phyllis for a second. Once the last mouthful had gone, he looked at her and hissed "Cat got your tongue woman? Seems to have as you don't appear able to answer your calls." "I told you Fred, I've lost my phone" Phyllis replied. "Stupid as well as useless" he sneered menacingly. "What do you want Fred?" Phyllis asked quietly. "I'm taking them paintings to be valued today down south" he said. "You can't...it's too soon. It's only been a matter of days" Phyllis said firmly. "Don't tell me what I can and can't do woman. This is getting too close for comfort now those blithering idiots Pete and Ray have been caught" he snarled. "They've been caught? How? When?" Asked Phyllis in horror. "The cops picked Ray up for trying to run her you work for off the road" Fred asked. "Lucy? Oh my god. Why did you tell him to do that?" Asked Phyllis shocked. "I didn't tell him woman, the man's an idiot! He appeared in court this morning I heard" said Fred. "So why aren't you there?" Phyllis said. "Are you mad? I ain't going that close to the filth" spat Fred in horror. "What's happened to Pete?" Phyllis asked. "All I know is the cops picked him up for questioning in town yesterday, and they've still got him" said Fred. "In town? I met him in town" said Phyllis in shock. "You did what?!" Exploded Fred, slamming his fist onto the table. "He was on the bus when I got on it, it wasn't planned. Keep your voice down" hissed Phyllis, realising everyone had turned to look. "This is getting far too close" muttered Fred. "What happens if they talk?" Said Phyllis worriedly. "They wont, they know the score" replied Fred confidently. "I hope you're right, I'm just glad Avril's away and can't get caught up in this" said Phyllis. "Yeah, so am I, cos if they had her, we would have a problem. That girl's a definite liability, not got the brains she was born with" sneered Fred. "You leave Avril alone" snapped Phyllis defensively.

"Now, like I told you, the paintings go today. Then once I've got the money I'll come for you. Be ready woman and we'll be out of here. I want what's mine and I will get it eventually, but for now the cash from those paintings will do nicely" said Fred, his voice full of menace.

"It's too early Fred" said Phyllis brazenly. "That's enough, be ready woman" Fred barked, as he pushed his chair back and strode out of the cafe. Phyllis ordered herself another cup of tea, she needed to think. This was all going very wrong, not how she'd planned at all.

Bill was wandering around the fairground, trying to pass the half an hour before he was due at work. As he passed the Snax Wagon at the edge of the fair, the enticing smell of bacon frying was too much for him. He gave in to temptation, ordered one and sat down to eat. "Hello Bill" said Lucy, noticing him there as she and Tom walked by. "Hello Mrs Reid, lovely to see you again" Bill smiled, hastily wiping his mouth with a serviette. "I don't suppose you've seen Phyllis around have you? She said she was going to the tea bar, and we've come to look for her as we're ready to leave." Said Lucy. "I have actually, and damn rude I found her too" said Bill. "Why, what happened?" Asked Tom. "I bumped into her at the parade" Bill replied, pointing towards the shops. "The parade? What on earth was she doing over there?" Lucy asked puzzled. "She was very rude and offhand to me, and told me she was in a hurry. Then when I looked back she was going into the cafe on the corner" said Bill. "How odd, we'd better go and meet her. She must have been sitting over there on her own quite a while" said Lucy. "Oh she wasn't alone" said Bill. "She wasn't?" Asked Tom, raising an eyebrow. "No she was with her Fred" said Bill pointedly. "Was she now? Let's go and meet her" said Tom to Lucy. "Okay, see you soon Bill." Lucy said with a wave. "No problem" he replied, turning back to his now cold bacon sandwich.

As Lucy and Tom neared the parade, Phyllis came hurrying towards them. "Oh sorry dears, have you been looking for me?" She cried. "Yes, we thought you were going to the tea bar" said Lucy. "Oh yes I was there, but had to nip to the cafe to use the toilet. Now where's those children?" Said Phyllis, scurrying off. "Another lie" said Lucy to Tom. "Certainly seems so" he nodded with sigh. Just as they were all getting in the car, Phyllis stopped suddenly and said "I'll meet you at the hospital, I nearly forgot there is something I need to do." "That's okay we can wait for you" said Tom. "No, no, no, certain people can't see this" insisted Phyllis, gesturing towards Lucy with her head. "Oh okay" said Tom. It was Lucy's 27th birthday in a few days, so if Phyllis was planning a present there wasn't a lot he could say. "We will see you at the hospital" said Lucy, climbing into the front seat. "Bye!" Said Phyllis, hurrying away. "Well I wonder what she's up to now" said Tom. "Oh Tom, that's very cynical!" Scolded Lucy with a grin. "Where that woman's concerned now, there's always doubt in my mind." Tom finished. "Can Nick come with us now?" Asked Emily, trying to pull her eldest brother into the car with her. "Of course he can" said Tom. Nick got in next to Jake and Emily. "Shall we make a video of the fair as we drive away?" He said, pulling his mobile phone from his pocket. "Ooh yes!" Cried Jake. "Yes, just like you did to show mummy we ate all our breakfast this morning!" Shouted Emily. Nick laughed at their excitement, he loved nothing better than seeing them smile.

"What's this?" He said, frowning at the black screen showing in his list of video recordings. He scrolled down to it and pressed play... "I told you never to ring me here. What on earth are you playing at?" Came Phyllis' voice. "No Fred, it's too dangerous, you can't come here...I told you, I'm dealing with it." "Oh my god, that's Phyllis" said Lucy, turning round from the front. "Fred, you've got the paintings, what more do you want?" Continued Phyllis. "That must be her on the phone this morning, I left my mobile on the table next to it and Morph must have pressed record somehow when he jumped up on the table." Nick said in disbelief. "No Fred, I can't meet you, it's too dangerous...No, you can't come here" Phyllis insisted. "I don't believe this, what a clever dog!" Laughed Tom. "Okay, they're going to the fair, I'll see if I can get a lift and meet you in the cafe on the corner... I'll be there as soon as I can" Phyllis growled. There was a click as the call was ended. "Just like a jigsaw, it's all coming together" smirked Tom.

CHAPTER 10

THE UNWELCOME VISITOR

When they got to the hospital carpark, Nick made sure there was no one around and played the video to Paul, Bruce and Amira. All three stood open mouthed in shock. "Oh wow, that woman is involved with everything that's happened it seems" said Amira. "I really hope they throw the book at her when they eventually pick her up" said Bruce. "Oh I'm sure they will" Paul reassured him. When they eventually reached Jeff's ward, Lucy took everyone else into the waiting room whilst Amira and Paul went in to see him. There was only really meant to be two people around the bed at a time. Nick would wait and go in with Jake and Emily, as the hospital staff had said that was okay, when Amira and Paul got back. They knew they wouldn't be allowed to stay long as Jeff still tired easily. Lucy felt her mobile start to vibrate in her pocket, she hadn't realised she hadn't turned it off. She looked at her phone and saw DCI Fields' number flash up on the front. "Hi, surely you're not still on duty?" She asked concerned. "No, I'm at home but I asked to be contacted as soon as the further checks I asked for on Phyllis came through." He replied. "Oh okay" said Lucy, pausing apprehensively. "I'd like to meet you later if that's possible, but not at Hilltop Manor" said the DCI. "Yes of course, is everything okay?" Said Lucy. "It's complicated, I'd sooner explain face to face" he said. "Er, alright. We're going to the Yew Tree when we leave the hospital for a meal. Do you know it? It's on Suffolk Road, near the stream" she asked. "Yes, I know it. Will Phyllis be with you?" Asked DCI Fields. "No, she didn't turn up to visit Jeff" replied Lucy. "That's good as it's her I need to talk to you about" said the DCI. "Okay we should be at the restaurant for six, is that too early?" Asked Lucy. "No, that's fine, see you then. Bye" said DCI Fields, and the line went dead. Lucy switched off her mobile and placed it back in her pocket. "DCI Fields wants to meet us at the Yew Tree at 6 o'clock, he says he wants to talk about Phyllis." Said Lucy worriedly. It was so lovely to get to see Jeff looking so much more like his old self. 'Mr Satoomi said if it carries on like this he will be home in no time' Lucy thought to herself.

As they drove into the carpark of the Yew Tree Pub, DCI Fields and DS Lowe were already sitting in their car in the corner of the carpark. Tom parked next to them so that they could talk through the window. "I'm sorry to keep you from your work DCI Fields" said Lucy politely. "We don't start until 9 tonight as we are working on a special assignment, we just came early to meet you" he replied. "In that case, why don't you both join us for dinner?" Asked Tom. "No, we couldn't impose" said DS Lowe. "Nonsense, you wouldn't be imposing at all, please join us even if it's only for a snack." Tom insisted. "In that case, thank you very much, we accept" said DCI Fields. "I'll just go over and make sure it's okay to change the booking, but when there's this many of us already, I can't see two more making any difference" laughed Nick. When he returned he said, "They're quite busy tonight, but said they will fit us in if we don't mind eating in the function room. I told them that would be okay as I thought there would be less chance of us being overheard in there anyway". "Perfect" said Tom. When they went in, they found the function room to be very homely, not too large, but with plush carpets and warm decor. Amira took the children to play in the soft play area once they had chosen their meal, Jake decided on chicken nuggets, chips and peas and Emily wanted fish goujons, jacket potato and beans.

Amira couldn't resist the home-made lasagne with a mixed salad. Everyone made small talk, chatting about everything imaginable while they chose what they would have to eat. Lucy decided on chicken kiev with new potatoes and mixed vegetables, Tom had rump steak with home-made chips and peas, Nick opted for spaghetti bolognese, Paul an all-day breakfast, while Bruce decided on good old British fish and chips. "I think we'll have something from the lighter bites menu" said DCI Fields. "Please, choose whatever it is you want" said Tom. DCI Fields settled on scampi in a basket and DS Lowe on New York Chicken and baked potato. Once the waitress had taken the order and everyone was settled with a drink, the discussion turned to Phyllis.

"As we now know, the married name of Phyllis is Reid. The question is, does she have any connection to your family Lucy?" Said DCI Fields solemnly. "Does she?" Asked Lucy, almost holding her breath. DCI Fields handed Lucy a photograph, "That's Fred Reid" he said. "Oh my god!" Said Lucy, clasping her hand to her mouth in shock. "What is it?" Said Tom, leaning over to get a better look at Fred's photo. "It's him! The man in the torn photo with Grandad" said Nick, looking over Lucy's shoulder. "Yes" said DS Lowe, nodding. "That means Phyllis and I are related" swallowed Lucy. "Yes it does I'm afraid. Fred Reid is Great Aunt Maud's nephew. So, your father in law's cousin" said DCI Fields. "I'm sorry, this is just so much to take in" said Lucy quietly. "We understand that Mrs Reid" said DS Lowe sympathetically. "But why? What does Phyllis want with my family, and why is she trying to hurt us? Why hasn't she said who she is?" Said Lucy puzzled. "I believe there was some falling out in the family years ago, long before you even met Ben. What's not clear yet is what it was over" said DCI Fields. "So are you saying this is some sort of vendetta?" Asked Tom. "That's definitely a possibility" the DCI replied. "Nick, I think you should let the officers hear your recording" said Lucy. Nick took out his mobile phone and both police officers listened intently to Phyllis' conversation with Fred earlier in the day. "I think that confirms it now Lucy. Fred wants what he thinks is his and he will stop at nothing to get it" said Nick, his face full of horror. "We need this recording to use as evidence please" said DCI Fields. "Yes, I'll sort that out for you" nodded Nick. Two waitresses arrived with the food, and Amira brought the children back to the table so that they could all eat. Lucy quickly filled Amira in on what had been said, and her face paled in shock.

At the end of the meal, DCI Fields was looking uncomfortable. "What is it? I can tell there's something else" Lucy asked. "Fred Reid has served time for assaulting a police officer, as well as convictions for other more petty crimes" said the DCI. Lucy gasped in disbelief. "That's awful" said Amira, visibly shocked. "He's also served time in prison for manslaughter Lucy. The victim's name was Edith Reid." He finished. Lucy visibly gagged as she tried to stop herself being physically sick. "What is it Lucy?" Asked Nick concerned. "Edith Reid was Great Aunt Maud's sister Nick" she replied gently. "Do you know anything at all about a family rift or any of the facts surrounding Edith's death Lucy?" Asked DS Lowe. "No I'm afraid I don't. Aunt Maud never mentioned her or Fred come to that" she said, shaking her head. "All we have is that Fred attacked Edith, who was a very frail elderly lady at the time, and she later died in hospital from her injuries. We have no idea of a motive for the attack" said DCI Fields. "Oh my god, that's horrendous. His own mother as well, the poor woman. No wonder Aunt Maud never mentioned anything!" Said Lucy. "Fred is clearly aggrieved that everything seems to have been left to Frank's side of the family, and I would say that's the motive we have been searching for for what's been happening to your family Lucy" said DCI Fields. "So, what do we do now?" She asked. "Well if Fred's selling the paintings today, my guess is Phyllis will leave Hilltop Manor either tonight or tomorrow when Fred comes for her, and we'll be waiting." "Well okay, if you think that's best" said Lucy hesitantly, her face full of uncertainty on what she should do next.

The rest of the meal passed with very little discussion, everyone seemed to have more on their minds, and their want for idle chit chat to fill the time seemed to have disappeared, along with their appetite for desserts. Lucy said goodbye to the two police officers and got into Tom's car with a heavy heart. Phyllis was her relation. She'd been living so closely with this woman and she hadn't said a word. Was she involved in Frank and Janet's disappearance? What about Ben? Did Phyllis know where he was? Lucy's head was in a spin, she was just so confused. By the time Tom turned off the car outside Hilltop Manor, Jake and Emily were fast asleep in their car seats.

Nick carried Emily, and Paul took Jake straight upstairs for Amira to get them ready for bed. Amira had insisted that Lucy go and have a cup of tea and take some time to unwind. When she walked into the dark kitchen she flicked the light on. "Oh!" She cried out, realising she was not alone in there. Phyllis stood at the kitchen window with her back to the door, she appeared to be staring out into the garden. "Are you okay Phyllis?" Lucy asked, when she didn't turn round. "Phyllis?" She asked again, walking over and putting her hand on the older woman's shoulder. Phyllis jumped and pulled away from Lucy's touch. "Phyllis" said Lucy softly, turning her round slowly to face her. Phyllis raised her head and Lucy gasped in shock.

Her lip was cut and bleeding, and her eye was going black along the bottom of the eye socket. "Oh my god! What happened?" She cried. Leading Phyllis over to the chair to sit down, Lucy called Tom. Moments later, he and Bruce walked into the kitchen. "What the heck!" Gasped Bruce, "What happened?" "I don't know, I found her like this" said Lucy quietly. "Phyllis, what happened?" Said Tom, bending down beside her. Although Tom had no time for her behaviour of late, the genuine concern in his voice was unmistakeable. "I'll call the police" said Bruce. "I fell" muttered Phyllis. "You fell?" Said Lucy incredulously. Phyllis nodded slowly, "Yes, I'm a stupid woman and I fell" she muttered, her eyes vacant and hollow. "Fell where, how?" Asked Tom. "I'm a stupid woman" repeated Phyllis sadly. "You can't have…" Tom began, but was silenced by Lucy shaking her head violently and putting her finger to her lips to try and stop him.

Amira came into the kitchen, took one look at Phyllis and gasped in shock, "What on earth happened?" "Phyllis said she fell" said Lucy, shaking her head again warning Amira not to say anything else. "Let's get you back to your cottage and get you cleaned up. Bruce would you come and make Phyllis a cup of tea please?" Said Amira, helping Phyllis up and walking slowly towards the back door with her. "Yes of course" said Bruce, following them out. "Fell my eye" said Tom once they'd gone. "Fred did that" said Lucy simply. "Fred?" Asked Tom, puzzled at how she'd come to that conclusion. "Didn't you hear her Tom? She kept repeating she was a stupid woman. From what the DCI said, Fred is a nasty piece of work. It all adds up" She said, looking Tom in the eye. He thought for a minute, "Do you know, I think you could be right" he declared.

"Any tea in the pot?" Asked Nick, as he and Paul came into the kitchen. "Is something wrong?" Asked Paul, seeing the look on their faces. Tom explained how they'd found Phyllis a short while ago. "Crikey!" Said Nick, shaking his head in disbelief. "Fred must have been here. That cut on Phyllis' lip was still bleeding, so far too fresh to have happened earlier today" said Lucy worriedly. Tom got up, "I'm going to check the CCTV to see if he's been here" he said determinedly. He was back ten minutes later, "There's no sign, I've rewound it, then watched the footage on fast forward, but nothing" he said. "Maybe she met up with Fred and he hit her then?" Said Paul. "But if Fred is back from selling the paintings, why hasn't Phyllis already gone?" Said Tom doubtfully. "I don't know, but

I just get the uneasy feeling that that lout Fred Reid was involved here somewhere" said Lucy. She decided to go to bed and bid Tom and Paul goodnight. As she got to the stairs, she heard Morph barking, she listened for a second, it was coming from the living room. Lucy opened the door and out raced Morph, tail wagging furiously. "Who shut you in there boy?" She said, scooping him up into her arms. She knew the answer to the question the moment it had left her lips, Phyllis. Why?… Maybe because there was someone Morph didn't know here…Someone like Fred. As Lucy got halfway up the stairs, Morph began wriggling vigorously. She put him down and he ran towards the study door and sat there growling. "No Morph, we aren't going in there tonight" said Lucy puzzled, but he still wouldn't move, even when she opened Jake and Emily's bedroom door. "Come on fella" she said, picking him up and placing him in his basket at the end of their bed. Morph ran past her and straight back to the study door again, and began a low continuous throaty growl. She followed him back out and picked him up for a second time. "What's up with you tonight Morph? We're not going in there" she said, putting him inside the bedroom and closing the door. "Night Lucy" said Amira, appearing at the top of the stairs. "Is Phyllis okay?" Lucy asked. "She wouldn't let Bruce or I into the cottage and got quite upset, insisting we leave" replied Amira. "Oh" said Lucy surprised.

As she walked past the study door, she had a sudden longing to see a picture of Ben. There was something about that room that really made her feel uncomfortable. Before she had chance to change her mind, she opened the door and went inside. Switching on the wall lights, she didn't know if it was her imagination, but they seemed to give out a dimmer light than usual. Lucy noticed the top drawer of the filing cabinet was open, 'That's strange' she thought, as she knew she hadn't left it open. 'Still, maybe Phyllis has been rifling, searching for her mobile again'. She was glad she'd remembered to give it to DCI Fields earlier, she had taken it with her this morning, intending to take it to him at the police station, but when they had arranged to meet at the Yew Tree, she gave it to him there. Lucy pushed the drawer shut and went to sit at the desk. She picked up the photo album and turned to the second from last page, this was the only photo she had access to of her and Ben, as it had been so chaotic, she hadn't had chance to unpack yet. She gazed at Ben's handsome face, staring into those deep sparkling eyes. She missed him so much.

Lucy noticed a movement from the corner of the room and looked up quickly. "You really think you're clever don't you bitch?" Growled a male voice. "Fred!" Lucy gasped in horror. "Don't even think about screaming bitch, I know where your kids are" he hissed. "You leave my children alone" said Lucy, in a voice much more forceful than she felt. "Oh I'll leave them safely tucked up in their cutesy little car bed, though I'm sure the little blonde princess should be in the bed fit for a princess next door" sneered Fred. Lucy shuddered, that man had been in her children's bedroom, he'd seen them, had he been watching them while they slept? The thought made her feel sick, she had to swallow hard to stop the bile rising in her throat. "What do you want Fred?" Asked Lucy. At that moment, the door sprang open and there stood Phyllis. "I knew you were here when you weren't at the cottage!" She cried. Quick as a flash Fred grabbed Phyllis by the wrist, pulled her into the room and tossed her onto the floor in the corner. "Shut up woman" he glared, after he had closed the door. "I told you to let me deal with it" said Phyllis, trying to get up. Fred glared menacingly as he strode towards her. "Leave her alone!" Cried Lucy. Fred towered over Phyllis as she cowered in the corner. "I've told you woman, it's my way now, so shut up!" He spat, delivering a hard kick to Phyllis' hip. "Ow!" She cried. "Get off her!" Shouted Lucy, starting to come round the desk to where Phyllis lay. "Stay there bitch!" Said Fred, coming towards her. "No Fred, leave her alone!" Cried Phyllis.

"Leave her alone?! Leave her alone?!" He mocked, "You've gone soft on this lot woman. Don't you understand, they've stolen what's rightfully ours?" He stormed. "Fred, we didn't even know you existed, Aunt Maud never told us!" Pleaded Lucy. "I'll bet she didn't, nasty, scheming interfering old hag. Always poking her nose in and if my mother hadn't listened to her so much, she would never have made me so angry that night" Fred declared. Lucy knew that he meant the night that he attacked his mother. Here she was trapped in the study with a clearly very violent and unstable man. She feared for hers and Phyllis' safety. There would be no point shouting for help, Tom and Paul had gone for a nightcap at Jeff's cottage with Bruce, and Nick and Amira had gone to bed. Their rooms were at the other end of the house, they'd never hear her. The only occupied room nearby was where her children were sleeping. An alarming thought struck Lucy, what happens if they woke up hearing the noise and they wandered in here? Oh my god no, that didn't bare thinking about. "What do you want Fred?" Lucy asked in as calm a voice as she could. "What do I want? I want what's mine! Where are the paintings?" He snarled. "You have the paintings Fred, you stole them" said Lucy, trying really hard to keep the calm edge to her voice. "I took them to sell them today, and do you know what they're worth? They're worth nothing, they're fakes. No better than a child's drawing". "Fakes?" Said Lucy, not understanding. "Don't mess with me woman!" Ranted Fred, starting to advance in her direction again.

"Leave her alone Fred, your argument's with me" said another male voice. Lucy looked up as Fred span round to look at the owner of this new voice. "Frank!" She gasped. "Hello Lucy" said Frank quietly. Lucy was relieved to see her father in law alive and looking so well, tired, but well. "Awh how touching, enough of the niceties" growled Fred. "Frank, I don't understand" said Lucy. "Shut up! Where's those paintings? If she don't know I bet you do" he sneered to Frank. "Actually Fred I do, and what I will tell you is they're way out of your grasp. Lucy knows nothing about it, so leave her out of it" said Frank authoritatively. "Why you...!" Shouted Fred, taking a lunge at Frank. With deft precision, Frank blocked the blow and Fred landed with a loud thud on the floor. "You just don't change do you Fred, always was much better at taking on the girls weren't you?" Said Frank, eyeing Phyllis' injuries. "You turned Aunt Maud against me so you got everything" said Fred bitterly. "I didn't do anything, you did that all by yourself. You beat a defenceless old lady who died from what you did to her. And why Fred? Didn't she have enough money to give you? Because money is all you've ever been interested in. You killed her sister then got away with a pittance of a sentence, who can blame Maud for despising you?" Said Frank, in a voice of pure loathing. "All the same, never wanted to part with any cash. I needed money" said Fred pointedly. "Then you should have worked for it like everyone else" Frank declared. "I want those paintings Frank, I'm warning you, I'll, I'll..." snarled Fred. "Warning me what? You'll do what? You don't scare me Fred, my family have been to hell and back these last few months and I only went along with this facade because I wanted to see you back behind bars where you belong" spat Frank. "You set me up, you...!" Roared Fred. At that moment the study door opened and Emily toddled in rubbing her eyes with tiredness. "Mummy I can't sleep, I need a drink" she said. "Emily go back to bed!" Cried Lucy urgently, but before anyone had chance to move, Fred had grabbed Emily and backed into the corner towards where Phyllis still lay, with her dangling under his arm.

"No!" Screamed Lucy running forward. "Put her down Fred" ordered Frank. "No chance, where are the paintings, or the kid will be sorry, won't you princess?" Said Fred, rubbing a grimy thumb along Emily's cheek. "Mummy!" She wailed, starting to cry. Suddenly Emily dropped to the floor and Frank leapt forward to grab her, as Fred collapsed in a heap. There, standing behind him was Phyllis, the ornamental cricket bat from the wall still raised above her head. "I couldn't let you hurt them Fred" she muttered dropping the bat. Frank passed Emily to Lucy as the door burst open and Tom, Paul and Amira rushed in. Amira grabbed Phyllis, "You're under arrest" she said, cuffing her hands behind her back. Fred was starting to stir on the floor, he was groaning and rubbing his head. Tom and Paul hauled him to his feet, "You're under arrest!" Shouted Tom as they snapped the handcuffs shut around his wrists. Lucy watched open mouthed, "Under arrest?... But I thought Paul was the police officer" she said in confusion. "He is, but so are we" said Amira.

DCI Fields appeared in the doorway, and as Fred and Phyllis were lead away, he turned to Frank. "I'm glad to see you're okay, but you really shouldn't have given us the slip like that" he said. "You put yourself in a great deal of danger and your wife is worried sick." he declared. "I'm sorry DCI Fields, but I know what that man is capable of and I couldn't see Lucy and the children in that kind of trouble, and you know what he's capable of as well" said Frank. "Janet? She's alive?" Asked Lucy. "Yes Lucy, she is. Janet has been in police custody under our protection" said DCI Fields. Lucy sat down in the chair in utter disbelief at what was happening. Nick appeared in the door way with DS Lowe, "Let me take Emily back to bed, DS Lowe has explained everything to me" he said, gently taking Emily from Lucy's arms. "Well I wish someone would explain it all to me" said Lucy. "We will I promise, I know it's hard but please bare with me a few more hours. I need to go to the station with Phyllis and Fred, and I'll need you to come and make a statement Frank. But I will be back in the morning" said DCI Fields. Lucy shrugged her shoulders in defeat. All she ever seemed to be doing was baring with DCI Fields, so what harm would once more do?

Frank came over to Lucy, he took her hands and gently pulled her to her feet. "I'm so sorry for what you have been through, I wouldn't hurt you for the world, but as ironic as it may sound, this is the only way I had of you being safe" he said softly. Frank hugged Lucy to him, tears of relief streamed down her face as she hugged her father in law back. "I'm so glad you're safe Frank, I really am" she said as she pulled away. "I know Lucy, I know" he said, kissing the top of her head and then following DCI Fields out of the room. Lucy trailed downstairs and went to sit in the living room. Nick had got Emily back off to sleep and was seeing the police out. "There's a visitor for you Lucy" he said, coming back into the room. She looked up, "Mrs Armstrong!" She cried. Margaret Armstrong didn't say a word, just took her in her arms and cuddled her tight. Lucy sobbed her heart out, she didn't know if she was crying tears of relief, fear, anguish, or all of them rolled into one. What she did know was the sight of a friendly face that she could trust was all that she could take. Mrs Armstrong held her until her sobs subsided. "You've been through so much Lucy, much more than anyone should have to endure in a lifetime, let alone a matter of days" she said "I really don't know what to think at the minute. I'm so happy that Frank and Janet are okay, it does make me miss Ben all the more though" said Lucy softly. "I know" said Mrs Armstrong sympathetically. "How long are you here for? How's your sister?" Asked Lucy. "She's much better thank you, and her husband is up and about again now. They both aren't up to speed yet though" said Mrs Armstrong. "Oh and I'm keeping you from them. You really should get back" insisted Lucy. "My niece has managed to arrange three weeks holiday from work so she can be there with her parents, so I can be here for you" said Mrs Armstrong, patting Lucy's hand. She smiled gratefully at the older woman, they hadn't known each other long, but Lucy could tell her concern was genuine. "Thank you Margaret." "Nothing to thank me for, it's good to be home" Mrs Armstrong grinned.

They looked up to see Nick was hovering in the doorway. "Is it okay to come in?" He asked warily. "Of course it is" Lucy smiled. She stood up and hugged her step son, he really was a good lad, she was very proud of him. "I really think we should all be getting off to bed, tomorrow is going to be a big day. I'm going to make the room up next to you Lucy, so I'm nearby if you need anything" said Mrs Armstrong. "Thank you" Lucy replied. "Margaret's right, I'll lock up while you get off to bed. Night Lucy" Nick said, leaning over and kissing her cheek. As she got ready for bed, there was a light tap on her bedroom door, "Come in" she called. Mrs Armstrong came in carrying a mug with steam billowing out of the top. "Cocoa for you" she smiled, placing it on the bedside table. "Thank you so much" Lucy said, smiling gratefully. "Now goodnight Lucy, sleep tight." Mrs Armstrong said, closing the bedroom door. Although Lucy had so much going through her head as she lay down, she slept surprisingly well and woke the next morning early.

Lucy thought she better get breakfast sorted as there was no Phyllis, she washed and dressed and went down to the kitchen. As she opened the door she was surprised to see the sight that greeted her. Jake and Emily were up and dressed, seated at the table, enjoying hard boiled eggs with soldiers and a glass of orange juice, Nick and Bruce were tucking into bacon and eggs, whilst Mrs Armstrong busied herself at the stove. "Good morning Lucy, I heard you moving about, your breakfast won't be long." Mrs Armstrong said smiling. "Oh thank you, I was just coming to do breakfast" said Lucy. "No need dear, that's my job." Mrs Armstrong replied. "We wanted you to rest, I've got Jake and Emily washed and dressed, I hope that what they're wearing is okay" said Nick. "It's just perfect, they look lovely. Thank you Nick." She said. "We're not going to craft club today mummy. Our teacher Miss Ball is coming here to play" said Jake. "Is she?" Said Lucy puzzled. "DCI Fields rang earlier and suggested it so we were all free to talk to him" said Nick. "I hope it's okay, but I agreed. I thought it might help you not having to worry about these two monkeys if you knew they were being looked after. I said here would be better and the DCI arranged it" finished Nick. "No that's very thoughtful, and you're right I would prefer them to be here" she replied.

Soon after breakfast the intercom on the main gate buzzed and Nick went to answer it. "Hello?" He said. "Hi it's Leah Ball, I'm one of Jake and Emily's teachers" said a female voice. "Oh hi, come on up to the house" said Nick. When the door knocked a few moments later, Nick went to answer it. Lucy came out of the kitchen and, wondering why Nick hadn't invited their guest in, went to see what was wrong. There, standing on the doorstep was Leah, while Nick gaped open mouthed at her. Lucy laughed at his smitten expression. She had seen that look before almost seven years ago when Ben started coming into the fish bar where they met. "Please come in Leah, it's very good of you to come" said Lucy. "Oh that's fine, I didn't mind at all when Suzanne asked me. Jake and Emily are lovely, it's great helping out in their class" Leah said. "Suzanne?" Said Lucy questioningly. "Oh sorry you probably know her as DS Lowe, she's my sister" laughed Leah. "Oh now I understand" she smiled. Leah was looking at Nick who was still staring. "Er, are you okay?" She asked. "Nick why don't you go and get Jake and Emily and bring them to the living room for me please?" Lucy said, trying to bring him back to reality. Leah was lovely though, tall and slim with beautiful brown hair cascading down her back. She was wearing grey capri pants and a white top with matching pumps. Nick trailed off without a word, "I'm sorry about that" said Lucy with a smile. Leah smiled back, "Please it's not a problem Mrs Reid."

"Miss Ball!" Cried Jake and Emily running into the room. "Hi guys!" Said Leah. "Mummy said you're allowed to look after us here today. Can we play games?" Asked Jake. "Most definitely" said Leah. "Can we play football?" Said Jake. "Of course!" Laughed Leah. "Would you like me to take charge of them now to give you some time to get organised Mrs Reid?" Asked Leah. "That would be great thank you, I'll show you where the kitchen is. Please help yourself to anything that you or the children would like. When my visitors arrive we shall be in the living room, feel free to go anywhere else in the house or garden" Lucy smiled. "That's fine Mrs Reid" said Leah. "Please call me Lucy, Mrs Reid is far too formal" Lucy said. Nick came into the living room and seemed to have found his composure again. "Would you like me to show you around Leah?" He asked. "Yes please" she said, flashing Nick a broad grin. "We'll help!" Cried Jake. "Come on then monsters!" Laughed Nick. Jake and Emily grabbed Leah's hands and began dragging her towards the kitchen. "I'm glad you're back with us again" Lucy whispered teasingly as Nick passed. "She's gorgeous" said Nick blushing. Lucy nodded in agreement, "Leah is certainly a very pretty girl indeed" she said.

CHAPTER 11

DCI FIELDS EXPLAINS

The gate buzzer sounded in the hall, "Hello?" Said Lucy. "Hi Mrs Reid, it's DS Lowe" said a voice. She pressed the button to open the gates and went to open the front door. The phone rang in the hall, "Hello?" She said, picking up the receiver. "Hi Lucy, guess who" said the caller. "Jeff! How are you?" She cried. "I'm feeling really good. PC Regan paid me a visit this morning, he told me what happened last night. I couldn't believe it, is everyone okay?" Jeff asked."Yes we're fine, we're waiting for the police to arrive this morning and hopefully fill in a lot of blanks" she said. "I just wish I could be there with you all" said Jeff sadly. "You will be very soon, keep your chin up Jeff". Said Lucy encouragingly. "I will do, you take care. Bye" he said. Lucy replaced the receiver and turned back to the front door, there stood DS Lowe and Frank. Lucy ran to her father in law and hugged him tight, it was even more amazing to see him alive and well in the light of day than it was last night. "Hi Lucy" said Frank, hugging her back. She said hello to DS Lowe, then went to close the door, as she did so another figure stepped into view. "Janet!" Cried Lucy. "Hello Lucy, it's so good to see you. I'm so very sorry you've been put through all this." Said Janet. Lucy hugged her mother in law and the tears of relief started all over again.

At that moment the kitchen door opened and Nick and Leah appeared, followed by Jake and Emily. "Nanny!" They screamed, bounding into Janet's arms. "Oh my darlings, I've missed you so much" she cried, dropping to her knees, tears streaming down her face. "Do I get one of those?" Asked Frank stepping forward. "Grandad!" Cried Jake and Emily throwing themselves at him, they hadn't seen him standing there. "Nick" said Janet, opening her arms to her eldest grandson. "Hi Gran, it's so good to see you" he said hugging her tightly. "What a strapping young man you've turned into" said Janet, stepping back to get a better look at him. "Gran!" Said Nick coyly, his face blushing bright red, remembering Leah was witness to all this. Nick turned to his grandfather and hugged him, they'd always been very close. "Good to see you my boy, you don't know how good" said Frank. "You too Grandad" said Nick, brushing away a stray tear before anyone saw it. "DS Lowe was kind enough to come and collect us" said Janet, trying to break the tension. "Would you like some tea?" Lucy asked. "I thought you'd never ask" grinned Frank. Mrs Armstrong was in the kitchen, clearing away the dishes. "Mr Reid, lovely to see you again" she smiled. "You must be Mrs Reid" she said, turning to Janet, shaking her hand. "Please, take a seat" said Lucy. "That's a fresh pot, I'll just get some more cups" said Mrs Armstrong, pointing to the tea pot on the table. "Shall I take the children out to play?" Asked Leah, who had been standing uncomfortably in the doorway. "Yes please" Lucy replied. "No we want to stay with nanny" said Jake, clinging to his grandmother, whilst Emily sat firmly on her grandad's lap. "Nanny and grandad will still be here when you come back" Lucy reassured them. "Will you? You promise not to go away again?" Asked Jake, his big eyes gazing from one grandparent to the other. "We promise" said Janet solemnly, whilst Frank nodded in agreement. Jake stood for a minute looking at them both, then seemingly happy with this promise, he took Emily's hand and they went off to the garden with Leah.

"There's so much I want to ask you, so much I need to know" said Lucy to Frank and Janet. "Of course you do, but let's just wait until DCI Fields gets here and we can start from the very beginning" Janet said. Lucy was going to protest but stopped herself, what was the point, and she didn't have the energy to fight anymore anyway. The intercom sounded, signifying there was someone else at the gate. "Shall I get that for you?" Said DS Lowe standing up. She returned a few moments later, "It wasn't DCI Fields I'm afraid, but I did find a surprise for you all. Well especially you Bruce" she said. "Really?" He replied, eyebrows raised. DS Lowe pushed the kitchen door wide open and stepped out of the way, "Jeff!" Cried Bruce. There, sitting in a wheelchair in the doorway, was Jeff. "But how, when, how will you manage?" Said Bruce. "I can live at the cottage with you until I get on my feet again, I just might need a bit of help getting into the house" Jeff laughed. "I'm Steve, Jeff's nurse" said the tall, dark-haired guy standing behind him. "His nurse? But how will we afford that?" Said Bruce, his eyes full of worry. "Frank sorted it all out for me" said Jeff, throwing him a beaming smile. Bruce turned to Frank with tears in his eyes, "Thank you so much, I really don't know what to say." "Nothing to say, the family should be together" smiled Frank.

Lucy swallowed hard, tears pricked her eyes and she blinked them back furiously. 'The family are back together, apart from Ben' she thought sadly. The intercom buzzed again and DS Lowe went to answer it. "It's DCI Fields, he said can we all sit in the living room please? It will be more comfortable for everyone. He's asked that you come as well please Mrs Armstrong". "Yes of course" said Lucy, getting up and leading the way. There was quite a gathering awaiting DCI Fields when he came in, "Hello everyone, I'm sorry to have kept you waiting, especially you Lucy" he smiled at her. Behind DCI Fields, Tom, Paul and Amira hovered in the doorway. "Are you not going to sit down? This was your home for long enough" said Lucy. "I hope you'll understand after DCI Fields has explained everything just why we had to keep you in the dark" said Tom. "We never wanted to deceive you Lucy, but truly it was for your own safety" said Amira softly. "We just wanted you and the children to be safe" added Paul. "I know that" she nodded. DS Lowe, Tom, Amira and Paul all took seats at the dining room table, whilst everyone else sat on the more comfortable chairs, waiting for DCI Fields to speak. "It's been a bit of a mission getting the background facts to the family feud between Great Aunt Maud and Fred until I got chance to speak to Frank himself. Mrs Armstrong was a great help filling in some of the blanks from what Maud had confided in her in the time leading up to her death. Maud looked after Fred a lot in his younger years as her sister Edith was often in poor health, she described Fred as a sullen unhelpful youth who always wanted his own way." Said DCI Fields. "No change there then" said Frank wryly. "No, none at all" said the DCI, nodding in agreement.

"Go on" said Lucy, eager to gain some answers. "Mrs Armstrong said the Maud had told her that Fred had set about his mother because she didn't have enough money left to buy him cigarettes. The old lady didn't stand a chance and although at one point it looked like she was on the mend, in hospital she eventually lost her fight. Edith died from her injuries two days after the attack. Fred pleaded that he was drunk and that Edith had set about him with her walking stick, medical experts ruled that out, citing her as far too infirm. Fred was convicted, after psychiatric reports, of manslaughter, serving just 5 years. Maud was distraught and vowed she would never have anything to do with him again" continued DCI Fields. "Poor, poor Edith" said Lucy sadly. "Fred was released on parole 7 years ago, and he met Phyllis soon after." "Two bad eggs together" said Frank. "I'm not so sure after interviewing Phyllis and Avril" said the DCI. "What do you mean?" Asked Nick.

"Phyllis has a younger brother, Jonathan, who lives in a care home. He has severe physical and emotional needs, Fred was paying the cost of his care from money he had accrued from a joint bank account with his late mother, and his love of gambling. He threatened to withdraw payment for Jonathan's care if Phyllis didn't go along with everything he demanded of her. He also threatened to hurt Avril, Phyllis' adopted daughter if she disobeyed him. Phyllis said Avril was always a model daughter, things only changed when Fred came to live with them. Upon interviewing Avril, I discovered that she was also a victim of Fred's abuse. Fred used to tie Avril up when her mother was out and burn her body with cigarette butts for his own warped pleasure. Phyllis knew that Avril was scared of Fred, but never knew he was actually physically hurting her" said DCI Fields. "Oh my god, why didn't she leave?" Said Lucy in horror. "Fred had convinced Avril he would hurt her mother if she did. The result was Avril reverted into her own shell, praying that her mother would eventually see this man for the monster that he was" finished DCI Fields. "I'm sorry but I actually can't help but feel sorry for Phyllis and Avril, even after all they've done" said Tom. "Me too" said Lucy. "The thing is, Phyllis always seemed so good with Jake and Emily. She seemed to really care about them" said Amira. "I think she did, that's why she was the one to stop Fred after taking the beating from him. I think it was all she could take hearing him threaten Emily" said Lucy. "So what was their intention?" Asked Bruce. "Fred is a thug, but he's not stupid, he knew he wouldn't get the house with Frank, Janet and Ben alive, so he set about trying to create a plan to eliminate them." DCI Fields continued. "Eliminate them?" Said Lucy fearfully. "He didn't get us though did he?" Said Frank patting Lucy's hand. "But, but, he must have got Ben" said Lucy, her eyes welling with tears once more.

Nick put his arm around her shoulder, "It will be okay Lucy, I promise" he said. "Fred's plan wasn't working how he had wanted it to when Frank, Janet and Ben disappeared, so he set his sights on the paintings as a taster to his lost inheritance." DCI Fields said. "But he has the paintings" said Lucy confused. "No, Fred has the fakes" the DCI replied. "But how?" Asked Bruce. "I think Mrs Armstrong can help again here" DCI Fields said. "Fred wrote to your Aunt Maud, demanding what he saw as his. Maud showed me the letter, it wasn't very pleasant at all. What Fred didn't threaten was very little, I'm afraid. He made threats in that letter against your family Lucy" said Mrs Armstrong. "So my children were always in danger?" Asked Lucy. "No, you, Nick and the children were never in that sort of danger. Before Maud died, she had written into her will that you had to be married 10 years and the children had to be 21 before you could inherit. It was the only way she could ensure you were safe. Fred demanded the paintings in the letter, so your Aunt asked me to replace them with copies" Mrs Armstrong explained. "My brother in law Bert is an astounding artist and he copied them. To the untrained eye you would never know the difference" She continued. "So where are the originals?" Asked Lucy. "I have them, they're in the attic at my sisters'" said Mrs Armstrong.

Nick laughed and everyone turned to look at him. "I'm sorry, but Great Aunt Maud was one clever lady, and can you imagine Fred's face when he realised all this had been for nothing, and he had been outwitted?" They all nodded in agreement. "Maud loved you all very much, that was very evident when she spoke of you" said Mrs Armstrong. "We loved her very much too and we miss her a great deal" Lucy said. "Maud was an exceptionally wealthy woman, her late husband George had been an extremely successful property developer, and he and Maud ran a thriving business both at home and abroad" said DCI Fields. "Oh my god, I never knew that" said Frank. "Maud was also very shrewd and guessed that at some point Fred would make his move, and she wasn't prepared to risk the safety of her family. For that reason she carried on living at the smaller house in Primrose Hill, and left here in the charge of Mrs Armstrong and Mr Benson, her solicitor" finished the DCI. "Now I understand a lot more" said Frank. "I spoke to Mr Benson this morning upon Mrs Armstrong's advice. There is a clause in Maud's will, that it should only be read once Fred was under lock and key. That's how sure she was that Fred would come after her estate. Mr Benson said this is the reason that nothing has ever been made official" said DCI Fields. "Well I never, Great Aunt Maud was a legend" said Nick. "So what happened to Frank and Janet? You said you had Janet in police custody" Lucy said.

"I may be able to explain that" said Frank. "Mrs Armstrong was given strict instructions upon her death to show this letter to the police. DCI Fields was assigned to the case, and realising the seriousness of the situation, and how violent Fred was, it was decided that we were better off in police custody. DCI Fields arranged safe places for us and waited for the right opportunity to remove us from our normal lives" said Frank. "So there never was a plane crash?" Asked Nick. "Yes there was, my plane did fail and I did have to bring it down suddenly. But it wasn't a crash in the sense of the word that everyone thought. On route to our safe place I asked to use the toilet and gave the police the slip there. I couldn't even tell Janet what I was doing as I knew she would try to stop me" Frank continued. "Yes I would" said Janet, nodding. "I knew of old what Fred was like, and I couldn't risk you all being in danger. I knew you and Ben would come to run the business as it was the right thing to do with a young family, so I came here to Hilltop Manor" said Frank. "You were here the whole time?" Gasped Lucy. "Yes" he nodded. "But where?" Said Lucy. "In the panic room off the study" Frank replied

"All those times when I thought I wasn't alone in the study, you were there?" Said Lucy suddenly understanding. "Yes I was, it was me that put the valuation for the paintings back in the album" said Frank. "I knew it, I knew there was someone there. And I knew that valuation hadn't been in the photo album when we looked before" she said turning to Tom. He nodded solemnly. "Where did you stay though? Where did you sleep, grandad?" Asked Nick. "I found the plans to the panic room Aunt Maud had built before she died. It's a pretty amazing place, it's a soundproof, self contained room, well small flat really, built behind the book case in the darkest corner of the study. That's how I was able to get in and out so quickly. I got a cab here, stopping off to get some clothes and some essential provisions, you know, tinned and packet stuff. I arrived with a suitcase I had bought on route, asking to stay for a while as I needed some time out. Mrs Armstrong was so kind, she agreed straight away. I waited for the first opportunity, which came when she went down to the field to call Jeff for his dinner, and left her a note saying I couldn't stay after all, I needed to get away properly. Then I slipped into the study" said Frank. "Well I never" said Mrs Armstrong in surprise. "I'm sorry for deceiving you, in fact I'm sorry for deceiving you all. I just knew Fred and what he was capable of" said Frank earnestly.

"So if the police had you and Janet with them, Ben did leave us after all" said Lucy sadly. DCI Fields nodded to DS Lowe and she got up and left the room. "Ben was a much harder cookie to convince Lucy. You were right, he wouldn't have left you and the children if it wasn't for a very good reason. When you left Primrose Hill you were being tailed. We had been watching you, waiting for the chance to speak to Ben alone. That chance came when he returned to the Pineapple Diner to get Emily's toy, I was one of the four men in suits that he left with, along with Rob Jeffers who came to see you at the store when you reported Ben missing. When you were shown the photograph of Ben and the four men at the airfield we had to make sure that Rob and I had our backs to the camera. I honestly didn't think Ben was going to agree, and it was only when he realised that by staying he could be endangering the lives of you and the children that he did. As a beneficiary, if Fred made any attempts to hurt him, you and the children could have been with him and hurt also. Ben's a really nice guy and a sensible one too. He only agreed to come along when we told him there would be police presence at Hilltop Manor and we would keep him informed on how you all were." Said DCI Fields. "I knew he wouldn't leave us, I just knew it" declared Lucy. "Yes you were right, Ben was faced with no other choice" the DCI nodded.

"I don't understand though, if you had Ben where is he now?" Said Lucy in confusion. "I'm here Lucy" said a male voice. She looked up, and there standing in the door way was DS Lowe with Ben. She stared at him in total disbelief as he walked towards her, he bent and tilted her face up towards him with his finger tip. "I love you" he smiled, that smile that lit up every inch of his handsome face. Lucy could hold the tears back no longer, tears of relief culminating all the events of late. Here was the last piece of the puzzle, the part to make her life whole again. Ben took his wife in his arms and they clung to each other like they would never let go. "I'm sorry Lucy, I really do hope you're starting to understand why things have had to be how they are" said DCI Fields. She nodded, wiping her eyes with a tissue that Mrs Armstrong had given her. Nick had given his dad a warm hug and then moved so he could have his place next to Lucy on the sofa. "Are you okay for me to continue Lucy?" Asked DCI Fields. "If it's okay with you I really would like to see my children first please" said Ben. "Of course" said the DCI. "Nick would you call them in from the garden please" He opened the patio doors and called out "Jake, Emily, you have a surprise visitor." The sound of small feet could be heard thundering around the side of the house, and moments later they appeared at the patio doors. "There's someone here to see you" said Lucy softly, taking their hands and leading them to the chair where Ben was sitting. "Daddy!" Screamed Emily, throwing her arms around his neck as he pulled her onto his lap. "Hello princess! I've missed you so much" said Ben, burying his face in her blonde curls and hugging her tight. "Jake it's daddy" said Lucy. He stood back from Ben and stared at him, uncertainty filling his eyes. "Can I have a hug mate?" Asked Ben softly. "You went away" said Jake in a small voice. "I know I did mate, but I promise I'm not going anywhere again" said Ben. Jake looked at his father, seemingly weighing up his promise, the way he had done earlier with his grandparents. "Really?" Said Jake. "Really" said Ben. A huge grin spread across Jake's face as he threw himself into his father's arms. Ben breathed a sigh of relief.

"How about I get everyone lunch while Ben spends some time with the children before we carry on?" Said Mrs Armstrong. "I think that would be a very good idea thank you Margaret" said Frank "Can I show you our room? I've got a racing car bed and Emily's got a princess one, but she doesn't sleep in it" said Jake excitedly to his father. "She likes to sleep in my bed with me and Morph" he went on happily. "Woah, I'd love to see them, but do you know what I'd like to do first?" Said Ben. "What?" Asked Jake. "I'd like to meet Morph" Ben replied. "He's outside" said Nick. Jake ran over to the patio doors and opened them, and Morph scampered in. "This is my daddy" said Jake proudly. "It's my daddy too Morph!" Added Emily, and everyone laughed. "Hello Morph, aren't you a cute little guy" said Ben, bending down to stroke him. Morph seemed to like Ben and bounded around licking him and wagging his tail furiously. In what seemed like no time at all, Mrs Armstrong was back with trays laden full of goodies. She had made sandwiches and salad, and had cut up the quiche from the fridge. There was pork pies, sausage rolls and bread sticks, as well as cakes and biscuits. It seemed she and Leah had made enough to feed a small army. "Lucy, will you be needing a nanny still now that Amira will be returning to work?" Asked DS Lowe. "Suzanne!" Scalded Leah, giving her a 'not-right-now-this-isn't-the-right-time' sort of look. "Well I've not really thought about it to be honest, but yes I suppose we will be, as now that everyone's home, we can actually concentrate on getting to grips with Bartons" said Lucy. "I know it's a bit cheeky, but I wonder if you might consider Leah? Now that her training has come to an end and her placement at the craft club, she'll be looking for employment" said DS Lowe. "Er, well I'd not really thought of Leah" said Lucy. "Honestly Mrs Reid, it really doesn't matter. Suzanne should never have asked you" said Leah blushing. "No Leah, you misunderstand me. When I said I hadn't thought of you, I meant because I didn't realise you were looking for a job. But if we talk terms later and if they're acceptable, I think it's a great idea" said Lucy smiling. "Really?" Said Leah. "Definitely" said Lucy with a firm nod. "Thank you so much Lucy" said DS Lowe. "No, thank you for suggesting her."

"All you need to sort now is someone to cover Mrs Armstrong when she goes back to her sister's" said Frank. "No need, my niece is going to move back home until her parents are both properly back on their feet." Mrs Armstrong replied. "Oh, are you sure?" Said Lucy. "Quite sure" she said nodding. "Well that's settled then, you will need someone to look after things until I get back on my feet though." Said Jeff. "Well actually, I've been doing some thinking on that one" said Bruce. "You have?" Replied Jeff, looking at his father in surprise. "My business partner is more than capable of running things while I'm away, and if it's okay with everyone, I thought I would stay here and cover Jeff's duties until he's fully able again." "That seems like a fabulous idea to me" said Janet, and everyone nodded in agreement. Once they had finished eating, Leah took the children back off to play in the garden.

When everyone was seated comfortably again, DCI Fields began to speak. "Please forgive me if I talk about events out of sequence in which they happened, but sometimes that's necessary to explain someone's involvement. The men you encountered with the scaffold lorry, Lucy, were Ray Martin and his dad Pete. Pete and Fred are buddies from way back, drinking and gambling together on a regular basis. Ray was a bit of a wheeler-dealer by all accounts, with his fingers in many pies. Fred caught them down on their luck and on a severe losing streak, and offered them money to carry out his orders" said the DCI. "So was it one of them that cut my break hoses?" Asked Tom. "No, their stature doesn't fit the CCTV footage of the guy on the scene at Bartons. Phyllis swears she never knew anything about it until you and Lucy came home after it happened. As for Fred, he's keeping completely tight lipped on who it was." The DCI continued. "Do you think it's another gang member?" Asked Lucy worriedly. "No, we think from the way Fred is talking, it's just someone he met along the way who needed money." Said the DCI. "However it's earned" said Bruce in distaste. "Ray Martin has admitted driving the car that first attempted to run you over with Tom." Said DCI Fields, looking at Nick. "So they were after me after all?" Nick asked. "No, Ray said Fred told him just to scare you that day." The DCI replied. "What about the day I was hit? I saw Phyllis on the phone just before I left the drive" said Jeff. "I asked Phyllis about that call and I've had her mobile phone checked. She's telling the truth, she didn't make a call. But she did receive an incoming one from an unknown mobile. A mobile that we found in Fred Reid's pocket when he was arrested" said the DCI.

"So she hadn't tried to get me run over?" Said Jeff. "Quite the opposite according to Phyllis. There had been a number of unpleasant texts that day from Fred, saying he wanted her to 'sort you', as you were getting too close for comfort when you overheard Phyllis' phone calls. She had replied saying she didn't want anyone hurt, and he had the paintings so leave it at that. Phyllis said Fred had rang her, threatening to come to the house after you and she told him you'd just gone out, thinking he wouldn't bother. What Phyllis didn't know was that Fred had Ray watching Hilltop Manor and doing regular drive-bys. Fred called him straight away, which is why he was on the scene so quickly, and was able to hit you and Tom." Said DCI Fields. "Oh my god, do you believe her?" Said Jeff, his face paling. "Phyllis didn't know anything about the drive-bys or the accident until Tom told everyone. Ray admitted this all himself" said the DCI.

"Seems Phyllis hadn't known as much as we thought" said Bruce.

"Exactly. I think Fred probably didn't trust Phyllis a hundred percent. He knew she was fond of you all and didn't want anyone hurt." Said the DCI. "So the scaffold lorry was just used as a cover to hold us long enough for my car to be marked?" Said Tom. "Yes it certainly seems so" said DCI Fields nodding. "So if Phyllis and Avril had so little knowledge of Fred's plans, why did Avril try to take Emily from the school?" Said Lucy. "This is another example of where Fred had Avril in his control. She said he had threatened to burn and torture Jonathan, in the way he had her, and he would stop paying for Jonathan's care" said DCI Fields. "The complete low-life!" Stormed Bruce. "Avril did get away by car when her identity was uncovered as not being you, a car driven by Fred" said the DCI. "What on earth were they planning to do with Emily?" Said Lucy shuddering. "Avril said Fred was planning to hold her hostage" said DCI Fields grimly. "What I don't understand though is did Fred ever carry out his threats to hurt Jonathan, or stop his fees?" Asked Lucy. "Yes, I'm afraid he did. When Phyllis met Fred, Jonathan was living happily at home with her and Avril. All that changed when Fred moved in. Jonathan's behaviour became unpredictable and violent at times. Fred wanted him in a home, but Phyllis fought hard against this, until Jonathan started referring to him as 'the bad man' and covering his head with his arms every time Fred came near. Phyllis agreed for Jonathan to move into the care home, vowing she would get her life together somehow and bring him home again." Continued DCI Fields. "Oh my god, I'm actually feeling sorry for her again" said Tom. "Me too" said Lucy.

"Why didn't she just leave Fred?" Asked Nick. "There are people in abusive and volatile relationships whose abusers manage to get them so scared and with no self-respect, they often feel they cannot escape" said DS Lowe. "How sad" said Mrs Armstrong. "I assume the burglary was staged?" Asked Paul. "Yes it was I'm afraid. Fred turned up here unannounced, saying he was taking the paintings. Phyllis couldn't make him see sense, and when Fred had left with the paintings, she called Avril to come and tie her up, to make it look like you had been robbed" said DCI Fields. "Well what about the CCTV footage? There was no one on that" said Nick confused. "That was Phyllis again. She rewound the CCTV once Fred had gone and once the part showing him had been recorded over, she switched the system off" said DS Lowe. "I still can't believe Great Aunt

Maud ever had such valuable paintings in the first place" said Ben. "Your great uncle George was a keen art lover and considered the paintings to be a very valuable investment for his family" said Mrs Armstrong. "Can I ask why you insisted we always travelled in Tom or Paul's cars, was it because they were police officers?" Asked Lucy. "Both Tom and Paul are highly trained response drivers, trained in pursuit and defensive driving. As for the vehicles, I don't know if you ever noticed the strange looking gold crests on the dashboards, did you?" Asked DCI Fields. "Yes I did, they look like an eye" Lucy replied. "That's it, they are state of the art tracking systems with on-board cameras" said the DCI. "Ah, now I understand. Paul used to tell Jake and Emily that it was an eye so I could see if they were being good in the car" said Lucy laughing. "It was a seeing eye, but not watching Jake and Emily" said the DCI with a chuckle. "So if you're a police officer, what's your involvement with Bartons, Tom?" Asked Janet. "I was put on a special assignment there as soon as Fred's letter to Maud came to light. It was my job to oversee things and make myself known as the manager to the staff, so I was on site if any trouble arose. I was there every day until you came Lucy, when it was agreed I'd be of more use here" said Tom. "I think that's everyone covered, unless anyone has any questions" said DCI Fields, looking round the room.

"All of them will be charged and we will let you know when they are due to appear in court" said DS Lowe. "I assume they will all receive custodial sentences?" Said Frank questioningly. "It's hard to say is the honest answer, but I would think so. I suppose Avril may escape with a suspended sentence, due to extenuating circumstances, and no previous convictions. Pete's involvement doesn't seem to be as much, so he may well receive a non-custodial sentence as well, but he has form so who knows" said the DCI. "What about Phyllis, and what will happen to Jonathan now?" Asked Lucy quietly. "Hmm" said the DCI thoughtfully. "Please, what do you think?" Asked Lucy. "Although Phyllis has no previous convictions, and there are some pretty extenuating circumstances, she does have involvement to a lot of serious crimes here. It depends if the court accept these circumstances, and it's in Phyllis' favour that she didn't want anyone hurt. She has also been very helpful to our enquiries and she was the one to eventually stop Fred. However, in my opinion, Phyllis could well be looking at a custodial sentence" said DCI Fields. "A suspended one?" Asked Lucy hopefully. The DCI shook his head, "I don't think so" he said solemnly. "What will happen to her brother?" Asked Lucy. "With the fees not being paid now he would have to come home or be found a suitable place in a council run establishment" said DS Lowe. "But if Phyllis goes to prison..." said Lucy. "If Avril receives a suspended sentence, she would be able to apply to be assessed as a suitable carer for Jonathan. But in view of his difficulties, without Phyllis I wouldn't hold out much hope" said DS Lowe. "That's so sad, that evil man has ruined so many lives, or at least tried to" said Janet. Lucy remained quiet, deep in thought. "There is something else, Lucy" said DCI Fields. "Yes?" She said, looking up in surprise. "Phyllis has asked to see you" said the DCI. "She's done what?!" Exploded Frank. "Calm down Frank, listen to what DCI Fields has to say" said Janet. "I wouldn't normally consider this Lucy, but in all that has happened, I wondered if it may help towards you finding closure" said the DCI. "Is she mad?" Spat Frank. "No, I'd like to see her, and Avril please if possible" said Lucy quietly. Ben cast a shocked glance sideways at his wife, but he knew not to argue with her when she had set her mind to something.

"You want to what?" Asked Frank in total disbelief. "Dad, Lucy knows her own mind, and if that's what she's decided, then I'm backing her decision" said Ben, giving Lucy's hand a quick squeeze. "But..." Frank started to protest. "No Frank, leave them be" Janet warned, giving him a stern look. Frank looked at Lucy and Ben, then back to his wife and threw his hands up in mock surrender. "I know when I'm beaten" he said with a shrug. "Thank you" said Lucy with a grateful smile. "We will be getting off and leave you good people to get on with reacquainting yourselves, but do you think you might allow me to see something before I go?" Said DCI Fields. "Of course, what is it?" Asked Lucy. "The panic room?" said DCI Fields, grinning like a small boy. Lucy laughed, "I think you'd better ask Frank as he's the expert" she said. "Be my guest, follow me" said Frank. Everyone seemed very interested in seeing that.

CHAPTER 12

LUCY GOES TO SEE PHYLLIS

There was a very long line of people that followed Frank upstairs. "I'll stay here with Jeff" said Leah. As Lucy opened the door of the study, she stepped to one side. "Over to you Frank" she said. He walked past the tall filing cabinets, towards the book cases in the corner of the room, and without warning, disappeared behind them. Lucy gasped in shock, she had never noticed that the bookcase was set off the wall, leaving just enough room to walk behind it. "Well I never, this corner's so dark you can't see anything different from within the room." Said DCI Fields. Frank nimbly keyed the code into the keypad next to the door in the wall. "This could have caused some problems, I was lucky that Aunt Maud hadn't got round to resetting the pin number, so it was still the same as the one in the plans" said Frank, pushing the door open. Once inside, everyone was amazed to see it looked like a very small flat. "As you can see there's everything in here I would need, including it's own air supply, electricity circuit and running water." He said, gesturing around with his outstretched arm. "Wow, Great Aunt Maud was not only a legend, she was truly amazing" said Nick in awe. "She certainly thought of everything" agreed Janet. "It's staggering to think that you were in here, Frank, and no one knew" said Mrs Armstrong. "Believe me I was very quiet, even though this place says it is fully soundproofed on the plans. I was always worried" laughed Frank.

"So where's this place built in line with in the house? It's hard to get your bearings in here" said DCI Fields. "This place is set into the back of the boiler room, at the far corner of the house. It's a much newer build as Aunt Maud had to have it replaced after a fire. She must have had the panic

136

room created at the same time. No one ever goes there unless needed, but even if they did, its has been sealed off with a solid steel door" said Frank. "This is fabulous" Nick replied, clearly very impressed. "There is a code system to open the door in the boiler room in an emergency. This place is also fireproof, able to hold a fire at bay with these doors for a considerable amount of time. Oh and it also has it's own phone system, I couldn't understand the plans for that bit. But the fact that it says that it's unable to be sabotaged was all I needed to know" said Frank with a dry laugh. "So why exactly did your Aunt Maud have this place built Frank?" said Tom. "I've no idea, but to Aunt Maud family meant everything and she wanted to keep them safe. Maybe against Fred's cronies, who knows? Maud was a very wise woman who always thought of every eventuality. It's just a shame she didn't live long enough to see it and tell us all about it" said Frank, the sad edge unmissable in his voice. No one actually said anything, but everyone in that room knew exactly what Frank meant.

"Anyway, we'd best be off" said DCI Fields, breaking the silence. "Okay I'll see you out, when do you want me to come to the station?" asked Lucy. "First thing tomorrow morning, say about 9, is that okay?" Asked the DCI. "If Phyllis will see me tonight, I'd really rather if that were possible" said Lucy. "Yes, that's fine. I'll stay on as I'd like to be there myself. I do understand why you'd prefer not to wait." Said the DCI. "Thank you, I do appreciate it" said Lucy, smiling gratefully. "Okay, see you at the station in about an hour?" Asked the DCI. Lucy shook hands with DCI Fields and DS Lowe and was just about to shut the door. "We better be on our way as well" said Tom, coming over with Amira and Paul. "Goodbye Lucy, you take care and once again I'm sorry" said Tom, giving her a hug. "You have nothing to be sorry about whatsoever Tom. Thank you for everything" said Lucy, hugging him tightly. In the short time they'd known each other, they'd become very close, and both knew they'd miss each other a great deal. Ben stepped forward and shook Tom's hand, "I will never be able to thank you enough for looking after my family. Don't be a stranger though Tom, any friend of Lucy's is a friend of mine. You'll always be very welcome here." He said. "Thank you, I'd love to stay in touch" Tom replied. Amira hugged Lucy goodbye, "I shall really miss you and the children. I've grown very fond of you all. Would you mind if I popped back and said goodbye to Jake and Emily another day? I just think they've had enough to take in for now" she said. "Me too if that would be okay" said Paul, leaning forward to give Lucy a peck on the cheek. "No, I'd rather you didn't" said Lucy straight faced. "Oh" said Amira, taken aback. "You can't come back to say goodbye, but you can all come back to visit any time you'd like" said Lucy with a broad grin. "Thank you" said Paul.

"There is just one more thing you don't know Lucy" said Amira warily. "Is there?" She said in surprise. "Er.. yes. I become Mrs Paul Henson 5 weeks from today" said Amira shyly. "Oh my god that's fantastic news! I'm so pleased for you both, congratulations!" Lucy cried. "There is something else though, but I'm not sure that this is the right time to ask" said Amira uncertainly. "Go on, what is it?" Lucy asked. "We would be really honoured if you and your family would be guests at our wedding, and even more honoured if Emily and Jake would be a bridesmaid and a pageboy" replied Amira. "Oh thank you both so much, I'm sure they'd absolutely love that. It's so kind of you to ask them, it's a lovely thought" Lucy said. "Not at all, they're fabulous kids" said Paul. Lucy glowed with obvious pride. "That's settled then, we'll be in touch very soon. Bye Lucy" said Amira. Lucy and Ben waved until their guests disappeared out of the gates at the end of the drive. "Did you want to go out somewhere tonight to celebrate you being home?" Asked Lucy. Ben draped an arm around Lucy's shoulder as they walked back up the steps to the house. "You know what my ideal first night back would be?" He smiled. "What?" Lucy asked. "Spending the evening at home with you and the children" he replied. "Me too" she smiled happily.

Ben played with Jake and Emily in the garden, while Lucy chatted with Leah about coming to look after the children full time. "So it's agreed then, you're happy with the salary, you'll move into Amira's old room, you get every other weekend off and a day in the week on the week in-between?" Said Lucy, looking at Leah for her decision. "That's fabulous, thank you so much!" Gushed Leah. "I'll be here a lot of the time working from home, and will often take the children to and from school, as the holidays will be over soon. I prefer to think of you as an extension to our family rather than an employee" Lucy smiled. Leah nodded furiously, she was very happy indeed. Nick poked his head around the door, "DCI Fields has just rung Lucy. He said if you want to come to the station now you can see Phyllis and Avril" "Thank you Nick, are you okay with the children?"

Lucy asked. "Fine, I was going to ask if you minded if Leah and I took them for a pizza" he said. "I'll need the car" Lucy told him. "Already got that one covered, Leah has her car here" said Nick with a cheeky grin. "In that case of course you can" said Lucy. Leah had gone out to get the children and tell Ben about the DCI's call. "Are we ready then?" Asked Ben coming in from the garden. "Yes" said Lucy, swallowing hard as she got to her feet. She kissed Jake and Emily goodbye, promising them both she would be as quick as she could.

"Did you see that pair?" Said Ben, grinning madly as he drove down the drive. "What do you mean?!" Said Lucy, feigning mock surprise. "I think Nick's found his Lucy there, don't you?" Said Ben with a chuckle. "So you noticed it too?" She said. "Still, he does have an advantage over me though" said Ben. "What's that?" Lucy asked, in genuine surprise this time. "At least he won't have to make himself broke eating all those chips" said Ben, laughing heartily. Lucy hugged herself inwardly, she was so happy to have Ben back. When they arrived at the police station, DCI Fields spoke to them in the corridor, "Phyllis and Avril are in two separate rooms, I'd rather you spoke to them alone" said the DCI. "That's fine" Lucy replied. DCI Fields opened the door of the room behind him, DS Lowe was seated at the table with Avril, whilst a uniformed officer stood silently behind. Lucy walked over to the other side of the desk to where Avril sat, still staring down at her hands. "Hello Avril, this is my husband Ben" said Lucy quietly. She slowly raised her head, her eyes full of tears,"Hello Mrs Reid, Mr Reid" she said, with a weak smile. "DCI Fields said you wanted to see me" said Lucy softly, "and I asked to see you anyway." "I just wanted to say I'm so very sorry, I never wanted to hurt you. Any of you. But he made me" said Avril through her tears. "I know he did" said Lucy. "He hurt me so bad Mrs Reid. He said he would do that to Jonathan, I couldn't let him do that" sobbed Avril. "I know that Avril, DCI Fields has explained" said Lucy. "He said he'd hurt my mum Mrs Reid, she's been through so much with him. She's not strong enough to take his violence and she's all me and Jonathan have got" Avril continued to sob.

Despite what this woman had been involved in putting her through, Lucy could not help but feel sorry for her. "I do understand Avril, and maybe you, Jonathan and your mum can all live together again one day. Now that that man is out of your life" said Lucy. Avril shook her head furiously, "I've got no job and I have learning difficulties. I caught a very bad bout of measles as a child and lost a lot of schooling. My mum used to keep me at home and hit me with a poker if I got things wrong when I did the shopping. But I couldn't read it Mrs Reid, I couldn't read the list" said Avril, huge sobs wracking her body. "Oh my god you poor thing" said Lucy, reaching across to hold Avril's hand. Ben hadn't uttered a word, but it was plain to see he was visibly moved by this mislead young woman's plight. "Please forgive me Lucy, and I would never have let him harm your little girl. I would have died first" said Avril, looking Lucy straight in the eyes. "You know Avril, I believe you" she replied. "Let's leave things there Lucy, you need to see Phyllis, as they are being moved to the holding centre soon before they appear in court on Monday morning." Said DCI Fields. Lucy stood up, "Goodbye Avril, and thank you for explaining it to me" she said. "Goodbye Mrs Reid, you're a lovely lady, my mum was right. Goodbye Mr Reid" said Avril, tearfully.

Lucy and Ben made their exit and stood in the corridor waiting for DCI Fields to speak to DS Lowe. "Are you okay?" Said DCI Fields, coming out of the room and closing the door behind him. "Yes" said Lucy quietly, and Ben nodded. DCI Fields led the way around the corner, and opened a door on the opposite side of the corridor. Inside was Phyllis. The female officer that Lucy recognised from the day of the burglary sat at the table opposite her and PC Regan stood behind. He nodded his head in acknowledgement to them, "Hello Scott" Lucy whispered as she passed. "Lucy, nothing I can say will ever be enough. I just wanted you both to know I'm truly sorry" said Phyllis, looking Lucy straight in the eyes. "Hello Phyllis, this is my husband Ben" said Lucy. "Hello" said Ben. "Mr Reid, I owe you an apology also. I know you'll never forgive me, but I want you to know why" said Phyllis sadly. "I'd like to hear that" Lucy replied, nodding. "When Fred came back into my life, I was in a terrible state, I'd not long lost my long term partner, Jack. Fred and I were married, but had been separated a long while, but had never got a divorce. Jack was a lovely man, so kind and caring, I'm ashamed to say it but I turned to drink. I never neglected my kids though" said Phyllis fiercely. "Your kids? I thought Jonathan was your brother?" Lucy said. "He is, but I've never thought of him any different to Avril, he has always needed my care" said Phyllis. Lucy nodded, now understanding the situation. "I was sober in the day time because I knew them kids needed me, but at night when they were asleep, no one needed me anymore. I was so lonely and drink just helped to numb the pain" said Phyllis sadly. "Go on" said Ben softly. Lucy glanced up at him, it was the first time he'd spoken more than one word. He gave her a reassuring smile and took her hand in his.

"The home Jack and I lived in wasn't fancy, and we didn't even own it but we were happy. Until that day when he didn't come home. Jack had a massive heart attack and he was gone, just like that" said Phyllis, a tear rolling down her cheek. "That's awful Phyllis, I'm very sorry" said Lucy sympathetically. "Fred caught me on the rebound, he could be so charming" said Phyllis. "Fred?!" Said Lucy, unable to hide her shock. Phyllis laughed wryly, "Yes, ironic isn't it? But as hard to believe as it is, it's true. One night I fell and broke my ankle, and I had no one else to call but Fred. He stayed with Jonathan and Avril until I got out of hospital and whilst Avril was at school and Jonathan at his day care centre, he moved us into his place. At first he was so attentive and helpful, but it didn't take long for his not so nice side to show through. My ankle didn't fix well and I had two operations to try and sort it. I counted the days until I was back on my feet and I could take Avril and Jonathan and escape back to our little house" said Phyllis, through the tears that were now falling. "So why did you stay with Fred?" Lucy asked. Phyllis bit her lip nervously, "Because when I did go home, one day when Fred was out, it wasn't home anymore. Well it was, just someone else's. Fred had forged my signature and given my house up" said Phyllis bitterly. "Oh my god" said Lucy. "What could I do? I was weak. Fred convinced me no one would believe a drunk, even though I wasn't drinking by then. We were trapped and we were still trapped right up until the police arrested him at Hilltop Manor. We were free. Except I'm not free anymore, Fred still managed to keep me prisoner, he still managed to get me locked up, maybe even Avril. Why? Because I'm a weak, stupid woman." Said Phyllis, starting to sob.

Lucy got up and walked round the table to Phyllis, she bent down and put her arm around her shoulders. "You're not stupid Phyllis, the only thing you've done is got involved with an evil, scheming manipulator" Said Lucy kindly. "I knew about Fred's Aunt, but never about any of you apart from Frank. Fred told me that Frank had framed him for a fire that he had caused, and his mother had died in it. He told me that's why his Aunt wouldn't have anything to do with him. I swear Lucy, I never knew the truth" said Phyllis earnestly. "Do you know Phyllis, I believe you, I really do" said Lucy. "I feel so guilty Lucy, not only for everything I've put you through, but for Jonathan and Avril too. Jonathan doesn't speak much and has never told me that Fred hurt him, but I know he did. I saw the way he recoiled in fear every time Fred went near him. The terror in his innocent eyes. He trusted me Lucy, and I let him down. I let him down in the worst way imaginable. That fear was the only reason I let Jonathan go into the home, I had no money, nowhere to live, and above all, no will power and self respect. He was safer there, but I will get back on my feet Lucy, I will build a home for us all again one day" said Phyllis, the determination in her eyes was unmistakeable. "For what it's worth, I think you did the best thing for Jonathan at the time" Lucy said. "I'll never forgive myself for Avril either, how did I miss the signs? I can't believe what that wicked, evil man was doing to her. That poor girl, and she took it all, never once complained. I just thought it was her age making her difficult. God forbid I never realised Lucy" said Phyllis, tears pouring down her face.

"Avril loves you very much, you and Jonathan, that's very clear" said Lucy kindly. "I just had to do as Fred said Lucy, I couldn't let him hurt them anymore. I never wanted anyone hurt, that's why I came to Hilltop Manor. I just thought if Fred could get the paintings without any violence, he may leave us all alone. I should have known though, known that I couldn't trust him. Nothing would ever be enough for Fred. I was very fond of you all Lucy, there was no way I would have ever agreed to be a part of harming any of you. I'd foolishly thought that if Fred had the money, he may have let me leave. He may have let me move out, but he was never going to let me go, I can't believe I thought he would" said Phyllis, shaking her head sadly. "I know Phyllis" said Lucy, the compassion overflowing in her voice. "Time to go" said DCI Fields. "Yes of course" said Lucy nodding. "Goodbye Phyllis, take care" she said softly. "Bye Lucy, Mr Reid" said Phyllis, tears still glistening in her eyes.

As DCI Fields walked her and Ben to the door, she couldn't help going over what she'd just been told. "Where is Jonathan?" Said Lucy. "He's in Marsdon Residential Centre in Whitelea." Said DCI Fields. "Okay, thank you for everything" Lucy replied. "Not at all, take care both of you" said the DCI. By the time Ben and Lucy were seated in the car, she still hadn't said a word. "You want to visit Jonathan don't you?" Said Ben quietly. "Please don't be mad with me, but yes I do" she replied. Ben sighed and turned to Lucy, taking her hand in his, "I could never be mad at you, I love you far too much for that. And to be honest, I'd quite like to meet Jonathan too" he said. "Really?" Said Lucy. "Really" said Ben. Lucy's mobile began to ring, "Hello" she said. "Hi it's Nick, just wanted to let you know we took Jake and Emily to the soft play area first, so we're running late for pizza". "No problem, that's fine" Lucy replied. "Have you been to the police station?" Nick asked. "Yes, we're just leaving there. I'll tell you all about it later" she said. "If you're just going home now, why don't you and dad come and join us?" Asked Nick. "That's a lovely idea, we'd love to. You know how your dad's never been able to resist pizza" Lucy chuckled. "Did someone say pizza? I'm on my way" said Ben. "Is it the one in the retail park near Bartons?" Lucy asked. "Yes that's the one, see you soon" Nick replied, before putting the phone down. "So that's settled then, pizza tonight and off to see Jonathan tomorrow morning" said Ben.

As Lucy sat round the table a short while later, she couldn't help but smile contentedly as she watched Nick and Leah gaze into each other's eyes, and Ben tease Jake and Emily mercilessly. 'This is how things should be' she thought happily. Once they had all eaten, she and Ben took Jake and Emily home, while Nick and Leah went to see the late night film together. It was strange that night, tucking the children into bed with Ben by her side, instead of alone as she usually did. As she closed the bedroom door behind her and opened her own, this time, for the first time in what seemed like an eternity, she had company. It was sheer bliss laying on Ben's chest, listening to his shallow breathing as he slept. Lucy didn't know what time she eventually fell asleep, but what she did know was that she was ecstatically happy. Maybe now she could finally look forward.

The next morning they set off straight after breakfast to see Jonathan, leaving Jake and Emily to enjoy a day with nanny and grandad. They arrived in Whitelea just after 10, Marsdon Residential Centre was set in attractive gardens with cut green lawns, and pretty trees overlooking a beautiful lake. The reception area was a plush sitting room, all expensive sofas and inviting decor. "Hello" said the woman on the desk frostily. "Hi we wondered if we could see one of your residents, Jonathan Kramer, please?" Said Ben. "Jonathan? Are you family?" Asked the woman. "No, we're acquaintances of his sister Phyllis" Ben replied. "It's only family or people with written permission of his next of kin that can see Jonathan" said the woman sharply. "Oh we didn't realise, his sister used to work for us. Is there no way we could see him, even just for a minute?" Lucy asked. "No permission, no visit" said the woman. Lucy and Ben were just about to leave when a smiling young girl in a nurses uniform appeared beside them. "Hello I'm Lily. I help to take care of Jonathan, I'm sorry I couldn't help but overhear, you wouldn't be Mr and Mrs Reid by any chance, would you?" She asked. "Er, yes we are. How did you know?" Said Lucy, taken aback. The young woman smiled again, "We received permission by email last night from Phyllis Reid, stating you may visit Jonathan whenever you like" said Lily. "Did you? I don't understand" said Lucy, puzzled.

Lily led them over to the corner of the room, and lowering her voice, she said. "We know about Mrs Reid and Jonathan's niece, we had to be informed. DS Lowe rang last night and said that she had a feeling you may decide to visit, so got permission from Mrs Reid just incase. "Well I never" said Ben. "That's wonderful news, so we can see Jonathan today?" Asked Lucy, hesitantly. "Of course you can, come with me and I'll take you to him" said Lily. As they walked along the lavishly carpeted hallways, Lily explained about how Marsdon operated its care system for residents. They were free to come and go with their families as they pleased, but whilst there, they tried to make things as homely and comfortable as possible. "This is Jonathan" Lily said, opening one of the many white doors along the corridor. On the far side of the room sat a man in his mid fourties, dressed in blue jeans and a smart shirt, staring out of the window across the lake. "Hello Jonathan" said Lucy, taking a step towards him. "Jonathan, this is Mr and Mrs Reid, they're friends of Phyllis'" said Lily. "Phyllis, is she here?" Said Jonathan, turning to face them with a broad grin. "No I'm afraid Phyllis couldn't make it today, but I'm Lucy and this is Ben" said Lucy, as they followed Lily over to where Jonathan sat. "Hello" said Jonathan to Lucy, but as she stepped aside for Jonathan to see Ben, he threw his arms across his head, "No the bad man!" He screamed. "No Jonathan, this is Ben. He's not a bad man, he's your friend" said Lily, putting her arms around Jonathan and brushing his hair down soothingly with her hand. Ben looked taken aback by Jonathan's sudden outburst, he hadn't expected that reaction at all.

"I won't hurt you Jonathan, my name is Ben" he said, sitting down gingerly in a nearby armchair. Jonathan peered at Ben nervously, still holding Lily's hand for all he was worth. "My friend? You won't hurt me?" He said warily. "No Jonathan, I'd never hurt you" said Ben. "You look like the bad man" Jonathan replied, still not convinced. Understanding now Jonathan's fear, Ben tried again. To Jonathan, Ben had a very similar build and look to Fred. "I'm not Fred Jonathan, I'm Ben. That bad man won't be able to come and see you again" said Ben softly. "He won't?" Jonathan asked, doubtfully. "No he wont" Ben reassured him. Jonathan relaxed, and Lily moved to sit on the stool next to him. "Phyllis told us all about you Jonathan, so we decided we'd like to come and see you" said Lucy. "Why?" Asked Jonathan. "Because we'd like to be your friends" Lucy replied. "Oh I haven't got any friends, except Phyllis" said Jonathan, his eyes shining at the mere mention of her name. "Oh and Avril of course". Lucy smiled, Jonathan was clearly very fond of Phyllis indeed. "I'm just going to go into the bedroom and hang up your clean washing, okay?" Lily asked Jonathan, "I'm just through that door" she said, patting his hand. "Do you have a car?" Jonathan asked suddenly. "Yes we do" said Ben relaxing now that Jonathan seemed a bit more settled in his company. "Phyllis doesn't have a car, she comes to see me on a blue bus" said Jonathan. "Oh that's nice isn't it?" Said Lucy. "I don't like buses, they're too big. I don't like big things" said Jonathan pointedly. "Buses can be nice mate" Ben said, smiling.

"I've got a boat, do you want to see my boat?" Said Jonathan, looking at Ben shyly. "Er, yes, where is it? Is it in a book?" Asked Ben. Jonathan laughed, "I can't keep my boat in a book" he said. "Oh where is it then?" Asked Ben. "It's in the cupboard" declared Jonathan. Lily had returned by now and laughed, seeing Ben's shocked face. She opened the cupboard by the window, "This is the Phyllis Rose" she said. "See it's in the cupboard!" Declared Jonathan excitedly. Ben and Lucy looked into the cupboard and there sat the most beautiful, motorised model speedboat they had ever seen. Lily picked it up, brought it over and handed it to Ben. "It's lovely" he said, admiring it's sleek white sides and contoured edges. "It's my boat" said Jonathan proudly. "It's beautiful" Lucy said. "It's got Phyllis' name on" said Jonathan, that unmistakable shine in his eyes returning. "I know, and I'm sure that makes Phyllis very happy" said Lucy. "Is Phyllis coming to see me with Avril?" Jonathan asked expectantly. "I don't know mate, but I do know that Phyllis will be here just as soon as she can. She's a bit busy at the moment" said Ben, smiling kindly. Lucy looked at her watch, "We have to be going Jonathan, but it's been lovely meeting you" she said. "Okay, bye" said Jonathan, admiring his boat that Lucy had put in his hands. "I'll see Mr and Mrs Reid out and I'll be back to take you to lunch" said Lily. Just as they got to the door, "Ben" Jonathan called. "Yes mate?" Said Ben, turning round. "Will you come and see me again and help me sail my boat?" Jonathan asked. Ben looked at Jonathan and smiled warmly, "I'd like that very much, see you soon" he said.

Lucy was so pleased they'd come today, that was a huge breakthrough for Jonathan to accept that not every man was like Fred. Lily walked them to their car, "Thank you for coming today" she said. "It was our pleasure" said Lucy. "Do you know, in all the time he's been here, we've never got that much out of him, he rarely says anything at all. He just sits there staring out of the window looking for Phyllis" Lily finished. "Oh that's so sad" said Lucy. "We'll definitely come and visit him again" Ben promised. "It might be best if you ring first, as Jonathan is due to be moved just as soon as we can find him somewhere suitable to go" Lily said. "Moved?" Asked Lucy in surprise. "Yes, his fees are due to run out" said Lily quietly.

As Lucy and Ben drove home she was very quiet, deep in thought. As they passed through the town centre, Ben pulled into a parking space. "What are we doing?" Lucy asked. "We need to talk" Ben replied softly. She followed him into a cafe and they found a small table in a secluded alcove. "What is it Lucy?" Asked Ben anxiously. "You didn't need to stop, I'm fine, it's nothing for you to worry about" said Lucy, nervously fiddling with the salt pot on the table. "Lucy if it worries you, then it worries me. Would you like me to take a guess at what's troubling you?" He said gently, taking the salt pot out of her hand and replacing it with his own. Lucy looked up at Ben, tears brimming in her eyes. "When you saw Phyllis and Avril yesterday, you were touched by their stories, and even more so, you believe they were both telling the truth. You think they're good people deep down and that they were both misguided by their fear of Fred. They got into something a lot deeper than they intended, and it was too deep for them to get out again. Is that right?" Ben asked. "Yes" said Lucy quietly, but this time not meeting his eyes. "You wanted to meet Jonathan for yourself so that you could try to understand some of Phyllis and Avril's fear for him, and their need to keep him safe." Ben continued. "Yes" said Lucy softly. "Lucy, look at me please" said Ben. Lucy raised her eyes slowly and looked into Ben's kind face, a stray tear escaping down her cheek. "Yes" she breathed. "You want to try and help them, don't you?" Said Ben gently. Lucy nodded, "Yes" she said. "Well so do I. I also think that both mother and daughter were telling us the truth. I thought Jonathan was a lovely guy, and deserves a life free from fear of that animal Fred" said Ben. Lucy nodded again, "Exactly" she said. "Come on Lucy, Mr Benson's due in half an hour to talk about the will reading. Let's speak to him about how we can help" said Ben, helping her to her feet. "I love you Ben, thank you for trying to understand me" said Lucy, hugging him tight. "I love you too, and it wasn't at all difficult to understand, as it mirrored exactly how I was feeling" Ben replied, opening the car door for his young wife.

CHAPTER 13
AUNT MAUD'S WILL

When they got home, Mr Benson was already there, having tea with Mrs Armstrong in the kitchen. He stood up to shake both of their hands, "Forgive me for being early, but I had a gap in my diary and thought I would use that to catch up with Margaret" he said, smiling at her. "Please, it's not a problem, you're more than welcome" said Lucy. Mr Benson was a short man, with a receding hairline and small, round silver spectacles, with the friendliest smile that Lucy had ever seen. "Shall we move through to the living room while we wait for my mother and father?" Suggested Ben. As they passed the front door, it flew open and in clattered Jake and Emily, with a rather tired looking Frank and Janet in tow. Jake and Emily ran to hug their parents, whilst the bedraggled looking Frank and Janet fought to regain their composure in front of their visitor. "Charles!" Said Frank, coming to shake Mr Benson's hand. "Hello Frank, and this beautiful lady must be Mrs Reid" he said, whilst Janet blushed furiously. "Hello Mr Benson, I've heard so much about you, please call me Janet" she said. "Is Nick here?" Asked Lucy. "Yes, he and Leah are sitting on the patio" Mrs Armstrong said. Lucy smiled to herself, Nick and Leah were together again. Seeing everyone now congregating in the living room, Nick and Leah came inside. After the introductions, Leah took Jake and Emily off to play. "Is everyone here that needs to be?" Asked Frank. "Er, Jeff needs to be here. Your Aunt Maud requested that he was present as well" said Mr Benson. "I'll go and see where he is" said Ben. He didn't have to go far.

As he opened the back door, Bruce was busy hammering nails in to re-fix the gate post under the watchful eye of Jeff. "Hi, Mr Benson has asked you join us Jeff, to speak about Aunt Maud's will" said Ben. "Me? Really? Oh okay then" he said, a little surprised. "Yes please, take him away. He's a slave driver! And a hard one to please at that" said Bruce, winking at Ben. "Er, I'm not that bad…" Jeff began, but he didn't continue, seeing the other two grinning like mad, he realised he was being teased.

Ben pushed Jeff up the makeshift ramp that Bruce had made to get his wheelchair up to the back door and through to where everyone else was waiting. "So what happens now Charles? Do we just get a date for the reading?" Asked Frank. "No, actually I'm going to do it now. Your aunt was most definite it was to be an informal affair" said Mr Benson. "Oh, okay" said Frank in surprise. Mr Benson finished setting out his paperwork and sat down at the head of the table. "We are here today to witness the reading of the last Will and testament of Maud Alice Read" he began. After reading through all of the other official requirements and legalities, he began to read out Aunt Maud's bequests. Everyone shuffled nervously in their seats. "I never thought this would be as scary as this, fear of the unknown" whispered Lucy to Janet. "Please remember your Aunt was quite a character, and she insisted these bequests were written in her own words" said Mr Benson. "Why doesn't that surprise me?" Said Frank with a laugh. Mr Benson began to read, "Hello everyone, if you're reading this then my clogs have finally well and truly popped, haha. But don't anyone be sad, I want you all, that's each and every one of you, to be smiling. Because I can still see you, you know, and I will be watching. Life is too short for regrets and sadness, it's for living to the full. Anyway, let's get on with this. Charles will deal with all the boring bits, like taxes. Heaven knows I pay him enough, haha. No seriously Charles, you have been a very good solicitor and a treasured friend, and I thank you from the bottom of my heart. In view of your loyal service at the end of this reading, I want my nephew Frank to read what's in the sealed white envelope. But remember, not until then! Anyway, on with the good bits. To my great great nephew and niece, Jake and Emily, I leave £100,000 to each of them, in trust until they are 21 years of age. I also leave a further £15,000 each to be released to them to be used for driving lessons, starting on their 17th birthdays. The remainder is to be used to buy them a safe, reliable, experience related car. There are enough inexperienced drivers on the road driving cars that are way too powerful for them, I want them to do it properly. These bequests to them comes with all my love. Such beautiful children, Ben, Lucy, they are a credit to you." "Oh how lovely and so kind and generous" said Lucy emotionally. Everyone nodded, murmuring their agreement.

Mr Benson continued, "To my great great nephew Nick, I also leave the sum of £100,000 in trust until he is 21. Nick, you've turned into a charming young man, who we are all very proud of. Mr Benson has the keys to the garage on the left at Hilltop Manor, the one with the blue door. Open it, there's a little something in there for you. As you are older than Jake and Emily and your trust won't have time to gain the interest that their's will, I am leaving you a further £10,000. Your great great uncle made a successful business from a fraction of that through sheer drive, grit and determination. I have every faith in you, Nick, that you can do the same. That £10,000 will be available to you now. Do me proud Nick, I know you will, my love will be there driving you on." "Wow, how amazing" said Nick, his eyes wide. "You're very lucky indeed" nodded Ben. "I wonder what's in the garage?" Nick asked excitedly.

"Oh and there's a ps here from your aunt" said Mr Benson smiling. "Is there?" Asked Nick in surprise. "Yes, she says, Oh and yes we will take a break for 10 minutes while you go and look in the garage haha" said Mr Benson, handing him the keys. Everyone laughed, trust Great Aunt Maud, always the dry sense of humour. Nick took the keys and raced out to the garage with everyone else following behind. He eagerly put the key in the lock and opened the door, "There's nothing here" said Nick confused. "Look a little closer Nick" said Mr Benson. Nick walked into the garage, it was completely empty, apart from a roll of paper and a photograph of a smart blue family hatchback. "Pick them up Nick and bring them back inside" said Mr Benson. Nick did as he was told, locked the garage, and followed everyone else back inside. "What have you got there?" Said Frank, unrolling the paper. "It looks like plans" said Ben. "They are indeed plans" said Mr Benson nodding. "Plans to what?" Asked Nick puzzled. Mr Benson picked up Aunt Maud's will again, and began to read, "Ah good, you're all back. No Nick, I've not completely lost it, your uncle bought the plot of land beside Hilltop Manor shortly before his death. The preparations have been done to make it suitable to build on, so that's what I want you to do. Charles has enough money set aside to allow you to plan a small house for yourself. The plans are what you now hold, for the layout of the land. There will also be enough there for one for Jake and Emily once they come of age. Charles' firm will look after things and arrange for it to be deposited in trust for them as well. There is enough money there for all three, not as grand as my beloved Hilltop of course, but comfortable none the less. As for the photograph of the car, that will be arriving at 5pm. Not too fast, but enough to impress the ladies. Be safe Nick, drive carefully." "Oh my god, I can't believe this!" Said Nick. "Your Great Great Aunt was a very kind person Nick. But also very wise and an extremely shrewd business woman" said Mr Benson. "I still can't believe she had all this and we never knew" said Frank.

"Your Aunt next speaks of Jeff and Margaret... You've both been loyal, hardworking employees, but have also become trusted friends. Jeff, even though you haven't been with Hilltop Manor anywhere near as long as Margaret, you are irreplaceable. I want you to have £10,000 as a token of my gratitude and the cottage you live in is now yours" said Mr Benson. Jeff gasped in amazement, "Thank you so much." Mr Benson continued to read, "Margaret, 35 years of reliability. How does one ever start to replace that, or to find a suitable reward? To you I leave £20,000 and your cottage in the grounds is yours. There will also be a car arriving at 5pm for you. A smart little runaround, so that you can finally let poor old Betsie retire" said Mr Benson. "Oh no, that's too generous" said Mrs Armstrong. "Maud wanted you to have these things Margaret, she was very fond of you" said Mr Benson. "I don't know what to say" said Mrs Armstrong, wiping a tear from her eye. "There is one clause though, to you both, whilst the cottages are yours, if you ever choose to sell them and move away, they must be sold back to the owners of this Manor. Maud was very definite she did not want strangers in the grounds" said Mr Benson. Margaret and Jeff nodded in agreement. "So who does own Hilltop Manor?" Asked Nick.

Mr Benson smiled a knowing smile, turned over the page and began to read again, "Hilltop Manor always had a special place in my heart. Although I never got to spend as much time as I would have liked to there. I made the decision to remain at Primrose Hill, as I was determined that under no circumstances would a rather unsavoury relative of mine ever be able to get his hands on the Manor. That's a lovely big house, but too quiet and empty. For that reason, I leave Hilltop Manor to my lovely great nephew Ben and his beautiful wife Lucy" said Mr Benson. Lucy gasped,

"Oh my god this place is ours!" She said in shock. "It certainly is" said Mr Benson. "I can't believe it!" Said Ben. "There's more" said Mr Benson. "You have a lovely family Ben and Lucy, all I ask is that you fill the house with love and laughter." "We will" murmured Lucy. "Your aunt also goes on to say, she would like you to have the house at Primrose Hill. She says rent it out, use it as a holiday home, just don't sell it. That house has far too many happy memories to let it leave the family" said Mr Benson. "Oh no we wont, we will keep it in our family. It would be an honour" said Ben earnestly.

"That must mean you get Bartons grandad" said Nick. "Your Aunt continues by saying, apart from 5% each to Nick, Jake and Emily from Bartons' yearly net profits, to go into trust until they are 21, she is also leaving Bartons to Ben and Lucy" finished Mr Benson. "Oh my god" said Lucy, in total shock. "What's left Grandad?" Said Nick quietly. The whole room fell silent with everyone looking at Frank. It seemed he had been omitted from the will of Great Aunt Maud, just as Fred had. Frank sat without uttering a word, his face giving nothing away to how he was feeling, but everyone in that room knew he must be in deep shock and bitterly disappointed. Mr Benson finished cleaning his glasses, and placed them back on his nose. "Your Aunt wants me to read this, but in her own words again. Ben and Lucy, you looked after me well for many years, and your little family brought me great joy. Hopefully now you will be able to enjoy a secure future as a way of a thank you. Now Frank, take that glum look off your face man, as if I'd ever leave you out! Charles has enough money in the pot to sort out a lovely place for you and Janet on the grounds next door too. I know how you like to plan, so planning your home should keep you busy. Oh, a question for everyone, have you ever heard of RIH?" Said Mr Benson. "RIH? Isn't that the development company that built Bartons and the flats in town?" Asked Jeff. "Yes it is, and I heard they'd recently won another contract for a mall in the United States" said Frank. "You are both right" nodded Mr Benson. "So what's that to do with the will?" Asked Janet puzzled.

Mr Benson straightened his glasses and began to read once more, "RIH stands for Reid International Holdings" he said. "Oh my god, they're worth a mint!" Said Ben in awe. "Reid International Holdings are a multi-million pound property development investment company, operating at home and in five different countries abroad. This is a business that your uncle and I built from the ground" Read Mr Benson. "No wonder Great Aunt Maud always took so many private phone calls!" Said Ben. "I never could understand why a woman of that age had a mobile phone that'd never stop ringing" laughed Frank. "Well Frank, I am leaving 10% to Ben and Lucy each, and 5% to Nick, Jake and Emily. That should give them a handsome income. The remaining 65% goes to you and Janet with my love and best wishes, and above all my gratitude for your love and care. Be lucky both of you" finished Mr Benson. Everyone looked at Frank, what a wonderful gift. Frank was sitting in the armchair with tears streaming down his face, "My God I miss that woman so much" he sobbed. "Come outside for a bit" said Janet, taking her husband's hand. "I think that would be a good idea, and we'll take a short break" said Mr Benson. "I'll go and make some tea" said Mrs Armstrong, hurrying off.

When everyone retook their seats 15 minutes later, Frank was his usual composed self. Mr Benson picked up Maud's will once more. "Again in your Aunts words" he said, looking around with a smile, "I think the final thing to sort with you all is the paintings. I would like them all to remain as family heirlooms and stay in situ at Hilltop Manor. Your uncle was very proud of that little gallery in the entrance hall and I hope that you all can be too. Well that brings me to my closing note, I won't say final because it will never be that. You're my family and close close friends and I love you all dearly. So I will always be right there with you. Take care, and be lucky, Maud" said Mr Benson. There wasn't a dry eye in the room after that, "I'm sorry it's only tea cups, but please raise them to Maud. May she rest in peace" said Frank. "To Maud" chorused everyone. "Er, isn't there an envelope for Frank to open Mr Benson?" Asked Lucy. "Oh that's right there is" he said, handing it to Frank. "Dear Charles, you didn't think I could forget you did you?" Frank began to read. "You've been far too good a friend firstly, as well as my solicitor for many years. I bought Barlow and Swain Solicitors two years ago, and today you are no longer the senior solicitor. From the moment this final will is read, you are now the owner. Your new sign will have been fitted by the time you return, courtesy of your colleagues who knew of my plans and were on standby to arrange it. I've taken the liberty of naming your new firm, Benson Reid Solicitors as a mark of our friendship. Please feel free to change it if you wish. Be lucky Charles, Maud" finished Frank. "Oh my, how very generous" said Mr Benson, clearly taken aback. "Are you going to keep the name Charles? Aunt Maud did say that she wouldn't mind if you changed it" asked Frank. "Keep it? Good grief of course, it would be an honour" said Mr Benson.

The intercom in the hallway buzzed just before 5, signifying there was someone at the main gate. "I'll get it!" Cried Nick, bolting out of the kitchen. "Just a little excited about his new car I think!" Laughed Lucy, following him out of the door. There was quite a welcoming committee standing on the steps of Hilltop Manor as the two shiny new cars made their way up the drive. A nippy Vauxhall Astra hatchback for Nick and a smart red Vauxhall Corsa for Mrs Armstrong. "Wow!" Said Nick excitedly, racing over to the blue car before the guy driving it barely had time to get out. He was behind the wheel in an instant learning where the controls were. Leah jumped into the passenger seat and they were soon admiring the interior together. Lucy smiled, they were really getting on well and Leah seemed like such a lovely girl. "Oh no! I won't be able to drive it until I get the insurance sorted out" said Nick in disappointment. "Yes you will, the insurance is all arranged for the first year. All I need to see is your licence and you could be on the road within the hour" said the guy who had driven Nick's car there. "That's amazing" said Nick happily. Mrs Armstrong was talking to the driver of her car, listening intently while he explained how everything worked. "I've never had a new car" she said "I'm thrilled". "Well I know Maud would be very pleased that you're happy" said Mr Benson.

Lucy and Ben managed to grab Mr Benson for a chat before he left and once he had gone, they cuddled up on the sofa. Jake and Emily sat between them, while Morph snuggled on Ben's lap. "Er I'm going to retire early if that's okay with you" said Mrs Armstrong appearing in the doorway. "Yes of course" said Lucy. "We were just about to watch a DVD, are you sure you wouldn't like to stay and watch it with us?" Asked Ben with a warm smile. "No, no, not at all. Mr and Mrs Reid have gone for a meal, Nick and Leah have gone into town in his new car and Bruce has taken Jeff back to his cottage. You all enjoy some well deserved family time" said Mrs Armstrong. "If you're sure" Ben said. "I am, but thank you for the offer. What I do have though is a lonely bag of popcorn and some marshmallows in the kitchen" she said with a laugh. "Oooh can we have some please?" Chorused Jake and Emily. "Coming right up" said Mrs Armstrong, hurrying off to get them.

Once Mrs Armstrong had gone to bed, they all settled down with popcorn and marshmallows to watch Oliver. Jake and Emily loved it and had seen it many times. By the time the film had finished though, Emily was already asleep and Jake wasn't far off. "Come on let's get you two off to bed" said Ben, picking up Emily in his arms. "I want mummy to come" said Jake sleepily. "I'm coming Jakey" she said, taking his hand. Lucy and Ben got the children ready for bed and they were both sound asleep virtually as soon as their heads hit the pillow. Hearing Nick and Leah come home downstairs, Ben said, "Shall we turn in too? It's been another long day." "It certainly has, an exciting one at that" Lucy replied. The next morning the bedroom door burst open, and Jake and Emily hurtled in. "Happy birthday mummy!" They cried. Ben came into the room carrying a tray filled with scrambled eggs, toast, jam and marmalade and a cup of tea. "Happy birthday honey" he said, setting the tray down carefully on the bed next to her, and the tea on the bedside cabinet. "Thank you all of you. Do you know something, with all that's been going on recently, I actually forgot today was my birthday" Lucy laughed. "We've got a present for you" said Emily. "Come on, let's get you both dressed while mummy eats her breakfast, and then we can come back to give mummy her gift" said Ben laughing. Jake and Emily charged out of the bedroom door, pulling Ben along with them. 'It is so lovely having him home' thought Lucy, listening to the fits of laughter coming along the landing.

Just as she finished the last mouthful, the door opened again. "You timed that just right" she said to Ben, Jake and Emily smiling. "This is for you mummy!" Cried Emily, handing her a present. "Well thank you sweetheart" said Lucy, opening the shiny pink wrapping. She gasped and stared at the contents of the small box, open mouthed. "Do you like it?" Asked Emily eagerly. "Like it? I love it!" She said, giving Emily a big hug. Inside the box was the most beautiful sapphire and diamond necklace that she had ever seen. "Here, open this mummy" said Jake, handing her a long, thin, gold envelope. "Oh how wonderful! Gift vouchers for my favourite store!" Said Lucy happily. "Yes, we thought it was about time you treated yourself" said Ben. "I can't go today though, it's too far to their nearest branch" Lucy said. "Of course you can, I've got the kids, it's your day. You go off and enjoy yourself" said Ben, leaning over to give her a kiss on the cheek. "Oh, okay then if you're sure, I will. And thank you again for my presents" said Lucy with a smile. "Hang on, you don't have mine yet" said Ben, handing her a silver gift bag. Inside was a beautiful white gold and diamond studded watch. "Oh my god it's so beautiful, this is too much!" Said Lucy, tears of happiness glistening in her eyes. "I've never had chance to spoil you before, please Lucy, let me do it just this once" said Ben softly. "I love you" said Lucy, throwing her arms around his neck. "Right back at ya" Ben replied, blowing her a kiss as he took the breakfast things out of the room.

A few seconds later there was a knock at the door, "Can we come in?" Janet called. "Of course you can" Lucy shouted back. "Happy birthday!" Janet cried, giving her a big hug. "Happy birthday Lucy" said Frank, bending down to kiss the top of her head. "Thank you" said Lucy smiling. "This is for you" said Janet, handing her a large parcel. "Can we help unwrap it?" Asked Jake and Emily. "Of course you can, I'll definitely need some help opening something this big!" Jake and Emily giggled excitedly as they eagerly ripped the paper away to reveal a beautiful black winter coat. "Oh it's gorgeous" said Lucy, jumping out of bed to try it on. "It looks lovely" said Janet nodding. "It certainly does, but maybe not with the pyjamas" said Frank with a grin. Lucy and Janet looked at Frank, then back at each other, raised their eyebrows and laughed. "This is for you as well" said Janet, handing Lucy a small purple envelope. "Thank you" she said, opening it up. "It's for today, Ben knows so he's not arranged anything" said Janet. "Ooh a spa day, sounds lovely!" Said Lucy, thrilled. "I thought you and I could spend some time together" added Janet hopefully. "That would be great" Lucy said, smiling. "Now come on Frank, let's take Jake and Emily and leave Lucy to get ready in peace" Janet said.

By the time Lucy came into the kitchen, everyone was in there waiting. "Happy birthday!" They all cried. "Thank you, thank you" said Lucy happily. "This is for you Lucy, dear" said Mrs Armstrong, handing her a present. Inside was a voucher for a year's subscription to her favourite magazine, and the latest issue. "Oh how thoughtful, I love this mag" said Lucy. "This is from dad and I" said Jeff, holding out a small parcel. Lucy ripped open the silky blue ribbon and tore through the matching gift wrap. Inside was a DVD of her favourite comedy show, two of the latest

CD Albums and two tickets to see the film of her choice at the cinema. "Thank you so much, these are great, and Ben and I were only saying last night how we'd like to see some of the recent films that have been released" "I got you this Mrs Reid" said Leah shyly. "Oh thank you Leah, how very kind" "I'm sorry it's not much" Leah said, as Lucy opened it. "Chocolates! Lovely! Oh and I love these bath salts, they smell heavenly. These bed socks are amazing" said Lucy, holding up the pink fluffy socks with the gold hearts on them. "I'm glad you like them" said Leah.

Lucy felt two arms drape around her neck and hug her from behind on the chair she was sitting, "Nick!" She smiled, grasping his hands and cuddling him round her. "Happy birthday Lucy, and thank you for everything" said Nick, kissing the top of his step mother's head and coming round to sit next to her, placing a present in front of her. Lucy opened the gift wrapping quickly, "Nick, thank you so much!" She exclaimed. Inside the wrapping was a large bottle of her favourite perfume, and the beautiful black designer handbag she had been admiring last time they were in town together. "Come on then Lucy, we need to be making track if we're going to have enough time to get fully pampered!" Said Janet laughing. "Have fun!" Said Mrs Armstrong. "Are you sure it's alright going today Ben? I don't like leaving the children on my birthday" asked Lucy worriedly. "It's fine" laughed Ben. "We'll only be a few hours" said Janet. Lucy kissed Ben and the children goodbye and hurried out to the car. She was taking their car as Nick said if Ben needed to go anywhere he'd take him. It was nice chatting to Janet as they drove along, Lucy had missed her very much. She did seem to have mellowed quite a lot though, but then Lucy supposed that what they had all been through recently would make you value your family more.

CHAPTER 14

HAPPY BIRTHDAY LUCY

Just over an hour later, they pulled into the gateway of the Blue Lagoon Health and Beauty Spa. "Heavens, this place is huge! It must have cost you a fortune" gasped Lucy, as the uniformed gateman came towards her. "Good morning madam, do you have a reservation?" Asked the man. "I have this booking card" she said. The man looked at the card, then handed it back to Lucy. "That's perfect thank you. Please drive up to reception and park in one of the gold parking spaces. You ladies have a lovely day" he said. "What a beautiful place" said Janet, gazing at the elegant glass panelled building in front of her. "Certainly is" Lucy replied. The two women followed the sign to reception, "Booking for Reid" said Janet to the pristinely dressed woman behind the counter. The lady looked down her list, "Yes of course Mrs Reid, and you are?" Said the woman, looking at Lucy. "Mrs Reid" she replied. The young woman clearly hadn't expected that answer. "Lucy is my daughter in law" said Janet. "Oh yes of course, I won't keep you a moment" said the woman, pressing a buzzer beside her.

Seconds later, a young man appeared. "Yes Polly?" He said. "Ah Jack, will you show these ladies to gold suite 5 please?" Said the receptionist. "Certainly, please come this way ladies" said Jack, opening a door to the right of the reception desk. They followed Jack down a long hallway, Lucy marvelled at the bronze coloured carpet on the floor, it was so soft and comfortable. As they reached the end of the hall, Jack stopped and pressed the lift button. Lucy noticed the corridor to her left was carpeted in the same soft pile, but this time in silver. The lift door opened to reveal the most luxurious golden carpet that Lucy had ever seen. "Oh how amazing is this? Your feet just sink into it" laughed Janet. Jack led Lucy and Janet along the golden carpeted corridor and stopped outside a door with a large gold 5 on it, swiped a card in the lock that he took from his pocket, and opened the door. Lucy gasped again, they had entered what looked like a plush studio flat. Kitchen area in one corner, sofa and tv in another, exercise machinery in a third and massage tables in the fourth. "This is fabulous!" Exclaimed Lucy. Jack smiled, "I'm glad you like it. There's fruit, vegetables, smoothies, mineral waters etcetera in the fridge. There are instructions on each piece of exercise equipment, you can use them yourself in line with that or Claude, one of our personal trainers, will be here at 2pm anyway. The controls for the TV and sound system are right by them, and if you select the treatments you'd like from the book on the table, I can arrange them for you. Most can be carried out here in the privacy of your own room. If you want to use the spa it is back downstairs opposite the lift, and the swimming pool is accessed from reception" finished Jack. "Thank you" said Lucy, picking up the treatment brochures. "There are fresh towels and robes in the closet over there" said Jack pointing. "I'll leave you ladies to pick your treatments and I will be back in 15 minutes to arrange them for you, if that's okay?" Said Jack, walking to the door. "That's great thank you, see you soon" said Lucy.

"Phew! You want to see all of the treatments available, I've never even heard of some of them" said Janet, smiling as she leafed through the other treatment brochure. "No, nor me" Lucy replied. "So what do you fancy?" Asked Janet. "Well I'd definitely like to try the spa and a full body wrap" Lucy said. "What about some form of massage? It's so relaxing" sighed Janet. "Ooh yes" Lucy agreed. "What else?" Asked Janet. The two women turned the pages of their brochures, carefully reading the description of each treatment. Lucy sighed again happily, it was funny how she hadn't had anything done yet, but still found it very tranquil already. Janet wandered over to the kitchen area, still reading her book. She picked up a banana and chose a smoothie from the fridge. "Would you grab one for me too please, and an apple if there is one?" Lucy asked. Janet brought Lucy an apple, grape, lemon and strawberry smoothie that she had found amongst the vast collection in the fridge. "It says these are all freshly prepared and replaced throughout the day" Janet read from the label on them. "Mmm lovely" said Lucy, taking a sip.

"Oooh Indian head massage, I've always fancied trying that and reflexology is so relaxing, shall we try those Lucy?" Asked Janet. "Lovely, what about a facial as well?" Lucy suggested. "Yes definitely" said Janet. "I'd love a manicure and pedicure as well." "I think that will use up all our time then, don't you?" Smiled Lucy. There was a knock at the door, and Lucy went to open it. "Hi Jack" she said. "Hello Mrs Reid, are you both ready to book your treatments?" He asked smiling.

Jack walked over to the wall next to the closet and took a small box off of the side. Lucy and Janet watched as he looked down their treatment list, pushing buttons on the box. "Does that book our treatments on it?" Asked Janet. "Yes, all at the push of a button" said Jack with a grin. "That's really clever" said Lucy impressed. "There, all done, and I've even managed to squeeze in a short session with the personal trainer as well, and still get you out of here with 10 minutes to spare of the time you want to leave" said Jack proudly. By the time Lucy and Janet left there later that day, they couldn't have been more relaxed. "I feel wonderful, thank you so much" said Lucy. "You're very welcome, and I've had a fabulous day" smiled Janet, "I'm so glad you enjoyed it".

"Not long now until we're home, I've had a great time but I can't wait to see Jake and Emily. And Ben of course" Lucy said. "I was thinking though, why don't we round the day off with buying you something for tea at the Yew Tree?" Said Janet. "That's very kind, but I do want to get home and spend the evening with the kids" said Lucy. "Of course you do, and we won't stay long. Maybe just something off of the bar snacks menu. What do you say?...Please?" Said Janet. Lucy didn't want to be rude, especially after Janet had spent so much on such a lovely day today, "Okay thank you" she said smiling. As Lucy pulled into the pub carpark, she struggled to find a parking space. "Dear me, it's busy tonight isn't it?" Said Janet. "Yes it is, I hope we can still find somewhere to sit" Lucy said. As they walked to the door, she was aware of a man dressed in black, leaning against his car bonnet, staring at them. Lucy didn't recognise him, but she shuddered uncomfortably. His gaze seemed quite menacing. As they stepped inside she couldn't help but feel relieved. The door opened again as they were standing at the bar waiting to be served. It was him, the man in black. He stood at the far end of the bar, staring, not taking his gaze from them. As Lucy looked up, his eyes met hers, they were so cold, almost as if full of hatred. 'Who on earth is he?' She thought, she was sure she didn't know him. "Lucy, Lucy, Neil said happy birthday" Janet said, nudging her. "Oh I'm so sorry. Thank you" she said, turning her attention to the Yew Tree manager who had just come to take their order. She and Janet chose what they wanted to eat, "Will you bring it over or shall I pop back for it?" Asked Janet. "I can do better than that, you're going to struggle to hear out here, let alone find a seat, how about I bring it through to the function room for you? The seating is far better out there for the birthday girl" said Neil with a smile. "Thank you, that would be lovely" Janet said. "Come on, I'll take you through" said Neil.

Lucy followed Janet and Neil across the pub to the function room, and as she did, glanced back towards the man in black. He had moved round to where they were standing moments earlier, his tattooed hand raising a pint to his lips in a slow methodical manner. Lucy couldn't help but notice he had a large snake tattoo slithering its way up his arm and he was still staring. She was quite glad that they wouldn't be sitting in the bar to eat. That man was really starting to make her feel very uneasy. "Whoops I forgot the key to the cupboard to be able to pop some music on in there. I won't be a second, go on through" said Neil. "After you" said Janet with a smile. Lucy pushed open the door, "SURPRISE!" Cried everyone. "Oh my god!" Lucy exclaimed, the room was full of all her friends and family. As she looked around she saw Ben, Nick, Jake, Emily, Mrs Armstrong, Leah, Frank, Bruce and Jeff. Then standing by Ben were Bob and Sue, their neighbours from Primrose Hill with their children Laurel and Adam, Bill, Lara and Penny, along with some of the other staff from Bartons, Jackie, Lisa and Meg her pals from school, and their partners and children. Then right at the back, she hadn't recognised him out of his suit, was DCI Fields, with him was DS Lowe, Scott Regan and last of all, Tom, Amira and Paul. Everyone was clapping and cheering. "There's two special guests we'd like you to say hi to" said Ben, leading her over to a table in the corner of the room. There sat Gladys and Bert, the elderly couple that ran the store that Lucy had gone to after Ben had first disappeared. Gladys got to her feet and hugged her tight. "Hello Lucy, it's so lovely to see you again looking so radiant, and to finally meet this husband of yours. He's quite a dish isn't he? I can certainly see why you were so upset at losing him" said Gladys with a wink, and everyone laughed. "Behave Gladys! Happy birthday dear" said Bert, kissing Lucy on the cheek. This time, when she looked Gladys in the eye there was no pity there, her eyes were filled with hope and genuine happiness.

"Mummy!" Cried two little voices, she turned round and bent down to hug Jake and Emily, she had missed them so much. "You look pretty" said Jake, "Pretty" repeated Emily. "Awh thank you" she said, hugging them both again. "Happy birthday Lucy" said Nick. "Happy birthday Mrs Reid" Leah cried. She thanked them both, and couldn't help smiling when she noticed that Nick and Leah were holding hands. Mrs Armstrong opened her arms wide and enveloped Lucy in a hug, like she did that night when she had been so upset. She didn't know what it was about Mrs Armstrong, but she always felt safe and cared for with her. "Happy birthday Lucy" she whispered. Lucy continued along the line of people waiting to greet her, "Happy birthday Lucy" said Bruce kissing her cheek, "Happy birthday, I would get up to give you hug, but on this occasion if you could come down to me it would be much appreciated" Laughed Jeff. Lucy bent down to his wheelchair and hugged him as tightly as she could without hurting him. Poor Jeff was still very tender. The next person in line took her hands in his, "Lucy you look sensational, not only do you look gorgeous, you smell gorgeous too" he said with a broad grin. "Thanks Frank" said Lucy smiling back. "Happy birthday Lucy!" Cried Jackie, Lisa and Meg, grabbing her in a group hug. "It's so lovely to see you, it's been ages" said Lucy. "It certainly has, we must all catch up a bit tomorrow" said Jackie, "We're staying here for a couple of nights" Meg added. "That would be fantastic" said Lucy with a big smile. "We did get you a present, it's on the table with the others" Lisa said. "Thanks girls" "Here she is, my favourite new boss. And I hear it's all official now" said Bill. "Yes it is, and I shall look forward to spending lots of time in the office" said Lucy. "Oh" said Lara, her face paling. "Yes I'm sure we can squeeze a third desk in there, don't you think Bill?" Asked Lucy with a wink. "Definitely" he chuckled. "Thank you all for coming" Lucy said, giving the Bartons crowd a little wave. "We were honoured to have been invited, happy birthday" said Bill.

Lucy walked over to where Bob and Sue were standing. "Hiya, it's lovely to see you" she said. "Happy birthday, we miss you already!" Said Sue, throwing her arms around her. "Happy birthday Luce" said Bob. Finally Lucy moved on to her last group of well wishers, "Happy birthday

Lucy" said DS Lowe. "Yes happy birthday, you deserve some happiness after the awful time you've had of late" said DCI Fields smiling. Paul bent down and kissed Lucy's cheek, "Happy birthday" he said, "We've left a gift or two over there" "Happy birthday!" Said Amira, giving her a hug. "Thank you all" said Lucy smiling. The final party guest stepped forward, "I've missed you all very much Mrs Reid, and Morph" said Tom. "I've missed you all too" agreed Lucy. "You know, when I started this assignment, whoever would have thought I would have made such a good friend? Happy birthday Lucy" said Tom sincerely. "Thank you so much" she said, hugging Tom tight.

Ben and Frank had ordered a huge buffet of pork, beef, gammon, ham and cheese sandwiches, sausage rolls, quiche, vol-au-vents, mini sausages and scotch eggs, with two fresh cream gateaus sitting proudly at the back of the table. Lucy was blissfully happy, dancing and chatting with her family and friends. Whilst everyone was busy eating, she decided to sneak off to use the toilet across the corridor opposite the function room, and was disappointed to find that they were out of order. "Sorry Lucy, you'll have to use the toilets in the bar" said Neil, passing by with a tray full of empty glasses. 'Oh no,' she thought, 'what happens if the man in black is still out there?' She paused by the door to the function room, seriously considering if she should get Janet to come with her. 'Pull yourself together Lucy' she told herself. 'You're twenty seven years old, you don't need someone to take you to the toilet, how ridiculous' she chastised herself. Lucy gingerly peered round the door into the bar, and breathed a sigh of relief. He must have gone. Hurrying across the crowded room she found the toilet and locked herself in the cubicle. She hummed happily to herself, she'd had the most wonderful day, things couldn't be more perfect. At that moment, a hand shot out from the cubicle next door and grasped her ankle tightly, pulling and wrenching, almost as if they were trying to pull her under the wall. Lucy looked down in terror and began to scream, 'Oh my god, that hand!', there, snaking up its arm, was the tattoo of a serpent, she could see now it wasn't a snake. It was him, the man in black.

Suddenly, the hand released its vice like grip, and Lucy heard the sound of the toilet door opening and running feet. She unlocked the door and stumbled back into the pub, running as fast as she could back into the function room. She fell through the door sobbing, crashing straight into Tom and Paul who were leaving the room. "What is it?" Asked Tom worriedly. "It was him, the man in black from the car park! He grabbed me!" Howled Lucy. "Grabbed you? Who grabbed you? Where?" Said Tom. "The man, the man from the bar, grabbed me in the toilet" sobbed Lucy hysterically. Tom and Paul raced out of the door, whilst Amira who had overheard ran to tell DCI Fields. "There's no one in there!" Shouted Tom, emerging from the toilet. "Outside!" Yelled Paul. Tom and Paul burst out of the pub doors just in time to see a black Mondeo roaring off up the road. "EY52 JDJ" said Paul, punching it into his phone. DCI Fields appeared behind them, "I got a licence plate" said Paul. "Tom ring the station quickly, I want that car stopped. Get the number plate run through the computer too" ordered DCI Fields.

When the DCI and Paul got back to the function room, Neil was there with Amira and DS Lowe, trying to comfort the still sobbing Lucy. Ben sat with his arms grasped tightly around her. "Is there anywhere else I can take the children?" Asked Leah. "Through the door at the end of the hallway, my wife Mandy is up there" said Neil, handing her a key. "Thank you" Leah replied, gathering up all the children. "They're putting everyone on the lookout for the car, the number plate is showing as a red Fiat" said Tom coming back into the room. "Thanks" said DCI Fields with a frown. He got a chair and placed it in front of Lucy, whilst Amira got ready to take notes. "What happened Lucy?" Said DCI Fields gently. She wiped her eyes and began to speak, "When Janet and I got here earlier it took us a little while to find a parking space, and when we did we didn't get out straight away as Janet was reapplying her lipstick. As we walked towards the pub I noticed a man with dark hair, standing leaning against his car bonnet. He was staring at us, well glaring in fact" said Lucy trembling. "What did he look like? How tall? Build? What was he wearing?" Asked Amira softly. "He had dark, almost black, hair, slightly wavy down to his collar" said Lucy, demonstrating with her hand. "Anything else?" Pressed the DCI, "How tall would you say?" "He wasn't really tall, not as tall as Ben, I'd say about my height, 5 foot 7" she said. "He was very thin with black jeans and a black t-shirt" Lucy added. "Is there anything else you can remember about this man Lucy?" Asked Paul. "Oh yes, he had a big serpent tattooed on his hand and running along his arm. I thought it was a snake when I saw it at a distance in the bar, but after seeing it close up in the toilet I'm certain it was a serpent."

"So what happened Lucy? Did this man follow you into the pub?" Asked Tom. "Yes, he came in and stood at the opposite end of the bar to us, just staring, staring all the time. His eyes were horrible, so cold, almost as if he hated me, but I've never seen him before in my life" said Lucy. "What happened when you came into the function room Lucy?" Asked the DCI. "He came round to where we were standing and just stood and stared drinking his pint" said Lucy with a shudder. "I didn't notice him, I'm so sorry Lucy. I'd never have let you out of the room alone if I had" said Janet, clearly upset at seeing her daughter in law this distressed. "What happened in the toilet Lucy?" Asked DS Lowe. "I was just about to unlock the door when this hand came under from the cubicle next door, it grabbed my ankle tightly, pulling me hard, it hurt so much" said Lucy, starting to cry again. "That's so awful, poor you" said Sue, patting her shoulder comfortingly. "He was pulling so hard, as if he was trying to pull me under the wall" sobbed Lucy. "Is there anything else you can tell us?" Asked DS Lowe in an encouraging voice. "No, nothing apart from I knew it was the man that had been watching me, as I saw the tattoo" said Lucy. "Are you sure the tattoo was a serpent? Was it coloured?" Asked Tom. "Er yes it was, bright red. How did you know, did you see him?" Asked Lucy puzzled. "Yes I think I may have, but not tonight. Can I have a word sir?" Tom said to DCI Fields. The two men went out into the corridor to speak privately.

"What is it Tom?" Asked the DCI. "About 10 years ago, I nicked a guy for armed robbery, Sean Lewis, he was a real nasty piece of work, held a pregnant woman hostage in a bank" said Tom. "Sean Lewis has an unmistakeable bright red serpent along his hand and forearm" said Tom pointedly. "Oh my word, what prison did he go to? Is he out? Do we know?" Asked the DCI. "He got 10 years, I gave evidence at the trial, with good behaviour he could be out. The worrying thing though sir is he was sent to Monkshall Prison" said Tom. "Isn't that where Fred was?" Asked the DCI. "Yes" said Tom quietly. "Hell, we need to find out if they knew each other, if there was any connection" said DCI Fields. "I'll make some calls" said Tom. DCI Fields went back into the function room, "Come on Lucy, let's get you out of here" he said helping her to her feet. "Ouch!" Cried Lucy as she tried to stand, sitting back down again into the chair heavily. Janet gasped, "Look at your ankle!". Everyone stared down at Lucy's left ankle, it was badly red and swollen and was starting to bruise. "No wonder you can't stand" said Paul. "If you look closely you can see hand prints where he was holding her so tight" said Amira. "You need to get that checked, we need to get you to the hospital" said Ben firmly. "I'll get Tom and Paul to go with you" said DS Lowe. "Give me the keys to your car and I'll see it gets home" said Amira. "Thank you" Lucy said, gritting her teeth in a pained smile. Tom came back into the room, "I've had word back sir, Fred and Sean were cellmates" said Tom quietly. DCI Fields ran a hand distractedly through his hair, "Suzanne, call the holding centre please. I want to see Fred and Phyllis tonight."Ben and Paul helped Lucy to her feet to start the slow hobble to the car. "I'm so sorry everyone" Lucy said over her shoulder. "You have nothing to be sorry for, go and get that ankle checked and I'll be in touch" said DCI Fields kindly. "Janet will you take Jake and Emily home for me please?" Said Lucy. "Of course I will, they'll be fine" Janet soothed.

When they got to the accident and emergency walk in department, Ben went off to find Lucy a wheelchair, her foot was swelling really badly now and she was in a lot of pain. They were very lucky and were seen almost immediately. The doctor moved Lucy's foot back and forwards, feeling all around the swelling. "I'm pretty certain there's no permanent damage, but you do have some nasty bruising and symptoms of a sprain type injury" said the doctor. "So no x-ray needed?" Ben asked. "No, not at this stage. I would suggest you visit the chemist for something to help with the pain and reducing the inflammation. However, because of where the injury is, I'm going to get the nurse to bandage it for you to give it some support when walking on it, and we can lend you some crutches, as I think you may well need them" the doctor smiled. Once the nurse had finished, Ben carefully helped Lucy back into the car. Mrs Armstrong came running down the steps as they pulled up at Hilltop Manor, "Oh Lucy dear are you okay?" She cried. "I'm fine Margaret, honestly" Lucy said.

Once she was settled in the armchair with her foot up on a stool, everything that had happened that evening came flooding back to her. "Oh my god it's all starting again" she said fearfully. "It may just be a horrible coincidence" said Mrs Armstrong in a hopeful voice. "I'm afraid I don't think so, not now we know there is a link to Fred" said Tom grimly.

"The thing I don't understand though is how he knew I was at the Yew Tree" said Lucy. "He was probably following you" suggested Paul softly. "Following me? I can't believe I was so stupid. All this time I've been so careful, watching over my shoulder at every turn. I dropped my guard because I honestly thought it was all over. But it's not is it?" Said Lucy trembling. "We will catch him, don't you worry about that" said Tom. Paul's mobile began to ring, "Hello…Yes sir, badly sprained and bruised… bandaged and on crutches…Oh right sir yes, I understand…I'll see you then…goodnight" he said, putting his phone back in his pocket. "What's up?" Asked Tom. "DCI Fields said he has been given permission to see Phyllis and Fred and he's just waiting to see them now. He said it will be far too late to come and see you tonight Lucy, but he will call tomorrow. He wants Tom and I to stay here tonight if that's okay please? He doesn't want to be taking any chances" Paul said. "Of course, if that's what he thinks" said Lucy. Mrs Armstrong got to her feet, "I'll go and make your rooms up." "We will find him Lucy" said Paul softly. "I know" she replied.

"DCI Fields, I'm sorry to keep you waiting, Mrs Reid is in here" said the officer at the holding cell. DCI Fields had to stop and think for a minute, as when someone said Mrs Reid he thought of Lucy. He kept forgetting that Janet, and in fact Phyllis, were also Mrs Reid. When DCI Fields and DS Lowe entered the room, Phyllis was sitting with her head in her hands. "I asked to see you Phyllis, there's something I want to talk to you about. Why have you not been completely truthful?" Said the DCI. "I was, I told you everything" said Phyllis. "Did you? Well I'm not so sure of that anymore. Today Lucy Reid celebrated her 27th birthday" "I know, I do hope all this didn't ruin it for her completely. I never meant to hurt her, I never meant to hurt anyone. I just thought that if Fred had money he would let me get on with my own life with Avril and Jonathan" Phyllis said sadly. "Lucy Reid's birthday was completely ruined when she was attacked this evening in the toilet of the Yew Tree pub" said the DCI. "Oh my god, Lucy was attacked, is she okay?" Phyllis asked, her eyes wide with panic. "She's very shaken and has received an injury to her ankle leaving her on crutches" said DS Lowe solemnly. "Lucy is hurt? No, why? Who would do such a thing?" Cried Phyllis. "I've no idea, that's what we were hoping you might be able to tell us" said the DCI gravely. "Me? But how would I know?" Asked Phyllis, shocked. "We suspect the man that attacked Lucy was Sean Lewis" said DS Lowe. "Sean? I didn't know he was still in the area" said Phyllis. "So you do know him then?" Asked DCI Fields. "Oh yeah, I know him. He's horrible. Only a young bloke, but one of the most scary I've ever met" said Phyllis. "He and Frank were cell mates Phyllis, but then I'm sure you know that already" said DCI Fields. "Yeah I know, he just turned up on the doorstep about 6 months ago, out of the blue. He was awful, rude, nasty and vicious a lot of the time. He used to put out his foot to trip Avril up as she passed him, and kick her if she was sitting on the floor. Fred used to just laugh, so in the end when he came round Avril and I would just sit upstairs or go out. He was always out with Fred, gambling I presume, and they wouldn't come back until the early hours, steaming drunk" said Phyllis grimacing.

"Was Sean involved in all of this Phyllis? Did you know he was still at large when we had the rest of you in custody? Did you leave him out there lying in wait for the chance to harm one of the Reid family?" Said DCI Fields. "No! Never! I wouldn't do that. If Sean was involved, I never knew. When he stopped coming round about a month before I came to Hilltop Manor, I thought he and Fred had fallen out, or he had moved away. I wasn't going to ask where he was, I was glad he was gone" said Phyllis. DCI Fields sat and looked at Phyllis, and he had to be honest, he really got the feeling she was telling the truth. "Could Fred have got Sean involved in this Phyllis? Offered him money maybe?" Asked DS Lowe. "Well I suppose that's possible, but if he did, I swear I knew nothing about it" said Phyllis, her eyes pleading. "Is there anything you can remember them saying? What did they talk about?" Asked DS Lowe. "Nothing, they were very careful not to talk in front of me and Avril. Although I did hear Fred say to Sean a couple of times that he would see him okay for money. I just thought he meant with their gambling. I never thought for a second Fred had told him of his plans" Phyllis said. "One last question Phyllis, do you know what Sean did for a living before he was locked up?" Asked DCI Fields. "Yes, he was a mechanic. Why?" She asked. "Nothing, thank you, you've been very helpful" he said. "Goodbye Phyllis" said DS Lowe, as she and the DCI got up and left the room. "What do you think sir?" She asked whilst they were waiting to see Fred. "Call it a gut feeling, but I believe she is telling the truth. I don't think she knew of any involvement of Sean in all of this" said DCI Fields.

"Would you like to come with me please?" Said the officer in charge. As they went into the room at the end of the corridor, Fred sat on the chair, slouched backwards, with the edge of one foot resting on the knee of the other. "Well, well, well, it's the hired help" sneered Fred. "Hello Fred" said DCI Fields. "How do you do sir? Pleased to make your acquaintance" said Fred, in a mock well-spoken voice. "I want to speak to you about Sean Lewis" said the DCI. "Who?" Asked Fred. "Sean Lewis, your cellmate from Monkshall" said the DCI coldly. "Was he? I can't remember" smirked Fred. "Don't mess with me, this is a very serious matter" said the DCI sternly. "Nah, I wouldn't want to mess with you. You ain't my type, but she is. I'd mess with you darlin'" Fred said, leering at DS Lowe. "That's enough" Said DCI Fields. "Ah sorry, is she yours then?" Asked Fred, still smirking. "I think you've said enough of the lewd comments, don't you Mr Reid?" Said DS Lowe curtly. "Ooh an authoritative one, I like 'em with a bit of fighting spirit" Fred leered, leaning forward across the table towards DS Lowe.

"That's enough!" Said DCI Fields, raising his voice. "Lucy Reid was attacked tonight in the toilet of the Yew Tree Pub, near her home, and we have reason to believe Sean Lewis was involved" said DS Lowe. "Way to go Seany-boy! She's a bit of a looker, is my cousin Frank's daughter in law" said Fred, grinning madly. "Do you know where Sean is?" Asked DS Lowe. Fred stood up, and as he did, the two police officers in the room stepped forward. "Calm down boys" Fred said, looking over each shoulder from one to the other. "Sit down" ordered the DCI. Fred looked in one pocket, and then in the other, "Nope he's not in there, so I guess I don't know where he is" said Fred with a smile, and sitting back down again. DCI Fields took a deep breath and swallowed hard, he knew that he had to keep calm as Fred was clearly out to rile him. "What's his involvement in all this? What did you pay him to do? Are you paying him to keep up this vendetta against Frank Reid and his family?" Said DCI Fields. Fred slammed his hand on the table and leant forward menacingly, "I ain't got nothing to do with that, okay? You ain't pinning that on me" he said. "So what is his involvement Fred?" Pressed the DCI. "I don't know what you're talking about" said Fred. "Was it him that cut Tom Baker's break hoses at Bartons Fred? He's about the right build" asked DS Lowe suddenly. The smile drained from Fred's face and just for a split second, DCI Fields was sure he could see fear in his eyes. "I've told you all I know, now I wanna go" said Fred. The DCI nodded to the two officers, who took an arm each to take Fred away. "Thank you for coming to visit, we must do lunch next time!" Fred called over his shoulder with a chuckle. "Did you see that look in his eyes sir? I think we've hit the nail on the head, I think Sean is our Bartons man" said DS Lowe. "You know Suzanne, I think you're right" said the DCI nodding.

CHAPTER 15

NOT AGAIN!

The next morning, Lucy woke bright and early. She'd had a poor nights sleep with her ankle hurting so much, despite Tom having stopped on the way home to get her some painkillers. She washed and dressed as best as she could, and then Ben helped her downstairs to the kitchen. Everyone was at the breakfast table already, apart from Tom. "Where's Tom?" Asked Ben. "He's in the living room on the phone" Paul replied. "Is everything okay?" Lucy asked. "He's just asking the DCI about arrangements for court" said Paul. "What do you think will happen?" Asked Lucy apprehensively. "They will just enter their plea and then have to wait for a Crown Court date, because these sorts of offences will not be dealt with in the Magistrates Court" Paul said. When Tom came back into the kitchen he gave Lucy a warm smile. "DCI Fields has suggested you don't come to court this morning, it will be too hard for you to get there with that ankle" he said. "Shouldn't I be there?" Asked Lucy. "No there's no need, all that will happen today is that they will enter their plea, then be bailed or remanded until a court date is set" said Tom. "Bailed? Is that likely?" Asked Frank in disgust. "I highly doubt it, not with all these offences and what happened with Sean" said Tom. "I should think not" said Bruce indignantly. "The DCI said he will come and see you later, as soon as he knows anything" Tom said.

"While everyone's here can I talk to you please? I need to tell you about when I saw Phyllis and Avril, and when we met Jonathan the other day. I've just not had chance to speak to you all together since." Said Lucy. "Yes of course" everyone chorused nodding their heads in agreement. "We just need a quick word with Mr Benson first, he has just arrived" Lucy said. "I'm sorry to drag you all the way up here Mr Benson, but it's probably the quietest place" said Lucy with a laugh. "That's okay" he said, placing his briefcase on the desk. Lucy was surprised how much more welcoming the study looked, now that she knew who the unexpected face in the shadows belonged to. "You know we saw Phyllis and Avril?" She said. "Yes I did, how did that go?" Asked Mr Benson. "I think they're telling us the truth" Lucy replied. "I have to admit I felt quite sorry for them" said Ben. "Please be careful Lucy, it would be well within Phyllis and Avril's interests to get you on side" warned Mr Benson. "Yes I realise that, but I believe them. Avril told us all about her learning difficulties, and about her fears of Fred and what he put her through" Lucy said. "I see" said Mr Benson, pushing his spectacles further up the bridge of his nose. "As for Phyllis, seems Fred led her a miserable life. She had a drinking problem and it sounds like Fred used her low self-esteem as a result of that, to manipulate her. She told us how bad she felt, not realising what he had been doing to Avril and to Jonathan at first. Then Phyllis put him into a home for his own safety. She insists she was hoping that if Fred had money he would leave her to get on with her life" said Lucy. "Yes he certainly doesn't seem a very pleasant character" agreed Mr Benson.

"We also went to see Jonathan, as Phyllis gave us permission to see him at the care home. He's lovely and adores Phyllis" said Lucy. Mr Benson smiled kindly. "When I went over to say hello, he completely flipped, covering his head, obviously panicking I was going to hurt him" said Ben. "Good grief, he must have thought you were Fred" said Mr Benson. "Exactly, Ben and I would like to help them despite what's happened. It's not Jonathan's fault, and we feel Phyllis and Avril got in way to deep with Fred and were too weak to get out" said Lucy. "Sounds as if you're probably right" Mr Benson agreed nodding. "We wondered if we could pay Jonathan's fees until we know what's happening with Phyllis and Avril" asked Lucy. "Are you sure? That's very generous. Especially considering what they did" Mr Benson said. "We know, but we want to help. Great Aunt Maud has given us the chance of an amazing life and we just feel that given half the chance, that family could turn their lives around" said Ben. "That's very amicable, but without somewhere to live, even on the remotest chance of either Phyllis or Avril receiving a non-custodial sentence, they wouldn't be able to apply for Jonathan to live with them anyway" Mr Benson said. Lucy shifted uncomfortably in her seat, "Yes we understand that and that's why we would like to let them live at Primrose Hill" she said. "Primrose Hill? Your Great Aunt's place?" Asked Mr Benson in disbelief. "Yes it makes perfect sense, it's already adapted downstairs from when Great Aunt Maud was alive and it could be rent free until they get on their feet" said Ben. "Well I don't know what to say" said Mr Benson, scratching his head in amazement. "It's also far enough away from here, where we won't keep bumping into them" said Lucy. "You certainly seem to have thought this through and who am I to stand in your way. It's your money and your house after all" said Mr Benson. "So we could do it" said Lucy hopefully. "You certainly could. You're amazing people both of you, big hearts and amazingly generous. Maud would have been very proud" said Mr Benson with a big smile. "Thank you" said Lucy and Ben.

When Mr Benson had left, Lucy and Ben re-entered the room with everyone else. "Sorry to have kept you waiting" Lucy said, before launching into the story. "When Ben and I met Avril, she was very apologetic" Lucy began. "So she should be" snorted Frank. "She explained to us her fears for her mothers' and Jonathan's safety, and the extent of Fred's bullying. Avril has learning difficulties and was also abused by her own mother as a child" Lucy continued. "That's awful, but no excuse" said Janet. "I don't think Avril was looking to make excuses mum, just explain." Said Ben. "Lucy and I have thought this through very carefully, and we think she was telling the truth" he continued. Lucy looked over at her husband and smiled, grateful for his support. "I know it's nothing to do with me, but for what it's worth, I've read a lot of background on Fred Reid, and that man is a monster" added Tom sincerely. "When we met Phyllis we had that fact further proved to us Tom" said Lucy. "How do we know what they're saying is true?" Frank asked. "It would be a benefit to both of them to get you on side I must admit" said Bruce, doubtfully. "Yes it would, but neither knew they were about to be arrested and neither have spoken to each other since, and yet they have both given the same story" said Ben. "Phyllis came across as very open, she explained about Fred's abuse and how she hadn't known what he was doing to Avril, and how she had only agreed to Jonathan going into a home to keep him safe from him. She admitted to resorting to drink at one point, and how, even though she stopped drinking years ago, Fred had convinced her she was worthless" said Lucy. "After what she did I think worthless is a good description" sneered Frank. "That's enough dad, you didn't see her. I think she was actually being very sincere" Ben said.

"Phyllis explained she came to Hilltop Manor trying to do things her way, she thought that by giving Fred the paintings, everyone would win. No one here would get hurt, and Fred would have money. Phyllis hoped that when he did, he would set her free from the life he had her trapped in to make a future for her, Avril and Jonathan" said Lucy. "I actually feel sorry for them again" said Tom. "So do we" replied Lucy nodding. "The next day, we payed Jonathan a visit. He's a lovely guy, the nurse said he spends all of his time sitting at the window in his room looking for Phyllis. His face lights up at the mere mention of her name" smiled Lucy. "Fred has clearly abused Jonathan as when I tried to go and say hi to him he threw his arms over his head, scared that I was 'the bad man' as he called him. He obviously mistook me for Fred" Ben continued. "Oh how awful" said Mrs Armstrong. "Jonathan asked us to come and see him at the end of the month, but the nurse said his fees run out then and he will have to be moved." Said Ben. "They don't know where yet, they need to look for somewhere with space to take him." "There, that's okay then" replied Frank. "No dad, it's not, as it's not going to be somewhere as well equipped for his care as where he is now. The best place for Jonathan would be with Phyllis, not moved to another new home" said Ben, looking his father directly in the eye. "I don't see what we can do, we aren't Jonathan's family" Frank replied. "No, we aren't, but Ben and I do want to help. We have talked it through with Mr Benson and he said we are able to do what we've decided" said Lucy. "Which is?" Asked Frank, eyeing them both warily. "We have decided to meet Jonathan's monthly fees until we know what's happening with Phyllis, and once we do, we will review it then" said Ben. "You're going to do what?!" Cried Frank. "That way Jonathan does not have to be uprooted as well as losing his visits from his family all at the same time" said Ben, unphased at his father's outburst. Lucy looked at Ben, he was able to hold his own in any situation once he had made his mind up, just like Frank really, she realised.

"What we have also decided to do is offer Phyllis a reference for helping towards any potential job if the court let her go" said Lucy. "Help her?

Have you forgotten what she has done?" Said Frank, shaking his head in disbelief. "No dad, not at all. But from what Lucy has said, Phyllis was a damn good housekeeper, and if our letter helps her get an income to get back on her feet, and support her family, that can only be a good thing can't it?" Said Ben. "What we have also decided to do" said Lucy, taking a deep breath. "Yes?" Said Frank. "We have decided to offer Avril and Phyllis a lease on Primrose Hill. It's already got adaptions from when Great Aunt Maud had them put in, so should be fine for her to have Jonathan return to her" said Ben. "Are you mad?!" Stormed Frank. "No dad, not at all, it solves everyone's problems" replied Ben determinedly. "I've never heard anything so ridiculous. Rewarding them after all they've put us through!" Frank raged. "Calm down Frank, actually I think it's a lovely idea" said Janet. Frank stared at his wife, totally unable to believe what he was hearing, "Good God! You've all gone stark raving mad" said Frank, striding across the room to the patio doors. "Ben and Lucy are sensible people, and if they believe Phyllis and her daughter, then I do too. This way Primrose Hill doesn't stand empty, Phyllis is a long way from this family and Jonathan could get to come back home. Oh and remember, Bob and Sue are only next door and can keep an eye on things" said Janet. "I'm going for a walk" said Frank, grumbling and moaning to himself. "Shall I go after him?" Said Nick. "No leave him to calm down" Janet said with a hopeful smile. "Thanks mum, we do appreciate your support" said Ben. Just then, Lucy's mobile rang, "Hello...Hello DCI Fields... yes this afternoon will be fine... oh my god you're joking...I can't believe it...I'll see you then...goodbye" said Lucy, replacing the receiver. "What is it Lucy?" Asked Tom. "That was DCI Fields, he said he has just come from the court. Phyllis, Avril and Pete have pleaded guilty, so he said hopefully we will just be waiting for a date for sentencing. We already know Ray pleaded guilty" said Lucy. "Well that's good isn't it?" Asked Nick. "Well yes it is, but it's Fred, he's pleaded not guilty, so there will be a trial" said Lucy despondently.

"Well of all the low-life things to do" said Frank, who had appeared back at the door. "How can he do that Tom? There's so much evidence against him isn't there?" Asked Ben. "Yes there is, but Fred knows he is going away for a very long time, he probably feels this is his last hit out at you and the rest of the family, Frank" said Tom. "Well I shall see that lying scoundrel behind bars if it's the last thing I do. I shall be there on that day in court to see it happen. Oh and Lucy, Ben? You get Phyllis and her family as far away from that animal as possible. Just let me know if there is anything I can do to help" declared Frank. "Thank you" said Lucy and Ben together. "He really is the limit isn't he?" Said Bruce angrily. "DCI Fields said he will come here as soon as he can because he wants to go through some things with us" said Lucy. It was a very somber group that greeted DCI Fields and DS Lowe when they arrived later that day, all still hardly able to take in what Fred had done. "DCI Fields, DS Lowe, please come in. I do feel guilty for taking up so much of your time again" said Lucy as she opened the front door. "Not at all, Suzanne and I are off duty now, but we both wanted to come and tell you what happened when we saw Fred and Phyllis. "Shall I take Jake and Emily to watch a DVD upstairs?" Asked Leah. "Yes please" said Lucy, smiling gratefully. Mrs Armstrong brought fresh tea through to the dining table and everyone sat down.

"Suzanne and I were both at court today, and it pretty much went how we expected it to. The evidence is overwhelming, so Fred's not guilty plea even knocked me for six" said DCI Fields grimly. "Does that mean we'll all be required to attend court?" Asked Nick. "I would think so" the DCI said nodding. "We've all done statements, is that what it's decided on?" Nick asked. "Yes, but the CPS will make that decision, not me" said the DCI. "CPS?" Asked Mrs Armstrong puzzled. "The Crown Prosecution Service" said DS Lowe. "Oh yes of course" replied Mrs Armstrong. "When DS Lowe and I met with Fred last night he was very unpleasant to say the least, he says he doesn't remember Sean Lewis, even though they shared a cell for a considerable time. He denies all knowledge of employing him to cut Tom's break pipes. He's not going to help at all. Phyllis, on the other hand, was totally the opposite. She matter of factly refutes knowing of any involvement Sean had in all of this. She said he used to come to their house and went off drinking with Fred until the early hours. She said he was abusive to Avril and she was quite glad when he stopped coming round." The DCI continued. "Dear lord, my cousin really is the pits isn't he?" Said Frank in disgust. "We've checked into Sean Lewis' background, he was released from Monkshall 2 years ago. He had his parole revoked after getting caught stealing from a local clothes shop. We have been to his flat, the address that is listed with the courts, he left there yesterday without any forwarding address. His land lady said he paid up until the end of the month, but just left suddenly last night. Sean also didn't turn up to sign on this morning, he obviously knows we are on to him" said the DCI.

"So why do you think he attacked Lucy if his gripe is with me? As I'm the one he thinks has inherited Hilltop Manor" said Frank. "I don't know Frank, I really don't" replied DCI Fields. "What we do want to do though, Lucy, is to have Paul go back to taking the children to school and staying there whilst they're there" said DS Lowe. "Okay yes of course, I think I'd rather that anyway" said Lucy. "We would also like to have Tom back with you again if that's okay. Without Phyllis to give anyone access, we feel you are all relatively safe at home, but if anyone goes out at all, we would appreciate if it was with Tom please until we have chance to track Sean down" said DCI Fields. Everyone nodded in agreement. With nothing more to tell everyone at that stage, DCI Fields and DS Lowe bid everyone goodnight and left.

The weeks passed, thankfully uneventfully, with everyone living a much longed for, normal family life. Well as much as you could with two police officers living in your home. But Lucy, Ben and the rest of the Reid household had come to think of Tom and Paul like family, so no one minded at all. Lucy had been shopping with Amira and had chosen a beautiful pale pink bridesmaids dress for Emily with a delicate headdress of flowers set in a tiny ring, and cute ivory satin pumps. Amira had said she would have to be careful as Emily was going to look too beautiful, and she would outdo the bride. They both laughed at this, but Lucy did have to admit she did look lovely. As for Jake he looked so smart in his little charcoal grey suit, and black brogues to match Paul and Tom's, who was to be the best man. When Amira came out of the dressing room wearing her wedding dress, Lucy gasped and tears sprang to her eyes. Her new friend looked sensational, absolutely stunning. Two days before the wedding, Lucy opened the door to Hilltop Manor to Amira, who was in tears. "Whatever's wrong?" She asked, taking Amira through to the living room and sitting her down on the sofa. "It's the hotel where we were holding the reception. They've had a flood and have had to cancel the booking. In two days we've got a hundred people coming to a wedding, and nowhere to hold the dinner and party afterwards" sobbed Amira. "What's the matter?" Cried Paul, noticing Amira as he came through the door. Lucy quickly explained, "Oh heavens, what do we do now?" Paul exclaimed. "I don't know, we'll never find somewhere else decent at this short notice" sniffed Amira. "We will, I'll go and get changed and we can start ringing round" said Paul, giving her a hug. "You could always have it here" said Lucy. "Here?" Asked Amira, wiping her eyes. "Yes, there's plenty of space for a marquee in the garden and the grounds are quite pretty for photographs. But I understand if it's not quite what you wanted" said Lucy. "Not what we wanted? It's an amazing offer! Hilltop Manor's a beautiful place and the grounds are stunning. This place would be perfect, wouldn't it Paul?" Gushed Amira. "It certainly would" agreed Paul, smiling broadly. "If you're sure that would be fantastic" said Amira. "Thank you so much". "You're welcome" Lucy smiled. "We had better start ringing round after all, we need to find a marquee, caterers and a whole list of other things" said Amira happily. "I'll leave you both to it" Lucy smiled.

"Tom I'm sorry to bother you, but is there any chance we could go into town please? I want to get Amira and Paul a wedding present" Lucy said walking into the kitchen. "Not a bother at all, when would you like to go?" Tom asked. "I'm ready when you are" said Lucy. "Give me five minutes and I will be right with you" Tom replied. Lucy, Tom and Ben arrived at Varnley Field shopping centre just under an hour later. "I've never been here before" said Ben. "It's quite big, Tom and I brought Jake and Emily here for some new clothes when we first arrived" said Lucy. They parked the car and took the lift down to the shopping area. Lucy bought Jake and Emily some new trainers, some perfume for Amira, chocolates for Mrs Armstrong, a jumper for Nick, a make up case for Leah, a t-shirt for Jeff, and a CD for Bruce and Paul. Everyone had been through such a rough time of late, she wanted to treat them all to a little gift. 'What am I going to get Ben and Tom?', she wondered, as they would be extra difficult since she was with them. She decided on t-shirts for them both as they were easier to hide within her shopping bags. Now was there anyone she had forgotten? 'Oh no Morph of course!' And she hurried off to find him a big chewy bone. With just the wedding present left to buy, Lucy, Ben and Tom stopped for coffee at the centre cafe. "Oh no I left the parking ticket in the car and we have to put it in the machine by the lift to get out of here" said Tom. "I want to just nip to the shop around the corner as well" said Ben. "Okay I'll come with you while Tom gets the ticket" said Lucy. "Oh but you can't" said Ben, giving Tom a knowing wink. "I'll wait here"

Lucy said with a smile. "Will you be alright?" Asked Tom frowning. "Stop worrying, I'm sitting outside a busy coffee shop, I'll be fine" Lucy laughed. The two men hurried off as she drained the last of her coffee.

"Deary me, you have been busy" said the little old lady sitting on the table next to her. "Yeah, feels like I've been Christmas shopping" said Lucy with a smile. "A couple of dashing young men you have with you, if only I was 30 years younger" the old lady chuckled. Lucy laughed, "Yes they are, that's my husband Ben and my friend Tom" "I'm Rose" said the old lady. "I'm Lucy and pleased to meet you" she said. "Are you off home now that you're all shopped out?" Said Rose, her eyes twinkling. "No, not quite, my friends are getting married the day after tomorrow and I'm hunting for a wedding gift" Lucy said. "Ooh a wedding, how lovely" chirped Rose. "My children are to be a bridesmaid and a page boy, so it's all very exciting" said Lucy. "Oh I'm sure it will be" Rose replied. "Where are your friends getting married? In a church I hope. Never thought those registry office places were quite the same" Rose said. "Yes it's a church wedding, and then a reception at my home" said Lucy. "That's lovely" smiled Rose, "I think that young man over there is trying to get your attention. Is he a friend of yours?" Asked Rose pointing. Lucy followed Rose's gaze and froze, there standing leaning casually against the wall of the shop opposite was Sean. "Oh my god, oh my god it's him!" Cried Lucy, frantically scrambling in her bag for her phone. "Are you okay dear?" Asked Rose. Sean stared at Lucy, pushed the sleeves on his sweatshirt back up his forearms, revealing the big red serpent, then turned and began to saunter away. Lucy's fingers wrapped around the phone in the bottom of her bag. She pulled it out and punched in Tom's number.

"Hello?" Said Tom. "It's him, he's here, Sean's here!" She garbled hurriedly. "I'll be right there". Seconds later Tom came running along the shopping centre as Ben appeared back round the corner. "Ben, Sean was there, he was right there!" Said Lucy almost hysterically. "Oh my god where?" Ben cried. "He walked off that way" Lucy sobbed, gesturing to where she had last seen Sean. "Come on Ben!" Tom shouted, and the pair ran off in the direction Lucy had told them. Ben was thankful that DCI Fields had insisted on showing them a photograph of Sean, at least he knew what he looked like now. "Lucy are you okay lovey? Whatever's wrong?" Asked Rose in a worried voice. The coffee shop manager had appeared by

Lucy's side now, and people at the other tables had stopped talking and had started to stare. "Yes I'm okay now, sorry" Lucy sniffed. "We lost him" said Tom, as he and Ben rejoined her. "Oh no" said Lucy. "Come on love, let's get you back to the car" said Ben, taking Lucy's arm as Tom picked up all the bags. "Bye Rose" Lucy stammered, smiling weakly. "Goodbye dear, I do hope you feel better soon" said Rose.

Lucy didn't even begin to relax until they were driving out of the exit to Varnley Field. Tom had rang the police station to alert them that Sean was in the area, giving them a description of what Lucy had told them he was wearing. "Oh Ben we still didn't get Amira and Paul's wedding present" said Lucy worriedly. "There's plenty of time for that, we'll sort something out" he soothed. When they got back to Hilltop Manor, a large white truck was parked in front of the house, starting to remove poles and sheets to erect the marquee. "That was quick" said Ben, getting out of the car and walking over to where Paul was standing, talking to one of the workmen. "It was wasn't it, we couldn't believe how lucky we were when Dan's firm said that they could do it" smiled Paul, introducing Ben to the man he was with. "Where do you want the tent?" Asked Dan. "Anywhere's fine" Ben replied. "May I have a quick word when you're ready?" Asked Tom. "Yeah sure" Paul replied as Dan walked away to tell his men what they needed to do. Ben took Lucy inside and settled her on the sofa. "Do you want a cuppa sweetheart?" He asked in a concerned voice. "No honestly I'm fine" Lucy said. "I can't believe the nerve of that guy" said Paul, coming into the room. "I know" nodded Lucy. "The station just rang, there's no sign of Sean" said Tom. Lucy sighed heavily, she really had hope that they would catch him.

That evening passed in a lovely relaxed manner, with everyone looking forward to the wedding. "Oh no!" Cried Mrs Armstrong at breakfast the next morning. "What is it Margaret?" Asked Frank. "I knocked the milk over and that was the last we had" Mrs Armstrong sighed. "Not a problem, I'll help you get this cleaned up, then Paul or I can nip to the shop to get some" said Tom. "No problem, I'll be five minutes" Paul said getting up from the table. "Oh thank you, you're both such kind boys" exclaimed Mrs Armstrong. "I'll come with you, save you trying to find somewhere to park" said Nick.

As Paul pressed his key fob to open the gate, it didn't budge. "That's strange" said Paul. "What's up?" Said Nick, who had been looking down at his phone texting a message. "The gate won't open" said Paul getting out. "No it's definitely stuck" said Nick trying again. "We'll have to get the key and open it manually" said Paul frowning. "I'll run back and get it and tell dad to ring the repair company" Nick said. "Thanks mate, but tell them it's urgent as we are going to have to leave the gates open until it's sorted" said Paul. "They can't get here to look at the gate until this afternoon" Ben told them when Paul and Nick had returned. "So what are you all up to today?" Asked Bruce. "I was thinking we may take Jake and Emily bowling and then onto Captain Marvo's" said Ben. "Oooh I wish I was coming" said Jeff wistfully. "Why don't you come along? The more the merrier" said Tom. "We would love to but Jeff's got a hospital appointment" Bruce told them. "Yes I'm taking them" said Paul. "Woohoo looks like I get to go bowling then!" Cried Tom to Jake and Emily. "Will anyone be here still as the caterers are coming to set up?" Asked Paul. "I can go to my sister's another day" offered Mrs Armstrong. "No you can't do that, I'll stay it's not a problem. I've got a headache to be honest and I've also got some paperwork to do. If I stay here I can do that and be here for the caterers and the gate repair people" smiled Lucy. "I can't let you do that Lucy" said Paul. "I wouldn't be happy leaving you here either" said Tom. "I'm fine, it's just all those clashing bowling balls banging wouldn't help, and Mrs Armstrong isn't going until this afternoon, when I will have a lawn full of people. I'll be up in the study, I promise" Lucy laughed. "Well okay if you're sure" said Ben doubtfully. "Quite sure, now you all get off and enjoy yourselves" Lucy said, walking over to give Ben, Jake and Emily a kiss goodbye. "Don't I get one of them?" Asked Tom cheekily "Me too!" Added Paul. "Well if there's a queue, but you'll have to come to me" Jeff laughed, gesturing to his wheelchair. "Form an orderly queue boys" Lucy laughed, blowing them all a kiss before she closed the door behind her. She smiled happily to herself, she was very lucky to have such amazing friends and family.

When Lucy reached the top of the stairs, she decided to go and have a lie down before she shut herself away in the study. She had taken some painkillers earlier, but her head really was hurting. Maybe a short rest would help. Lucy sat up with a start and looked at her watch, she had fallen asleep and had been there nearly 2 hours. If she didn't get her paperwork started, she wouldn't be finished before the children came home. She did hope she didn't miss any callers as Mrs Armstrong would have probably have left by now. Lucy decided to go and get herself a drink before she began the mammoth task of getting to grips with Bartons' sales figures. As she walked into the kitchen, she saw Mrs Armstrong hadn't gone yet after all. She was sitting at the kitchen table chatting to a man in a high vis jacket. The man had his back to her, all she could see was his long blonde hair in a pony tail and he was wearing a black baseball cap. "Hello dear, this is Lee who has come to repair the gate. It's so cold out there I offered him a nice cup of tea before he started" said Mrs Armstrong. "Hello Lucy" said the guy, turning to face her. "Oh my god no! Get out of this house!" Lucy screamed. Even with that died blonde hair she could see this was Sean. Sean threw back his chair and fled out of the back door. She heard his van start up as she grabbed the hall phone to call the police. "Margaret lock the back door!" She shouted as she waited for them to answer, she wasn't taking any chances.

The poor operator must have had their work cut out understanding what had happened as Lucy frantically tried to explain. She was shaking so much at times she must have been almost impossible to decipher. When she had finished her call she came back into the kitchen and sank down onto the chair, "I'm so sorry Lucy, I didn't know. I didn't realise" said Mrs Armstrong. "It's okay, it's not your fault" she said. "I just never thought he would come that close, not into the house" Mrs Armstrong said in shock. "No Margaret, neither did I" added Lucy gravely. "Do you want me to call Ben and tell him what's happened?" Asked Mrs Armstrong. "No thanks I'll do it or he'll only worry" said Lucy, picking up the phone again and dialling Ben's number. "Hi sweetheart" he said. "Ben, I don't want you to panic, but Sean's been here" she said as calmly as she could. "He's done what?!" Cried Ben. "Margaret and I are fine, I've called the police…" "I'm coming home now!" Ben interrupted her. "No don't do that, you'll ruin the day for everyone" Lucy insisted. "Tom and I will drop Nick, Leah and the kids to Captain Marvo's and I'll ring Paul to collect them. He should be finished at the hospital soon" said Ben. "There's really no need, we're fine" said Lucy. "I'm on my way" Ben insisted. "Okay" Lucy finished, deciding to give in as this was one fight she wasn't going to win. "Oh and Lucy," said Ben. "Yes?" She replied. "I love you" he added. "I know you do and I love you too. I'll see you when you get here, please don't rush. Tell Tom to drive carefully" Lucy said, replacing the receiver.

CHAPTER 16

THE WEDDING

There was a knock on the door and Mrs Armstrong went to answer it. "Who is it?" She called nervously. "Police" answered a male voice. Lucy watched as Mrs Armstrong pulled the chain across the door, she'd never seen her do that before and felt terrible that her family being at Hilltop Manor had made her feel that nervous. Over 35 years Margaret had lived there and now animals like Sean had made her worried to open the door of her home. Mrs Armstrong opened the door slightly, "Can I see your ID?" She said, peering nervously at the two men that stood on the doorstep. "Certainly" they both said, passing her their cards. Mrs Armstrong unchained the door, "I'm sorry gentlemen, but I'm not taking any chances" she said inviting them in. "Not a problem madam" said one of the police officers. "I'm DC Lytton and this is DS Mitchell" said the taller of the two men. "Hello, thank you for coming so quickly" said Lucy. "DCI Fields called us as we were in the area, and told us to come straight here" added DS Mitchell. "We had a look at your gate on the way in, there's clear signs of vandalism and it looks like every available gap in the outer casing has been smeared with a clear hard coating. Probably superglue" said DC Lytton. Lucy gasped, "So this was all completely planned? Sean sabotaged the gates so that he could get in here freely?" She said in shock. "Yes it certainly seems that way" DC Lytton agreed. "Would you gentlemen like a cup of tea?" Mrs Armstrong asked. "No thank you, we're fine" they said. The front door swung open and Ben and Tom charged in, "This is my husband Ben" said Lucy. "Hello Mr Reid, Tom" said DC Lytton. "Mark,

Ryan" said Tom, greeting his fellow officers. "We need to take a statement from you ladies if we may please" DC Lytton said.

Lucy led the way through to the living room. "So what exactly happened please?" DC Lytton asked. "I'd stayed home to do some paperwork and to see the caterers as we've got a wedding reception here tomorrow. We also had the gate repair company due this afternoon" said Lucy "So were you at home as well madam?" Asked DC Lytton, turning to Mrs Armstrong. "Yes, I wasn't going to my sisters' until this afternoon" she said. "I've had an awful headache all morning, so decided to have a lie down before I got started with my paperwork that I had to do." Lucy continued. "Lucy fell asleep, as I looked in on her when I didn't find her in the study. I went to see if she wanted anything to drink" said Mrs Armstrong. "Ah I see" said DC Lytton, scribbling non-stop in his notebook. "Anyway, as I came back down the stairs, there was a knock at the door, and the man there said he had come to mend the gate" Mrs Armstrong told them. "Did you see ID?" Asked DS Mitchell. "Well no, to be honest I didn't think he would have known the gate was broken if he wasn't from the company Ben called to fix it. I didn't know it had been tampered with then" said Mrs Armstrong, starting to get upset. "No, no, of course you didn't" soothed Tom, putting his arm around her. "What happened next Mrs Armstrong?" Asked DC Lytton kindly. "I was making a cup of tea anyway, and I asked the man if he wanted one before he started work on the gate. It's so cold out and he seemed so nice, I didn't think I was doing anything wrong" sniffed Mrs Armstrong. "No of course you didn't, you were just being your usual kind helpful self" Tom said, hugging her tighter.

"So how was Sean Lewis discovered?" Asked DS Mitchell. "When I woke up I wanted a glass of water, and he had his back to me when I came into the kitchen. Mrs Armstrong introduced us, but didn't use my name, and when he called me Lucy I looked more closely. He's dyed his hair blonde, but it was definitely him" said Lucy with a shudder. "What I don't understand is why he took such a chance of actually coming right into the house" said Ben. "How soon after we went out did Sean arrive Margaret?" Asked Tom. "About 20 minutes I think" she replied. "Yeah I thought so, he must have been watching the place. Saw us all go out, then gave us long enough to come back if we forgot something before he knocked" Tom said. "Sean Lewis is very clearly playing a very daring cat and mouse game" said DS Mitchell. "Did he threaten either of you in any way?" Asked DC Lytton. "No, he was perfectly charming to me" Mrs Armstrong said. "When he realised I recognised him he ran" said Lucy. "Well at least that's something" DC Lytton said. "I'm going to take a look at the CCTV for a registration" Tom interjected. "Okay thank you" nodded DS Mitchell. "No luck, the van's listed as scrapped, so he must have changed the plates" said Tom. "Mrs Reid, I'm going to report all of this back to DCI Fields, and I'm sure he will be in touch. For now though, keep doing everything you've been doing. Just be extra careful with visitors" said DS Mitchell. "We will be, thank you I'll see you out" said Ben.

The real gate repair people turned up later that day, much of the gate mechanism had to be replaced and it was confirmed large amounts of superglue had been used to clog up the system. The caterers had set up as much as they could do for the next day, so it seemed that the party at Hilltop Manor was all systems go. "I can't thank you enough for letting us hold the reception here" said Paul, as he put down the phone from Amira that evening. "It's really our pleasure" said Lucy and Ben together. "Amira is just so happy, she's really grown to love this place in such a short time" Paul said. "You know, so have I. It has a real hypnotic charm" Lucy laughed. The next morning everyone was up bright and early so that they could enjoy breakfast before the caterers took over the kitchen. Bruce and Jeff weren't coming to the wedding, they were staying behind to oversee things at Hilltop Manor. "Is this the day I get to be a princess mummy?" Asked Emily, as Lucy was getting her dressed. "Not a princess silly, a bridesmaid" said Jake knowingly. "But daddy said I look like a princess. I don't want to be a maid" Emily cried, her bottom lip starting to quiver. "You look like a princess everyday sweetheart. But today you get to wear that beautiful dress and shoes for Amira and Paul's wedding. You get to walk up the aisle at the church in front of Amira, just like we practiced, do you remember?" Asked Lucy. "Oh of course you do don't you Em? Because you're a big girl" said Jake, giving his sister a high five. Emily nodded solemnly.

"You look gorgeous" said Ben, coming into the bedroom. "Thank you" Lucy replied. She wasn't a hundred per cent sure on the lilac lace shift dress when she bought it, but now seeing it with the matching shoes and accessories, she was very pleased. There was a knock at the door, "Can we come in?" Called Janet. "Of course you can" Lucy shouted back. "Woah don't you look the beautiful family? You look amazing" said Janet with tears in her eyes. "You look fabulous too mum" said Ben. Lucy had to agree that Janet, in her cream dress and hat, and Frank, in a smart grey suit, certainly made an attractive couple. "The cars are here" said Nick from the doorway. "Thank you" Lucy replied, coming round the door to face him after a final check in the mirror. "Mum, you look amazing" Nick said. Lucy placed her bag on the bed and turned back to face him, "You called me mum" she said, taken aback. Nick smiled shyly, "You don't mind do you? I love my mum dearly, but you have always been like a second mum to me" he said quietly. "Mind? I'm delighted Nick, thank you" Lucy said. "No, thank you for everything you've done" said Nick, walking over and placing a kiss on her cheek.

"Come on before we all end up in tears" said Frank with a smile. As they came downstairs Mrs Armstrong was waiting by the door with Leah. "Ladies you look lovely" Frank said. "As do all of you" Mrs Armstrong said with a grin. Leah's cheeks flushed, "Thank you" she said with a shy smile. At that moment, Paul and Tom walked through from the kitchen. "Wow, you both look so handsome" said Lucy. As they came down the steps of Hilltop Manor, two beautiful cars stood waiting. A stunning stretch Silver Wrath II Rolls Royce for Lucy, Emily and Jake, and a sparkling shiny white limousine for everyone else. The chauffeurs stood by the open door of each. "See Emily, a car fit for a princess" whispered Paul as he lifted her inside. "Thank you" said Emily in awe, as she threw her arms around his neck. Bruce and Jeff had come to wave them off and snap plenty of photographs to remember this wondrous day by.

When they arrived at the church, quite a crowd had already gathered, Lucy waited outside for Amira with Jake and Emily. Finally, another Rolls Royce came to a halt, the chauffeur opened the door, and out stepped Amira. "Wow! A princess" gasped Emily. Amira looked amazing in a long white gown that showed off her perfect figure, her long dark hair swept up into a beautiful bun with tiny pink flowers set into the headdress. "You look beautiful" whispered Lucy. "Thank you" Amira breathed. "Where's your dad and your sister?" Asked Lucy, noticing that Amira was in the car alone. "I waited as long as I could, my brother's at the airport waiting to collect them, and their flight has been delayed" said Amira worriedly.

"They've been on holiday and were due back from Tunisia last night, but the air traffic strike is delaying everything" said Amira sadly. "Oh no" said Lucy, distraught for her friend. "I wondered Lucy, would you do me the biggest favour and be my matron of honour please? I'd have asked you anyway if it wasn't for Grace" said Amira hopefully. "Oh Amira I'd love to" Lucy replied. "Who's going to give me away though?" Said Amira unhappily. "I've got an idea, give me two seconds" she said. Lucy dashed into the church, her eyes scanning the rows of pews, 'Ah there he is'. Lucy rushed over to him and bent and whispered something in his ear. He rose immediately and followed her outside. "DCI Fields" gasped Amira. "It would be an honour to stand in for your father if you will have me" he smiled. "That would be fantastic, thank you so much" Amira said.

Suddenly the sounds of 'Here Comes The Bride' filled the air. "Come on, your big moment is here" smiled Lucy. Amira crouched down to Emily, "Would you do me a very special job please? My niece Sadie isn't here, so I don't have a flower girl. Do you think you could do that for me?" She said. "Oooh yes please!", Said Emily excitedly, "…what's a flower girl?" Amira laughed and handed Emily a basket full of tiny peach and white petals. "All you do is walk up the aisle with Jake sprinkling tiny handfuls of petals, like this" she said. "I can do that" said Emily in a grown up voice. "I know you can sweetheart" said Amira with a smile. "Are you ready Amira?" Asked DCI Fields. "Yes" she replied, standing up, taking a deep breath and following Jake, Emily and Lucy to the door of the church. "Go on" said Lucy, gently pushing Jake and Emily forward and then following them herself.

Emily toddled along, expertly throwing tiny handfuls of petals in front of her, she and Jake looked so cute, and Lucy glowed with pride. As she reached Ben, he looked surprised to see her in the wedding procession instead of Amira's sister. "Long story" she mouthed with a smile as she passed him. The ceremony was beautiful, and very soon they were walking back down the aisle as husband and wife. The photographer gathered guests into all different shots and poses, then everyone was back in their cars and on the way to Hilltop Manor. As they walked in to the huge marquee, Lucy couldn't help but gasp, it looked amazing. Soft white drapes adorned the doorways, and the windowed areas, and everything was decorated in tasteful soft peach and white. It looked like something out of a fairytale.

Lucy watched as Amira and Paul mingled with their guests, they looked so happy. When everyone sat down to dinner, the food was out of this world. Beautifully cooked and presented, they started with a lobster and prawn mix, with king scallops on a bed of mixed salad leaves. Then there was rack of lamb, a choice of two types of potato accompaniment and a medley of vegetables. The meal finished with blackforest or strawberry gateau and cream. There was a sensational nut cutlet with all the trimmings for any vegan guests, and everyone received coffee, tea and after dinner mints. There was even a children's option, of tomato soup, chicken nuggets, chips and beans, with jelly and ice cream, which Lucy thought was a really lovely touch and very individual. She had never heard of a children's menu at a wedding before.

After everyone had eaten they all moved to the adjoining marquee, this time beautifully decorated with soft blue and baby pink balloons and delicate white lillies. When it came time for Amira and Paul to leave for their honeymoon in the Seychelles, a crowd gathered in anticipation as Amira tossed her bouquet high into the air. As the bridal spray fell, long slender arms reached up to grab it, Leah smiled shyly at Nick as she hugged the bouquet to her. At the end of the evening it was a very tired Jake and Emily that Lucy put to bed, the only problem was Morph hadn't seen them much all day, as he had been in the house most of the time due to so many people milling about. So Morph wasn't ready to sleep, he wanted to play. Eventually, he decided though, that if they wouldn't play, he would have to sleep, and hopped up on the bed and snuggled down between Jake and Emily.

The next afternoon, Lucy was sitting in the car outside the butchers with Tom, waiting for Mrs Armstrong to come out. Suddenly, there was a tap on the window, she looked up and there was Rose. "Hello dear" she said, as Lucy put the window down. "Hi Rose, it's lovely to see you again" Lucy said with a smile. "Oh you've only got one of those good looking young men with you today, I see" said Rose with a chuckle. "Ben's at home" Lucy grinned. "How did your wedding go at your house?" Asked Rose. "Very well thank you, my friends had a lovely day" Lucy replied. "Oh that's good, I'm so pleased. It's good to see you looking better than you did the other day. You looked so pale" said Rose in a concerned voice. "What are you doing right out here?" Asked Lucy. Mrs Armstrong had come out of the shop and Tom had got out to help her load the bags into the car. "I've been to see a friend and on the way back on the bus I was feeling a bit rough. I'm diabetic you see, so I was coming to get a chocolate bar" Rose told her. "Oh no poor you, do you not have one of those insulin pens?" Lucy asked in concerned. "Yes but I think it must have dropped out of my bag at my friend Hillary's" said Rose. "The shop's shut for half day closing" said Mrs Armstrong, obviously over hearing. "Oh no, now what am I going to do? The next bus isn't for an hour" said Rose in panic. "It's okay, come back to Hilltop Manor with us and we can get you a nice cup of tea and a piece of homemade cake" said Lucy kindly. "No, no I can't put you to that much trouble" Rose said, shaking her head. "It's no trouble at all, and I'm sure one of the guys can drop you home afterwards" said Lucy. Rose got into the car next to Mrs Armstrong, and they were soon chatting away about the rising price of bacon and sausages. Lucy smiled to herself, listening to them putting the world to rights.

"Are you feeling better?" Asked Mrs Armstrong, half an hour later after Rose had polished off a cup of hot sweet tea, two slices of cake and a biscuit. "Yes very, thank you" smiled Rose. Lucy couldn't help but think that that was rather a lot of sugar for a diabetic. "Would you like anything else?" Asked Mrs Armstrong. "No thank you, but if I could just use your bathroom please" Rose asked. "Of course, I'll show you where it is" said Lucy. She took Rose to the toilet at the back of the main entrance hall, "Thank you dear" said Rose. Lucy returned to the kitchen to help Margaret clean up. "Er, hello, can I help you?" Asked Nick, looking up from the TV programme he was watching. "Oh I'm sorry pet, I was admiring the beautiful array of paintings in the hallway when I came out of the bathroom. Must have lost my bearings, I was looking for the kitchen" Said Rose, in a flustered voice. "Let me show you" said Nick kindly, getting up. He guided Rose out of the living room, down the hallway and to the kitchen. "Thank you dear, sorry to be a nuisance" said Rose. "It's not a problem" Nick replied as he helped to settle Rose back onto the kitchen chair.

"Oh, er, hello again" said Ben as he came in from the garden with Bruce and Jeff. He was obviously surprised to see Rose sitting there. "Hello dear" she greeted him with a cheery wave. Just then the kitchen door opened and Jake and Emily came in with Tom and Leah. Tom had taken over transporting the children to school and home again whilst Paul was away and PC Regan stayed there during the day to ensure there was always an officer on site. "Jake, Emily, everyone, this is Rose" Lucy said. "What lovely children, and my Lucy you are lucky having all these handsome young men in one place" Rose said. "Handsome I thank you for, but I'm hardly young" Laughed Bruce. "Well you are to me dear" Rose chuckled. "We're all going to watch the England game on TV if that's okay Lucy" said Tom. "Yes of course it is" she replied. "Never could see the point in football" declared Rose. "No, me neither" said Lucy with a smile. "Give me a call when you're ready to go Rose" said Tom cheerily. "Why doesn't Lucy drop me home if you're busy?" Rose suggested. "No that's fine" said Tom quickly. "I just didn't want to disturb your game and I thought Lucy and I could have a girly natter on the way" Rose chirped. "Er, I don't mind" said Lucy hesitantly. "No, it's really not a problem. Just give me a call" Tom insisted.

"Seems so silly dragging him away from his match, I don't live very far, you'd be there and back within 15 minutes" said Rose. "Well, yes I suppose you're right" said Lucy thoughtfully, surely it would be okay dropping Rose home, she wouldn't even get out of the car, so it would be perfectly safe. "Come on, they'll never know. And Leah here can come with us if she likes" smiled Rose. "Okay" said Lucy. She knew Tom was tired and he deserved a night off. Lucy, Leah and Rose set off, with Rose giving directions. Lucy was sure she'd passed some of the places twice, they appeared to be going round in circles, but she didn't like to say anything. She didn't want to hurt the old lady's feelings if she was getting confused. "That's it dear, pull up there behind the truck, that's my grandson's" said Rose. "Oh I didn't know you lived here" said Lucy, eyeing the expensive looking apartment block that they were parked outside of. "Yes dear, I'm staying with my grandson. He has his own business and has done very well for himself" she smiled. "So I see, well, goodnight Rose" said Lucy. "You get off now" Rose called, waving from the pavement. "Oh no I can't leave you out here" said Lucy. "Oh, oh er, okay" Rose said, walking slowly towards the entrance.

"What's she doing?" Asked Leah, as Rose seemed to hesitate by the doors, and then began to rummage in her bag. "Maybe she's lost her key?" Suggested Lucy. At that moment the door opened and a young couple came out and walked off up the road into the night. Rose grabbed the door before it closed and slipped inside, waving cheerfully as she went. As Lucy and Leah let themselves back in through the kitchen door of Hilltop Manor, Tom was sitting at the kitchen table. 'Oh dear' Lucy thought, 'He doesn't look very happy at all'. "Why Lucy?" Asked Tom, his voice full of disappointment. "I'm sorry Tom but you've been so tired lately, you're always running around after one or other of us. I just thought you deserved the time to watch the game in peace" she said. "Lucy, you and your family are never a bother. Not to mention it's my job. Imagine what DCI Fields would have said if something would have happened to you and you had been out without me. I'd have been in big trouble" said Tom. "Oh I never thought of that, I won't do it again, I really am sorry. I didn't mean to make you worry" Lucy said quietly. "We'll say no more about it" said Tom, giving her a hug. She smiled at him gratefully. "Oh no, Rose has left her bag" said Leah, picking it up from under the table. "I do hope she isn't worried about it. I don't suppose you have a phone number for her do you?" Asked Leah. "No I don't I just hope I can remember where it is when I take it back tomorrow" said Lucy.

"Oh no you don't, it's not late. We'll take it back now. I've got to take the kids to school tomorrow, then take Jeff and Bruce to the hospital and Ben to drop some paperwork to Mr Benson" said Tom. "I think Nick's arranged to spend the day with his mum tomorrow too" Leah added. "Well it will definitely have to be tonight then, as it looks like I'm going to be extremely busy tomorrow" said Tom. "Oh okay, are you coming Leah? I might need your help in finding the place again" Lucy laughed. "I think we're lost" said Lucy a short while later, as she, Tom and Leah passed the same petrol station for the third time. "No we aren't, isn't that Rose's grandson's truck?" Leah asked pointing. "Yes, that's it. Well done Leah" Lucy clapped. "Come on then" said Tom getting out. "I don't know the number" Lucy said worriedly, looking at all the buzzers in front of her. "Nothing for it then" said Tom, pressing the first one. "Hello?" Said a male voice. "Is this where Rose lives please?" Lucy asked. "No you have the wrong flat, sorry" said the man. "Oh I'm sorry to have bothered you" she said. Tom pressed the next buzzer. "What?!" Snapped the man that answered it. "Oh er, I'm sorry to bother you, but is this where Rose lives?" Asked Lucy, taken aback by the man's abruptness. "No!" He snapped back, and cut the buzzer off. "What a charmer!" Said Tom sarcastically, pushing the next buzzer. "Bonjour!" Said the lady that answered. "Hello is this where Rose lives please?" Lucy asked. The lady began speaking hurriedly in French, "I'm sorry I don't speak French" replied Lucy in despair. The lady said something else in French and then, "Au revoir" and replaced the buzzer. "Oh dear we don't seem to be getting anywhere here" sighed Leah. "Three more left to try" said Tom, pushing the buzzer of flat four. "Hi!" Said a cheery male voice. "Hello, is this where Rose lives please?" Lucy asked. "Sorry I don't know anyone here yet as we only moved in today" said the man apologetically. "Thank you anyway" said Lucy. "I do know that flat 5 is empty if that helps at all" said the man on the buzzer. "Yes it does, and thanks again" Lucy replied.

"Well that narrows it down then, doesn't it? Rose must live at number 6" smiled Tom, pushing the final buzzer. They waited, and no answer, so Tom pushed it again. Still nothing. "How strange, we didn't drop Rose off all that long ago, and the truck's still there" said Lucy puzzled. "Maybe they've gone to bed?" Suggested Leah helpfully. "Nothing more we can do" said Tom, heading back to the car. Lucy glanced along the street and spotted the couple coming towards her that had let Rose into the block earlier. "Er, excuse me. Do you know if someone called Rose lives at number 6 please?" She asked running up to them. "No I'm afraid she doesn't, we do" said the man. "Oh, we've tried all the other buzzers" Lucy told them. "I'm sorry but I don't know anyone of that name" said the man with an apologetic smile. "She said that was her grandson's truck" Lucy added, pointing at the black pick up that they were parked behind. "No I'm sorry she must have been mistaken, that's my truck" said the man. "Oh I'm sorry to bother you" said Lucy in shock.

"What do you make of that then?" Asked Tom as they got back in the car. "I don't know" said Lucy puzzled. "Do you think we may have the wrong block?" Asked Leah. "No, this is the right block and the truck's here, so that proves it" said Lucy. "Well there's nothing else we can do, let's go home" Tom said. The next day when Lucy went down to breakfast, Bruce was happily cooking away in the kitchen. "Where's Margaret?" She asked. "Poor Margaret's not well at all, she called me as Jeff and I came by her cottage this morning. She looks awful, she thinks that she may have some type of bug" Bruce said. "Oh no, poor Margaret, does she need anything?" Asked Lucy concerned. "No I already asked her that. She said she was just going to go back to bed. She asked me to pass on her apologies" Bruce said. "Would you like me to take over breakfast?" Lucy offered. "No you take a seat, I think I've got everything under control here thanks" said Bruce. "Well okay, if you're sure" said Lucy, sitting down and pouring herself a cup of tea.

Soon after breakfast, Tom set off to take Jake and Emily to the school. Even though Leah no longer officially worked there, Miss Timms, the head, had agreed for her to be a classroom assistant in Jake and Emily's class. Once they were all safely delivered, Tom would take Nick and his grandparents to visit his mother for a few hours. Although Ben and Julie were divorced, Frank and Janet had remained close to her. It was just after 11 when Tom arrived back to pick up Jeff and Bruce for Jeff's hospital appointment and to take Ben to the solicitor's office. "I can't leave you here" said Ben. "Nonsense, we can't leave Margaret alone. Someone's got to be here incase she needs anything" said Lucy. "Well what about Sean?" Asked Ben worriedly. "You've got to go and pick the paperwork up from Mr Benson today, as remember he is on holiday for a week tomorrow. And I promise I won't be opening the door to any workmen, in any case the gate's fixed now, so I'll be fine" Lucy insisted. "Well okay" said Ben doubtfully. Lucy stood on the steps and waved them all off, and then went back into the house. She noticed her favourite magazine laying open on the hall table. '10 minutes to enjoy a well-earned read' she thought, going into the living room and settling herself on the sofa.

CHAPTER 17

ROSE PAYS LUCY A VISIT

No sooner had she opened the first page, the buzzer from the gate sounded in the hallway. 'I wonder who that is' thought Lucy, she wasn't expecting anyone. "Hello" she said into the intercom. "Lucy, it's Rose" said the voice. "Oh hello Rose, have you come for your handbag?" Lucy asked. "Yes dear, can I come in?" Rose asked. "Yes of course" Lucy said, pressing the button to open the gates. As Lucy opened the front door, the phone began to ring on the table behind her. "Come in Rose" she called cheerily as she went to answer it. "Hello?...Hello..."she said into the receiver. "That's strange, there's no one there" she said. Lucy turned back round smiling brightly, "Hello Lucy" said a male voice. Instantly the smile dropped from Lucy's lips. There stood Rose and Sean. As she looked down, she noticed he was holding a gun in his right hand, and it was pointing straight at her. "Hello Lucy, I believe you've met my grandson Sean" Rose sneered. Lucy stared open mouthed, gone was the sweet little old lady and in her place, a woman with the hardest eyes she'd ever seen. "What do you want with me?" Lucy stammered, finding her tongue. "Want with you? Why money of course. The same as we've always wanted" said Rose sarcastically. "I don't understand, what money? And where do you and Sean come into this?" Asked Lucy puzzled. "Very simple, Sean had the misfortune of sharing a cell with that useless oaf Fred. When he got out Fred promised to make him rich. 'Just one job' he said" Glared Rose. "The break pipes" said Lucy quietly. "Clever girl" Rose said. "So if Sean got his money, what do you want with me?" Lucy asked. "That's just it, he never did get his money. That idiot got himself banged up before he paid up" Rose spat. "So Sean was under Fred's orders after all when he cut the breaks" said Lucy. "Fred's orders? Are you kidding? I'd be surprised if that fool has enough brains to order a takeaway" Laughed Rose.

"So it was Phyllis after all?" Said Lucy in horror. Rose threw back her head and laughed out loud, "Poor sweet, innocent, trusting Phyllis. She was right, when Fred went out, he did come to the Lewis household. But not to see Sean, he came to see Charlotte, my daughter" Rose smirked. "Fred was having an affair?" Gasped Lucy. "Got it in one" Rose sneered. "So Phyllis wasn't involved like she insisted all along" said Lucy. "Of course she wasn't. I only agreed to let her come here because I could gain inside knowledge of the place and your movements" said Rose. "You agreed? You're behind this?" Said Lucy incredulously. "Go to the top of the class Mrs Reid" laughed Rose hysterically. "So you planned all this?" Said Lucy, sitting down on the stairs in shock. "Every last detail" said Rose proudly. "I don't have any money here" said Lucy nervously. "Maybe not, but you have the paintings" snapped Rose. "I don't have them, Fred stole them" Lucy said.

Suddenly Sean lurched forward, he had been standing there all this time saying nothing, just staring that cold hard stare. "Don't mess with me bitch. I was with Fred when he tried to sell the paintings, I know they were fakes" he snarled, pressing the gun into her neck. Lucy screamed in terror, "The paintings aren't here, the police have them as evidence" she stuttered. "Jesus grandma, what do we do now?" Asked Sean. "Nice house like this? Our host Mrs Reid had better find us something else of value, hadn't she?" Barked Rose. "I've not got anything and the money isn't through from the will yet either." Said Lucy. "This is all going wrong grandma" said Sean, in panic. "Shut up and let me think!" Roared Rose. Lucy looked at Sean and even though he had a gun, in an instant she wasn't scared of him anymore. At the pub he'd looked menacing, but here with his grandma he was just like a small boy waiting to be told what to do. Lucy felt she had far more to fear from Rose herself. "I don't have much in the bank but I could arrange to get that transferred to you" Lucy offered. "How much?" Asked Sean immediately. "A couple of thousand" said Lucy. "Don't insult us Mrs Reid, that wouldn't last us five minutes. Sean take care of the CCTV, it's in the large cupboard at the end of the hall" ordered Rose. "What about if she tries to make a run for it while I'm gone?" Said Sean, eyeing Lucy. "She's not going anywhere, because she's coming with us" said Rose.

She took Lucy's arm and they followed Sean down the hall. He opened the door and went inside, Lucy heard four shots being fired before he came back out, her blood went cold. He really did have bullets in there, she'd been praying he'd been bluffing. "All done grandma" said Sean. "Good boy, now let's get all the doors locked" said Rose, as she went to bolt and chain the front door. They went into the living room to make sure the patio doors were locked and then into the kitchen to bolt the back door. "Sit down" Sean ordered Lucy, pulling out a chair from the kitchen table. Rose walked over to close the kitchen blind, "Go and close the curtains across the patio doors" ordered Rose. "What about her?" Sean asked. "Give me the gun, Lucy and I will be fine" Rose smiled. Sean handed the gun to his grandmother, there was something about the way Rose ran her bony fingers along the gun's contours that made Lucy feel she really did have much more to fear from Rose indeed.

As Sean came back into the kitchen, there was a knock at the back door. "Who's that?" Cried Sean. "Probably Margaret" said Lucy nervously. "The housekeeper?" Said Sean, his eyes wild with panic. "Get rid of her" spat Rose to Lucy. "But how?" Lucy asked. "I don't care, tell her you're ill. You'll think of something. But no tricks, understand?" Said Rose, digging the gun into Lucy's ribs. Lucy opened the door, aware that Rose was holding the gun only inches away. "Hello Margaret" she said. "Hello dear, I thought I'd come and see everyone as I'm feeling much better" Margaret replied. "Oh I'm so glad" Lucy said. "Are you okay dear?" Margaret asked, obviously sensing that something was wrong. "Yes I was er…just going to have a lie down while everyone else is out. I'm not sure if I'm coming down with something and I wouldn't want you to catch it" said Lucy. "You're on your own? Where's Ben?" Asked Margaret. "He had to go into town, he wanted to get Jake and Emily's snake for them before they got in from school" Lucy said. "Their snake?" Asked Margaret in surprise. "Yes you know the coloured one the man had on his arm in the shop the other day?" Lucy continued. "Oh okay that one, I remember. That will be nice, I hope you feel better soon Lucy" said Margaret. "Thank you, bye" said Lucy closing the door.

"Good she's gone, interfering old busybody" said Rose, gesturing for

Lucy to sit down again. "I'm hungry grandma" said Sean. "Dear me boy, you would manage to eat whatever the situation was that was going on at the time wouldn't you?" Said Rose fondly. "Do you want me to make you both a sandwich?" Asked Lucy nervously. "Yes that's a good idea, how very kind of you. Two cheese sandwiches please" said Rose in a sarcastic tone. "Okay" said Lucy, getting up to get what she needed from the fridge. "Cut it in four" Rose ordered. "No problem" said Lucy. When she'd made the sandwiches she put one down in front of Rose and the other in front of Sean. "You not hungry?" Said Rose, eyeing her suspiciously. "No" said Lucy quietly. "Eat it" Rose demanded, pushing her plate towards her. "Oh no, thank you" said Lucy. "Eat it I said, just one quarter." Rose continued in a menacing voice, the gun still in her hand.

Lucy picked up the sandwich and gingerly took a bite. "Can I eat mine now grandma?" Said Sean. "Leave it, put it down" Rose snapped. "Why grandma? I'm hungry" Sean protested. "Swallow it" Rose demanded, not taking her eyes off of Lucy, who was still chewing. Lucy did as she was told, "I really can't eat anymore" she said meekly. "That's fine, you can eat it now Sean. Just wanted to make sure our host hadn't administered any unrequested added extras" said Rose. "I wouldn't do that!" Said Lucy in horror. "You never know who you can trust nowadays" said Rose with a menacing grin. Ben and Tom had just come out of Mr Benson's office when Ben's phone rang. "Hello?" He said. "Ben, it's Margaret" Mrs Armstrong said. "Oh hello, is everything okay?" He asked worriedly. "No I don't think so" said Margaret. "Why, what's happened?" He asked in panic. "I was feeling better so I thought I'd go and see everyone but Lucy had the back door bolted. When I knocked she came to the door but didn't want to let me in, she was acting really strangely. She said she was going for a lie down, but she was going on about you having gone to get Jake and Emily a snake?" Margaret continued. "Gone to get a snake?" Asked Ben confused. "Yes she said it was the coloured one the man had on his arm in the shop the other day" finished Margaret. Ben went quiet on the other end of the line for a moment,

"Oh my god he's got her! Sean's in there with her!" He blurted out suddenly. "I think you're right but I don't think it's only her. As I walked up the path to the door the blind wasn't quite closed properly, and I'm sure it was Rose I saw standing there" said Margaret. "Rose? What on earth is she doing there?" Asked Ben. "Probably come to pick up her handbag I suppose" Margaret said. "Sit tight, I'm going to phone DCI Fields." Ben replied. "Oh my god, I hope they're okay" said Mrs Armstrong worried. "I'll call you back. Stay in the cottage Margaret and don't open the door" said Ben firmly. Hurriedly he explained what had happened to Tom whilst searching for the number of DCI Fields' mobile, he had given it to them a few days ago, as he said it would be easier if they needed to speak to him rather than ringing the station.

"DCI Fields' phone" said a female voice. "Hello is DCI Fields available please? It's Ben Reid" he said. "Hello Ben, it's DS Lowe, is everything okay?" Said the voice. Ben quickly explained what Margaret had told him. "I'm going to speak to the DCI and I will call you straight back" said DS Lowe. "I want to get back to Hilltop Manor now" said Ben. "Come on, I'm sure the DCI will ring back any minute" Tom replied, starting the car. A few minutes later, Ben's mobile rang again. "Hello" he said. "Ben, it's DCI Fields. DS Lowe has told me what's happening and I agree, it does seem like Lucy was trying to tell us something. How far are you from home?" He asked. "Ten minutes" Ben replied. "Okay, I want you to ring Lucy at the house. Just talk to her, see if you can get any clues. But don't let on we know what's happening. Above all, don't tell her you're coming home. We don't want Sean to get suspicious" said the DCI. "Okay, I'll do that. Surely when you get there though it's just one man, you can raid the place?" Asked Ben. "That's a possibility" answered the DCI. "A possibility?" Ben exclaimed in disbelief. "Ben please remain calm for Lucy's sake, and Rose if she's in there, as something is making Lucy behave how she is. Did you not say that Lucy is a karate black belt?" Asked DCI Fields. "Yes she is" Ben answered. "Then suitably able to take care of herself against a man of Sean's stature we hope" said the DCI.

"So what's the problem?" Asked Ben. "Try to stay calm, but with Sean's background, we cannot rule out the possibility that Lucy is behaving how she is because he's got a gun" finished DCI Fields. "A gun, oh my god!" Cried Ben. "Call her now, I'll meet you outside the gates of Hilltop Manor" said the DCI before he ended the call. Ben scanned through the numbers on his mobile and pressed call when he came to his wife's name. Lucy's phone began to ring in her pocket. "Who's that?" Demanded Sean as Lucy removed it. "It's my husband" she replied in a small voice. "Don't answer it" snapped Rose. "Gimme it" ordered Sean. Lucy placed her phone onto the kitchen table, so that Sean who was sitting opposite her, could reach it. The phone stopped ringing, then seconds later began to ring again. "Leave it!" Thundered Rose. The mobile stopped ringing for a second time, then instantly began ringing for a third. "Shall I answer it Rose?" Asked Lucy. "No!" She barked. "If I don't answer it he'll come home" said Lucy, as the phone stopped ringing for a third time, and this time the phone in the hall rang out. "Persistent isn't he?" Sneered Rose. "Shall I answer it gran?" Asked Sean. "No of course not. Answer it Lucy, and remember, no tricks" said Rose, her eyes flashing.

As they all walked out into the hallway, they were met with a barking and growling Morph, who had been asleep under the table. Sean shot a well aimed kick at him, narrowly missing his head. "No, don't hurt him please!" Cried Lucy. A slow wide-spread grin appeared on Rose's face, "Any smart tricks Lucy, and Sean will shoot the dog" she said. "I wont" Lucy promised. "Now answer the phone" Rose snapped. "H-h-hello" said Lucy. "Hi sweetheart, just wondered if you wanted me to pick anything up for tea with Mrs Armstrong not feeling well?" Ben asked brightly. "Er, no thank you. I don't think so, and Margaret's feeling better I think" Lucy said. "Oh is she there with you?" Asked Ben. "No, just Rose, she came to pick up her handbag" Lucy said. "Ah that's good, at least you have some company" Ben replied. "I must go now" said Lucy, as Rose gestured to her to end the call. "Why is Morph barking so much?" Asked Ben. "He's waiting for me to let him out" she said. "Oh okay, I won't be long anyway" Ben answered. "No, you can't! I mean, why not meet the kids and you all take them out for tea somewhere?" Suggested Lucy. "Okay, but I'll pop home and pick you up first" said Ben. "No, I'm not feeling too good. I don't want to come, and in any case I told Rose she could stay for tea, and you could shoot her home later" said Lucy hurriedly. "Oh okay" said Ben. "You don't mind shooting her home later do you?" Pressed Lucy.

Rose leant down and pulled the phone from the wall. "I told you no tricks didn't I?" Spat Rose, her eyes flashing menacingly. "I didn't!" Said Lucy. "I said you'd shoot her home, you don't mind shooting her home do you?" Said Rose in a sarcastic voice. "You bitch!" Roared Sean, grabbing Morph by the scruff of the neck and dragging him into the kitchen. A moment later, Lucy's blood went cold as she heard the sound of the back door opening, a gunshot rang out, then the door slammed shut again. "No!" She screamed, bursting into tears. "He won't be barking no more grandma" said Sean proudly as he came back to join them. "Good boy" said Rose with a chuckle and a triumphant glance at Lucy. "Morph" sobbed Lucy deflated. "Now let's move through to the living room and carry on getting acquainted shall we?" Said Rose. "Rose, what is it you want with me? Ben won't stay out for long. Especially not if he thinks I'm ill" warned Lucy. "Awh, how very touching" Rose replied. "What are we going to do if she's got no money grandma?" Asked Sean. "You will ring her precious Ben and tell him you want those paintings, and you want them now. Tell him you want them in the van and you'll be taking Lucy with you until you're safely away from here. Then you'll let her go" snarled Rose with a snigger. "Take me with you?" Asked Lucy in horror. "Well you didn't think they were just going to open the gates and let us drive off into the sunset did you?" Jeered Rose.

"What about you grandma? Where will you be?" Asked Sean. "You're going to let me go, releasing a hostage will look good for you" said Rose, rubbing Sean's arm reassuringly. "I don't know gran, you never said it would be like this" said Sean uncertainly. "Sean my boy, I've got to go separately so that I can get home to get all of our stuff together. You just be ready when I call you" soothed Rose. "On second thoughts Lucy, you ring that handsome husband of yours, and you tell him our demands. Warn them no tricks, I've got nothing to lose, remember that" said Rose. Lucy noticed a sinister look, almost like one of excitement, in her eyes as she ran her hand round the gun's barrel. "What are you going to do grandma?" Asked Sean worriedly. "Shut up both of you, and give me chance to think!" Said Rose in a menacing tone.

When Ben and Tom arrived back at Hilltop Manor, DCI Fields was waiting for them. He led them into the back of what looked like an oversized transit van, "Take a seat please" he said. Inside the van was carpeted and resembled a small office, chairs and a table on one side and computers and other high-tech equipment on the other. "This is like a makeshift incident room" said Tom, seeing Ben's confusion. Ben's mobile began to ring and he hurriedly grabbed its from his jacket pocket. "Hello" he said. "Ben, it's Margaret" said the panicked voice. "What is it Margaret, what's happened?" Asked Ben frantically. Tom signalled to him to put the phone on speakerphone, the man sitting at the computer wanted to record the call. "Ben, I heard a shot, and then Morph appeared at my door" Margaret said in tears. "A shot?! Oh my god" cried Ben. "I didn't know what to do, I took Morph and we're in the panic room" sobbed Margaret. "How did you get in there?" Asked DCI Fields. "I chose the original code when it was set up and it's never been changed" said Margaret. "But how did you get into the house?" Asked the DCI. "I didn't, I went in through the disused entrance" she said. "Okay Margaret, you're doing great, stay with the phone and I'll call you back" said DCI Fields.

"DCI Fields, I need to speak to my wife. I need to make sure she and Rose are safe" said Ben insistently. "Of course, but when is your father back?" He asked. "Not for another week yet" said Ben. Frank and Janet had flown out to America to meet with the people organising RIH's new development there. "I need to speak to him, he will have a better idea of what's in the panic room than anyone" added the DCI. "I'll call him while Ben rings Lucy" Tom said. "Okay, thanks Tom. Now Ben, when you ring Lucy, we're going to record that call as well" At that moment, Ben's mobile rang. "It's Lucy" he said, seeing her name flash up on the front. "Answer it, but on speakerphone if you can" said the DCI, nodding to the man at the computer to be ready. Ben took a deep breath, pressed answer and flicked it straight onto the speakerphone. "Hi honey" he said brightly. "Ben, please listen carefully" said Lucy hesitantly. "What's up? Are you okay?" Ben asked, trying to hide the anxiety in his voice. "Sean's here and he's got a gun" said Lucy, her voice shaking. "A gun? Oh my god are you and Rose okay?" Ben cried. Rose dug Lucy forcefully in the ribs with the end of the gun, further reminding her to be very careful how she answered that question. "Yes we're fine" said Lucy quietly. "What does he want with you?" Said Ben. "He wants the paintings, he was with Fred when he tried to sell them and knows they're fakes. I've told him the police have them, but he says you've got to get them and put them in the van" said Lucy, her voice unsteady.

"Ask Sean to speak to me" whispered DCI Fields. "Lucy, DCI Fields wants to speak to Sean" Ben said. She turned to look at Rose and Sean, they'd been listening on the speakerphone on Lucy's mobile. Rose nodded to Sean who walked over and took the phone. "What?" He barked. "Hello Sean, my name is DCI Fields" he said. "I know who you are, what do you want? You know my terms" said Sean in a cold, hard tone. "We can get you the paintings Sean, but it will take a long time. There's a lot of red tape to go through to get them released" said the DCI calmly. "I don't care how you do it copper, but you get them here and you don't have hours. I have a gun and I'll use it if I have to. I've already shot the dog" Sean said. "Let the ladies go Sean, I'll get you the paintings, but you don't need them" said DCI Fields. "Don't treat me like I'm stupid, you know my terms!" Roared Sean, switching the phone off angrily. "Well done boy" said Rose, clapping excitedly. "Oh my god, what are we going to do? He sounded really angry" said Ben fearfully. "Try not to worry too much Ben, Sean knows he needs Lucy" DCI Fields reassured him. "Sir, I have Frank Reid on the phone for you" said Tom. DCI Fields took the phone, "Frank, I need you to tell me all you can about the panic room. Margaret Armstrong is in there at the moment, but she's obviously very frightened and may not be thinking straight" said the DCI. "Of course, but how is my daughter in law, where is my son?" Asked Frank. "I'm fine dad, I can hear you as the phone's been put on speakerphone. Sean has Lucy and Rose and he has a gun" Ben told him. "Good lord! Are they okay? The children aren't in there are they? Please tell me they're not" said Frank. "No, Jake and Emily are with Leah. I've arranged for them to stay with Bob and Sue overnight" Ben told his father. "What about Nick?" Asked Frank. "He's with his mum still" Ben replied. "Thank God for that!" Said Frank, the obvious relief clearly evident in his voice.

"Now Frank, what exactly is in that panic room? I'm assuming the house is well and truly bolted up, so that may be the only way in" said the DCI. "How do we know that Lucy and Rose are okay? Is Margaret watching them on the monitors?" Asked Frank. "Watching them? There's CCTV in the panic room?" Asked the DCI in shock. "Yes, there's a camera on the front and the back of the house and four more inside. That's how I knew what was going on when I was there" Frank said. "Ben, get Margaret Armstrong back on the phone for me please. Is there anything else Frank?" Asked the DCI. "No nothing, other than everything in there, electricity, phone, heating, etcetera, work's independently of the main house" Frank said. "Mr Reid, you have been a great help" said the DCI. "You're more than welcome. Ben, please keep us informed" Frank said. "I will dad, take care" Ben replied. "Margaret's on the phone for you, DCI Fields " Ben said.

"Okay thank you, hello Margaret" said the DCI. "Frank Reid says there are monitors in there with you that allow you to see certain places in the house" he continued. "Yes there are, I've found them. Sean has Rose and Lucy in the living room" said Margaret. "Are they okay?" Ben asked. "They both look fine" said Margaret reassuringly. "That's good, now I want you to keep watching for me and call Ben or Tom straight away if anything changes please" instructed DCI Fields. "There is one thing, there's a separate monitor here marked main house, and it's black. No matter what I do with it there's just a fuzzy screen at best" said Margaret. "It sounds as though Sean has disabled the CCTV system in some way" Dean, the guy at the computer, said. "Well that's very interesting. That may mean he can't see what we are up to outside unless he's looking directly out of the window" said the DCI thoughtfully.

"What do we do now then sir?" Asked Tom. "Time to speak to Sean again I think" replied DCI Fields. Ben dialled Lucy's number and waited for her to answer. "Hello" barked Sean after only the first ring. "Sean, it's DCI Fields. The paintings' release is being organised, but my superior wants you to let Lucy and Rose go" he said. "I told you no" said Sean. "I just want to let you know that we're moving inside the grounds Sean, just onto the front lawn. We won't come near the house" added the DCI. "What for?" Snapped Sean. "This is a country lane Sean, it's too dangerous to be out here, and we will need to come in when the paintings arrive anyway" said DCI Fields reassuringly. "Okay" Sean agreed. "Please think about what I've said Sean" said the DCI. "I've said no copper" said Sean, ending the call. "What now?" Ben asked. "We'll move inside like we said, and then wait for him to call us" said DCI Fields. Once the police van, Tom's car and a police car were installed safely on the lawn, DCI Fields rang Mrs Armstrong back again. "What's happening Margaret?" He asked. "Nothing I'm afraid. Lucy is sitting on the sofa, Rose is in the armchair and Sean keeps going to sneak a look through the curtains of the patio doors" she said.

Suddenly Ben's mobile began to ring, "Hello" he answered. "Let me speak to that cop" Sean demanded. "Yes I'm here" said DCI Fields. "The old lady's got chest pains and she's starting to go to sleep" he said. "Sean, Rose is an elderly lady, you've got to let her out of there" said DCI Fields. "No one's going nowhere" Sean replied calmly and firmly. "Sean, you have to let me call her an ambulance. She could die, and you don't want to be blamed for that do you? That would be murder" pressed DCI Fields. The line fell silent for a minute, "Okay, take her. She's only a hindrance anyway. But Lucy stays with me" said Sean. "That's it, that's the right decision. Let Rose come out" encouraged the DCI. The line went dead, "He's put the phone down again" said Ben in desperation. A moment later, the door opened and Rose stumbled out slowly, holding her chest. "Walk towards us Rose, just keep walking" called DCI Fields. As Rose got within feet of the police van, she stumbled forward and Scott Regan quickly stepped forward to catch her. "Sit her down in the police car" said DCI Fields, the ambulance is on its way." Ten minutes later, an ambulance, with blue lights flashing, sped along the drive and onto the grass. "This is Rose, she's 71 and has been suffering chest pains" Tom told the paramedics. "Hello Rose I'm Johnny, let's get you into the ambulance and see what's going on shall we?" Said the older of the two paramedics. "Thank you dear, I'm sorry to be so much trouble" said Rose in a frail voice. "Not at all, spending time with beautiful young ladies like you is what I come to work for" Johnny said with a wink as he and his colleague Phil helped Rose up the steps of the ambulance.

A short while later, Johnny came over to the police van to speak to DCI Fields. "How is she?" Asked the DCI. "We can't find anything visibly wrong, but Rose is still complaining of chest pain. In view of her age and the stressful situation she's been under, we're going to take her into A & E, just to let them take a look" said Johnny. "Okay thank you, I'll get someone along there soon to have a chat to her." Said the DCI. "Just after Rose had gone, Ben's phone rang, "It's Lucy...Hello" he said. "Ben, Sean wants to know where the paintings are. He said remember he may not have Rose anymore, but he has me. He said don't mess with him" Lucy said, her voice shaky. "Sean, can you hear me?" Asked DCI Fields, as he had been listening in. "Yeah I can hear you" snarled Sean. "Rose has gone to hospital, you've helped her, you've done the right thing Sean. Now why not let Lucy go, do the right thing again Sean. It's not too late to stop this. I can put in a good word for you if you let Mrs Reid go" said the DCI. "I said no, I want those paintings!" Shouted Sean. "Yes I know you do, but I don't have them, and it takes time to organise getting them here. All this time you hold Mrs Reid doesn't look good for you" coaxed the DCI. "Good for me? You're treating me like I'm stupid copper, I ain't going back to prison" Sean spat. "I know you don't want to go back there for long, and you might not have to. Even if you did it won't be for anywhere near as long if you let Mrs Reid go" said the DCI in a calm voice. "Then maybe I won't let her go…or me for that matter" snarled Sean. "Aargh!" Screamed Lucy. "Lucy, Lucy are you okay?!" Cried Ben in horror. "She's okay for now" said Sean in a threatening voice, ending the call.

CHAPTER 18

YOU NEVER KNOW WHO YOU CAN TRUST

Ben jumped to his feet, "You've got to do something, you've got to get Lucy out of there!" He exclaimed. "We will Ben, we will. Tom, we need to get in there" said the DCI. "But how?" Asked Ben. "Through the panic room. At least if we're in there, we can watch what's happening, and try to get Sean where we want him to spring a surprise attack" said the DCI. "Get Margaret Armstrong and Frank Reid back on the phone please" he ordered. DS Lowe had arrived about an hour ago and rang Mrs Armstrong, while Tom tried Frank. "Mrs Armstrong on speakerphone for you sir" she said. "Hello Margaret, can you see what's going on?" Asked DCI Fields. "They're still in the living room, but it looks like Lucy's crying and Sean is pacing around. He keeps going to look out of the window" said Margaret. "Okay, I'm going to need your help please. We're still waiting on the arrival of the armed division. They have said they will be here within 30 minutes. When they arrive, we need to get them into the panic room with you, but we've got to get them across the grass without being seen. What I'm going to need you to do is tell us when Sean isn't near the window" said the DCI. "Okay I understand" said Mrs Armstrong. "I can't get a line to Frank's mobile sir" said Tom. "Don't worry now, I think we will be fine with just Margaret's help" he said.

"DCI Fields, DCI Fields! They're moving" said Margaret. "Moving where?!" Cried Ben, up on his feet again, the anxiety clear on his face. "They're in the kitchen, and Lucy looks like she's making him a sandwich" Margaret said. "Hang on, armed back up is here" DCI Fields told her. "Right Margaret, we have three officers coming to join you. I need the code to open the door please" said the DCI. "31751" Margaret told him. "Now it will take these men around 30 seconds to clear visibility of the living room window. Where's Sean, Margaret?" Asked the DCI. "He's eating in the kitchen" she replied. "Okay, that's great. GO GO GO!" Shouted DCI Fields. Minutes later, the men were with Margaret in the panic room. "We're here" Said Steve, the officer in charge. "That's great. Margaret thank you so much. You have been amazing. Now sit back and let these guys take it from here" said DCI Fields. "I will do, thank you. Sean has taken Lucy back into the living room" Margaret said. "Okay, thank you again" said DCI Fields before ending the call.

Ben's mobile began to ring again, "Hello honey" said Ben. "Why hello sweetheart" said Sean's mocking voice. "Sean, I thought you were Lucy. What have you done with her?" Ben demanded. "Done with her? Nothing yet" said Sean. "If you so much as hurt her…" said Ben angrily. "You'll do what? When the paintings come, your wifey and I are out of here" said Sean smarmily. "That's enough Ben" warned DCI Fields. "Yeah, listen to the cop Benny Boy" mocked Sean. "You won't be so sure of yourself when you're banged up again" said Ben. "I'm not going to prison. I'm not going back there" said Sean, growing angry. "That's enough. Tom, take Ben outside to cool down. Now Sean, have you thought anymore of going the right way and letting Mrs Reid go?" Asked DCI Fields. Bruce and Jeff had just come home by taxi and were now at the police van as well. They couldn't go home as the police wouldn't let them that close to the house. "Where's my paintings?" Demanded Sean. "How's Mrs Reid Sean? Bring her to the phone, I need to hear she's alright" said the DCI. "I told you she's okay. Come here bitch!" Cried Sean. "Argh get off my hair!" Screamed Lucy. "Leave her alone you animal!" Shouted Bruce. "Shut up! I'm in charge here, understand?!" Screamed Sean. "Get him out of here!" Shouted DCI Fields. "In charge? You're not in charge you fool!" Cried Bruce. "Bruce that's enough! Come away" said DS Lowe urgently. "I'm in control! When I get out of here.." Shouted Sean. "You're not getting out of there!" Interrupted Bruce, "The only place you're going is to prison!" "No I'm not, you don't know what you're talking about! I'm not going to prison, grandma said I wasn't before I let her go!" Roared Sean, but stopping the moment he uttered the words.

Everyone in the police van had fallen silent, Lucy stared in horror.

"Your grandma? Rose is your grandmother?" Asked DCI Fields in shock. "Yeah, she's my gran, but she's smarter than all of you put together, isn't she? Cos she's out of here" said Sean, throwing his head back and laughing for all he was worth. "Are you telling me Rose wasn't ill?" Asked the DCI. "Of course she wasn't ill copper, she's just gone to get things ready" said Sean. "What things Sean?" Asked DCI Fields. "Just things okay? Now get me my paintings. I'm getting fed up with this" said Sean angrily, as he ended the call. "Oh my god" said Ben, "Well I didn't see that one coming" "Suzanne, ring DC Phillips and see if he's arrived at the hospital yet to interview Rose. Tell him to arrest her" ordered DCI Fields. DS Lowe took her mobile from her pocket and went off to make the call. "What happens now DCI Fields?" Asked Ben anxiously. Before he had chance to answer, DS Lowe came running back into the van. "She's gone sir" she said. "What do you mean gone?" Asked the DCI. "DC Phillips said that when he got to the hospital he was told that Rose had gone to the toilet, and to wait in her room. She never came back and when the toilets were checked there was no sign of her" DS Lowe said. "Sean was obviously telling the truth, there was nothing wrong with Rose after all. It had all been a ploy to get her out of there" She continued.

"Sir, Steve said they are watching Sean on the monitors and he's showing signs of becoming very edgy" said Tom. "The paintings are here" said a uniformed officer, poking his head through the door. "Thank you. Tom, get me Steve on the phone please" asked the DCI. Tom dialled the number and a few moments later, Steve's voice filled the van. "Yes DCI Fields?" He said. "Steve I'm going to call Sean and show him the paintings, I want to try and get him to the study. You and the boys take it from there. I'll leave the call connected so you can hear what's going on, but please mute the phone your end" said the DCI. "Of course" Steve replied. "How are you going to get him to the study DCI Fields? He's got a gun and he could shoot Lucy before they have the time to stop him" said Ben worriedly. "Steve and his men are the best in their field Ben, they know what they're doing, believe me" the DCI replied. "I really hope so" said Ben quietly. "Can you call Lucy please Ben, so that I can speak to Sean?" Said DCI Fields. Ben did as he was asked, "Hello" said Lucy softly. "Lucy can I speak to Sean please?" Said the DCI. "Have you got my paintings?" Said Sean gruffly. "Yes, they're here, but we need the keys to put them in your van" said DCI Fields. "How do I know you've got them?" Sean demanded. "Look out of the window Sean, and I'll show you" said the DCI. "This better not be a trick copper!" Shouted Sean. DCI Fields nodded to Tom to get the paintings, "Sean I've got the paintings here. If you look out of the door, my officer will be standing on the grass with them. He'll hold each one up in turn" said DCI Fields. Seconds later, the curtain was pulled back slightly at the patio doors and Lucy's face appeared.

DCI Fields couldn't see Sean from this distance, but guessed he would be standing behind her. Sean let out a triumphant whoop and a laugh, "See I knew you'd see things my way" he said. "Okay Sean, now I'm going to need the keys" said the DCI. The sound of scuffling could be heard on the line, and then Lucy's voice, "Ouch my arm!" She said in a scared tone. "Shut up bitch" said Sean angrily. "Sean there's no need to hurt Mrs Reid" said the DCI. "She does as she's told and I won't...for now" he added. Ben looked livid, but he knew he mustn't lose control as he had earlier. "She's going to throw the keys out, then post them back through the letterbox. Remember copper, no tricks. I ain't got nothing to lose" warned Sean. "There won't be any tricks" said the DCI. Everyone outside watched as the front door opened and Lucy came into view, she threw the keys as far as she could, before she was dragged back inside and the door slammed shut. Sean took Lucy back to the far end of the hallway by the living room door, and minutes later, the keys clattered through the letterbox. "Pick them up" ordered Sean, pushing Lucy forward. She did as she was told and Sean snatched the keys from her and pushed them deep into his pocket.

"Sean are you still there?" Came DCI Fields' voice. "I'm here" Sean replied. "I need to speak to Mrs Reid, her family want to know she's okay" said the DCI. "Speak to him bitch" said Sean. "H-hello" stammered Lucy. "Mrs Reid, you've been very brave. I want you to continue being so. Please try not to panic, I know you're nervous, but panic in any room doesn't help the situation. Just do what Sean says" said DCI Fields. "Oh okay" answered Lucy quietly. "What now Sean?" Asked the DCI. "All of you, move to the furthest corner of the lawn, I want clear passage out of here." Sean said. "I gave you my word that I won't stop you. These paintings will set you up for a new life, it's just a shame there's no certificate of authenticity with them. They'd be worth so much more" said the DCI. "A what?" Asked Sean. "A certificate to verify the paintings are genuine, proves you own them really" said the DCI. "Where's that?" Sean demanded. "I don't know, I'd imagine Mrs Reid has it" said DCI Fields. "Where is it?" Sean barked, turning to Lucy. "It's in the filing cabinet in the study" she said nervously. "Get it!" Roared Sean. Lucy walked up the stairs, aware at every step that Sean had the gun in her back. As she opened the door, the study was eerily black. She noticed immediately that the blinds were closed, and they never were. The lighting was so poor in the study that they left them open. The extra glow from the light of the room was always very welcome.

Lucy flicked the switch to turn on the wall lights but nothing happened. She tried again, but still nothing, "The lights aren't working" she said. "Brilliant" said Sean nastily. "There's a light on the desk" said Lucy quietly. "Put it on" demanded Sean, digging her in the ribs with the gun. Lucy edged her way across the room in the dark, while Sean waited just inside the door. She felt her way round to the far side of the huge desk to switch on the table light, suddenly a hand shot up and pulled her down. "Lay flat on the floor and don't move" a male voice ordered. "The room filled with white powerful beams, "Armed police, get on the floor! Drop your weapon!" "Drop your weapon!" Ordered another voice. "Get on the floor! Drop your weapon!" Said the voice again. Lucy could just see Sean's startled face illuminated in the bright lights through the gap under the desk. For a second, she thought he was going to run, but he tossed his gun to one side and threw himself on the floor. "All clear, all clear" came the authority voice again. Lucy sighed with relief and promptly burst into tears, she just couldn't stop herself.

Moments later, she felt a gentle hand on her shoulder. "Lucy, get up pet. It's all over" said a soothing female voice. She sat up slowly, "Oh Margaret!" She cried, collapsing into her outstretched arms. Mrs Armstrong slowly helped Lucy to her feet and hugged her tightly. "Are you okay Mrs Reid? I'm Steve Barnette, the officer in charge" said a tall uniformed man. Lucy nodded her head, "Yes thank you" she said. The study burst open and Ben rushed in, "Lucy!" He cried, taking her in his arms. Lucy, Ben and Margaret watched as a struggling Sean was led out, still protesting he wasn't going to prison. "That's exactly where he's going" said DCI Fields, coming through the door. "For a very long time" added Tom, following him in. Ben helped Lucy downstairs and into the kitchen, she said she wasn't hungry, but he insisted that she have something to drink. She hadn't had anything in all the time she had been held prisoner by Rose and Sean. Once Lucy was seated at the table with a cup of hot sweet tea, she began to shake violently, she seemed to have no control over it at all. "That's shock dear, drink the tea" soothed Margaret. "It will help" agreed DCI Fields. "Please Lucy, let me do you something to eat, even if it's just some toast" begged Margaret. Lucy nodded, "Toast would be lovely" she said. "Lucy, when you're feeling better, we're going to need a statement from you" said DCI Fields. "That's fine I'll do it now. Then I want to see my children" said Lucy softly. "They'll be in bed by now, we can go and collect them tomorrow" Ben said. "No I want to see them tonight, I just need to be with them. I won't wake them up" said Lucy.

Tom had gone off to the airport to wait for Frank and Janet, the reason Tom hadn't been able to get a connection to Frank when he had tried earlier, was that he and Janet had left to come home straight away. "Okay Lucy, as soon as I've got someone free to take you to Primrose Hill, you can go" said DCI Fields quietly. "I can take her" said a voice. Everyone turned to see who it was, and there, standing in the doorway, was PC Regan. Lucy hadn't noticed him there, she had been too busy cuddling Morph for all she was worth. She was so relieved to see him alive, she really thought Sean had killed him. "Would you Scott? Oh thank you" said Lucy gratefully. "Aren't you just going off duty Scott?" Asked the DCI. "I am, but it's fine" Scott replied, with a warm smile. Just over half an hour later, Lucy and Scott set off from Primrose Hill, Ben hadn't been able to come as they would need the three rear seats to bring home Leah and the children in the morning. Lucy had telephoned Bob and Sue, who had agreed that she and Scott could sleep in a chair each in the living room, for what would be left of the night by the time they got there. "Thanks for doing this" said Lucy, as she and Scott drove away from Hilltop Manor. "Not a problem, I've always thought you were a good person Lucy. The way you clearly cared about Jeff and the way you looked after me with coffee and sandwiches at the hospital, very kind. Just such a shame you had to get mixed up with this" said Scott.

Lucy and Scott chatted easily as they drove along the deserted road that led to the town, when suddenly Lucy spotted someone lit up in the car's headlights. "Oh my god, it's Rose" she said in horror. "Where?" Scott asked. "Just there, at the road side" said Lucy pointing. "Well I never, so it is" said Scott. "Quick, put your foot down then call the police" said Lucy urgently. She had no wish to come into contact with that horrible woman ever again. As Scott passed Rose, her hard eyes bore into Lucy and a shiver ran down her spine. "That's definitely her" said Scott. Without warning he jammed on the breaks and began to reverse. "Scott, what are you doing?!" Lucy screamed in terror. The car came to a halt, the back door opened and Rose got in. "Hello Lucy" she smiled, a slow menacing grin. "What's going on here, why did you stop?" Asked Lucy in panic. "Because he's a gentleman, aren't you Scott?" Said Rose. "Go easy on her Auntie Rose" said Scott, driving off again. "Auntie? Oh no please tell me this nightmare isn't true?!" Cried Lucy in despair. "Oh it's true, very true" said Rose with a chuckle. Lucy sat in the front seat, tears silently running down her cheeks. There was no point in trying to jump out and run, they were back in the middle of nowhere, she didn't know what was about to happen, but what she did know is that she had to pull herself together, gather her thoughts so she was thinking clearly. She had to be ready for any chance to escape, or to at least notify someone as to where she was.

A short while later, Scott turned off the road between the trees, onto a track that lead to the old disused quarry. Lucy's heart pounded, 'Are they going to kill me and leave me here?' She thought in horror. No, she quickly reasoned, they wanted money from the Reids, and if they didn't have her they had nothing. She was safe for the minute, she thought. Scott's car bumped along the uneven track, down as far as they could go, and came to a halt by an old grey stone building. Lucy thought this must have been an office or a gatehouse where the lorries that used the quarry in its day had to be booked in and out. Scott got out, came round and took Lucy by the arm. Rose opened the door to the grey building, "Put her on the floor down there, where we can keep an eye on her" she spat. "No Auntie Rose, it will be freezing on that stone floor. Lucy can sit on the chair, she won't try anything, will you Lucy?" Said Scott. "No" said Lucy quietly. She sat in the chair and began to shake violently. Scott walked back out of the door and returned a moment later with a blanket, "Here Lucy I always carry this in the car" he said, gently wrapping a blanket round her. "Dear god, what is wrong with all the men in this family? Sean doesn't have the brains he was born with and you're going soft over her." Said Rose with obvious distaste.

"Why did you leave Sean in there?" Asked Scott. Rose threw back her head and laughed, that cold callous laugh that Lucy had heard before, "He was never going to pull that off, so I bailed. No point us both being locked up" said Rose matter of factly. "He trusted you" Lucy blurted. "I've done him a favour then haven't I? Don't trust anyone in this life. You should know that" said Rose, looking at Scott with a smirk. "I'd try to get some sleep if I were you Lucy, Rose wants to be moving from here again soon, and you'll need some rest" said Scott. "I don't know if we need to move too quickly, we've got enough food here to last for a few days, and that should be plenty of time for the Reid's to sort out some money for us" laughed Rose. Lucy put her head down on the desk in front of her, how was she ever going to get out of here? Yeah she knew self defence, but she couldn't be sure that Rose didn't have a weapon and Scott had a car. How would anyone ever find her right down here? This quarry didn't look like it had been used for years. Lucy was so scared.

Outside, everything was eerily quiet, there was nothing or no one around, it seemed. The concrete covered ground empty, splayed out in every direction, the huge cliff faces on three sides and vast trees concealing the quarry from the road on the other. Worried green eyes peered down from the shadow of the bushes that lined the road, glad that they at least knew where Lucy was. What Lucy, Rose, nor Scott knew, was that when they'd left Hilltop Manor, they'd been followed. You see after Bruce had lost his temper with Sean on the phone, and DS Lowe had escorted him away from the police van, he'd gone for a walk to cool down. As he leant against a post at the main gate, he'd heard a male voice whispering. Wondering who it was and who they were talking to, he'd edged round to the other side of the huge pillar, and there, just outside the drive, was Scott. He had his mobile pressed to his ear, and seemed to be talking in a whispered, urgent tone. "I didn't even know you were involved until Sean blurted it out…Blood is thicker than water…Where will you go? You're on foot and everyone will be looking for you…I'll pick you up in the lay-by just outside town on the main hospital road…as soon as I can get away" Scott said. Bruce hurried off when he realised Scott would be off of the phone any second. He didn't want to be seen, he would be keeping a close eye on Scott though.

Bruce had been in the living room when Scott left with Lucy. In a panic that he had lost them, he borrowed Nick's car and drove off in pursuit. All he could do was head for the lay-by in the vague hope that he would catch up. He got there just in time to see Scott pull out again. Bruce hadn't known for definite Rose was in that car, until he had seen her get out inside the quarry. "Is she asleep?" Hissed Rose. "Yes I think so" said Scott, coming over to look. Lucy kept her eyes tightly closed. "What made you change your mind?" Asked Rose. "I couldn't see you get arrested, could I? Whatever's been said or done, you're still my dad's sister" said Scott. "Your mother gave you my number then?" Said Rose. "Yes I've had it a long time, but never had any intentions of ringing it. Dad brought me up drumming it into me that you were no good. He never said why, but I hadn't seen you for so long, I had no reason to disbelieve him. All I knew was that he hated you and he was my dad, so that was good enough for me" Scott told her.

"Yeah he always did overreact, did your father. Your mother's met me in secret for years, and it was only when your father died six months ago, that we've been able to meet freely" said Rose. "Dad would never have your name mentioned and I never knew about Sean. Not until mum saw it in the paper, that the police were looking for him after he grabbed Lucy at the Yew Tree. That's when she explained everything" said Scott. "It's all water under the bridge now, but your father blamed me for coming between him and your mum and causing a break up in their relationship. I didn't do anything, and they got back together anyway. But he wouldn't listen" said Rose wryly. Scott was quiet for a moment, "I didn't know if you were going to be in that lay by, after all, I am a cop…was a cop" he finished, somewhat sadly. "I wasn't until I spoke to your mother, I rang her after you called me and she said you'd spoken to her earlier when you found out I was involved. She said she'd begged you to help me. She said that you rang her before you rang me and told her to get on a plane to your sister's in Spain before the police came looking" said Rose cockily. "I'd do anything for my mum" said Scott wistfully. "I'd gathered that. Your mum's very proud of you. Always telling me of your achievements in the police force" said Rose. "I love her very much. Anyway, what's the plan? Are we meeting up with anyone else to get us out of here?" Asked Scott brightly. "Anyone else?" Said Rose with a manic laugh. "Surely we aren't on our own?" Asked Scott in horror. "Yes, just you and me left against the world. All the other buffoons have gone and got themselves arrested" said Rose bitterly.

"So what are we going to do? Are we going to contact the Reids?" Asked Scott. "No I think we'll let them sweat a bit" said Rose with a grin. "Okay, if you think that's best" agreed Scott, taking a seat at the rickety old table. "Pass me over that bag of hers, better make sure there's no phone in there" said Rose. "She wouldn't do that, Lucy's not stupid" declared Scott. "I said pass it to me" said Rose glaring. Scott picked up the bag and passed it to Rose, "What are you doing?" Asked Lucy sitting up. "Well you won't be needing that" said Rose, taking Lucy's mobile out, putting it in her pocket and tossing the bag itself back down the table towards Lucy. "How are we going to get out of here? We don't even have Sean's gun anymore, the police took it" said Scott. Rose looked thoughtful for a minute, "Yes they did didn't they…but they didn't get this one" she said, slipping a gun from her pocket. Rose's eyes locked onto Lucy's, her fingers tracing the outline of the gun lying on the table. Lucy recoiled in horror, Rose was still armed after all. "Well done you, talk about prepared!" Laughed Scott. "You know I really can't believe this of you Scott, we trusted you, why?" Said Lucy in anguish. "Nothing personal Lucy, it's just Auntie Rose's way is much easier than day in day out in the police force" said Scott. Lucy could not believe what she was hearing.

"You Rose, we've shown you nothing but kindness" said Lucy quietly. "Like he said, it's nothing personal" mimicked Rose, her voice full of sarcasm. A couple of hours passed, Lucy's mobile seemed to ring continuously. Ben, Tom, Sue and Bob, but Rose just stared at the screen, chuckling at every passing call. DCI Fields and DS Lowe had rang Scott, but he too hadn't answered. "DCI Fields, how sweet" said Rose, when his name appeared on the front of Lucy's phone. "Should we answer it, or even text back do you think?" Asked Scott. "No, the fool thinks we're miles away" said Rose, roaring with laughter. What Rose didn't realise though, is that DCI Fields didn't think that at all, he knew exactly where they were, and he was closer, much closer than Rose could ever imagine. DCI Fields was standing at the top of the quarry, shielded by the trees looking down at them. Bruce had called him immediately and he had come straight there.

"Are you going to move in on them? We don't know Lucy isn't in danger" asked Bruce. "No, not yet. I want to wait for them to contact us" said DCI Fields. "Damn, this phone won't work" snapped Rose. "The signal will be very poor down here" Scott said. "I want to hear the news on it" said Rose angrily. "Walk around a bit or try the other end of the room" Scott suggested. Rose walked up to the other end of the concrete passage that linked that room to the next, keeping firm hold of her gun. "Keep a close eye on her" she ordered as she walked off.

CHAPTER 19

THE TRIALS BEGIN

"Lucy, please don't be afraid. I'll get you out of here" Scott whispered. "What?" Asked Lucy in surprise. "I had to get Rose here, I couldn't risk her being able to come after you or your family. I had to make sure she wasn't working with anyone else" said Scott, still paying extra care to keep his voice down. "So you're not helping her?" Asked Lucy apprehensively. "No of course not, I had to text DCI Fields once I knew for sure Rose was working alone. Then he'll come and get us, but I didn't bargain on another gun" he said, sitting as close as he could to Lucy without drawing attention to himself. He cast an anxious glance over his shoulder, Rose seemed to be engrossed in listening to the radio. "So you won't get into trouble? I'm so glad I wasn't wrong about you after all. Please, send the text" begged Lucy. Scott took his phone from his pocket and quickly typed in 'All clear…but she has a gun!'

Suddenly, something caught Lucy's eye. "Noooo!" She screamed, but she was too late. Rose brought the brick down hard on Scott's head. Lucy watched in horror as he slumped forward and fell from the chair into a heap on the floor. "Can't have him sending that now, can we?" Cackled Rose, picking up Scott's phone. Lucy watched open mouthed as Rose laid it on the table, then brought the brick down on it over and over again. "Oh my god Rose, he's not moving! You must call an ambulance!" Insisted Lucy, staring in horror at the pool of dark red blood collecting by Scott's head. "No, he should never have betrayed me" said Rose coldly. "Rose, it's DCI Fields. Can you hear me Rose? I just want to talk to you, no one's going to hurt you" Came the DCI's voice. Rose rushed to the slit that was

217

left un-boarded on the window. "Jesus, the coppers. That text must have gone through!" Cried Rose in panic. "Rose, can you hear me? Came the DCI's voice again. "Rose please, give yourself up it's over. Scott needs an ambulance" sobbed Lucy. "I said no!" Rose roared. "Rose, DCI Fields is a good man. You can trust him" pressed Lucy. "No you can't, you can't trust any copper!" Shouted Rose, gesturing to Scott as if to prove her point. "Rose, can you hear me? I just want to talk to you" shouted DCI Fields. "Come here" ordered Rose, grabbing Lucy roughly by the arm and pushing her towards the door. "Ow! You're hurting me!" Cried Lucy.

Rose threw open the door and pushed Lucy into view, taking extra care to stand behind her, "What do you want?" She shouted. "Rose, just let Mrs Reid go and come quietly with us" said DCI Fields. "I said no, I want my paintings!" Rose roared. "Just let me come and talk to you" said the DCI, taking a step forward. "Stay back!" Rose screamed, taking the gun and pointing it at Lucy's head. DCI Fields stepped back immediately, "Rose, there's no need for the gun" said the DCI. "There's every need. You can't trust anyone" said Rose coldly. "Where's Scott?" Asked DCI Fields. "You don't need to worry about him, he won't be causing anymore trouble." She said, with a callous laugh. "That's not true Rose, there are people you can trust. What have you done to Scott?" Asked DCI Fields calmly. "Let's just say he's sleeping" Rose replied, nodding proudly. "If he's hurt, he needs help" urged the DCI. "Get him all the help you want when we're out of here". Rose leant back inside and snatched Scott's car keys from the ledge. Grabbing Lucy's shoulder she edged towards the car. "Rose please don't do this" Pleaded Lucy. "Shut up" snarled Rose.

Without warning Lucy felt the tight grip on her shoulder release, "Get off me!" Roared Rose, struggling wildly and pushing Lucy to one side in the process. Lucy turned to see Scott swaying unsteadily, but doing his best to restrain Rose. Suddenly Rose slipped free and ran towards the low wall at the edge of the building. With blood still seeping from the gash on his head, Scott advanced towards her. "Get back or I'll shoot!" Rose roared, her eyes glinting with amassed adrenaline. "You won't shoot me" said Scott, shuffling closer. "Get back, I'll shoot I tell you!" Screamed Rose, enraged. "You won't shoot Rose, you may need these first" slurred Scott, swaying even more and opening his hand to reveal four silver bullets. Rose opened the gun in horror, and seeing it was empty she threw it to the ground in uncontrolled temper. Before anyone could stop her, Rose grabbed an old spade from beside her and ran at Scott, screaming obscenities. Lucy leapt to her feet and grabbed Rose, having nothing to fear as she was no longer armed. For an elderly lady, she was very strong. Then there was the sound of running feet and Lucy felt powerful arms wrenching Rose away.

She turned round to look for Scott, who was now slumped against the door frame. She raced over to him and guided him back inside to sit down. "Are you okay?" He slurred, as the sound of an ambulance siren filled the air. "I'm fine thanks to you" she said, tears rolling down her cheeks. "That's good" nodded Scott, as his head dropped forward. "No, stay with me Scott!" Screamed Lucy, dropping to her knees by his feet. Lucy let the paramedics take over, "Now they'll look after him" said DCI Fields gently, helping her to her feet. She watched in desperation as the paramedics tended to Scott, then wheeled him on a stretcher to the back of the ambulance.

"Ben!" She cried, as she turned round and spotted her husband's outstretched arms. The pain and worry in his eyes said it all, there was no need for words. As Ben helped Lucy into the second ambulance, then got in behind her, she couldn't help but go over in her head all the things that had happened of late. DCI Fields had insisted she go to the hospital, just for a check up, even though she had insisted she was fine. An hour later, they were sat around Scott's hospital bed, with his mum Jane, his wife Louise and DCI Fields, waiting for him to wake up. Scott had taken a very nasty blow to the head and had lost a lot of blood, but thankfully he was going to be okay. "Oh Scott" sobbed his mother as he slowly opened his eyes. "I'm fine mum, honestly" he said in a low voice. "Well done Scott, what you did there was very brave, and it must have taken a lot to do the right thing against family. I'm very proud of you" said DCI Fields. "Thank you sir" Scott replied. "I don't know how to ever thank you, when I first heard what was happening I was so angry that Lucy had been involved in it, but now I understand" said Ben gratefully. "It was nothing. You and your family have been through so much, and you have a pretty amazing wife there. So strong and kind, look after her mate" Scott said, smiling weakly. "Oh I will do" nodded Ben, as he hugged Lucy tightly. Lucy stood up and took Scott's hand, smiling down at him "Thank you, thank you so much" she said softly. "You're welcome" whispered Scott. "Can I just ask you something please?" She said. "Yes of course" Scott replied. "How did you know there were no bullets in Rose's gun?" Lucy asked. "Because I took them" he replied. "When you had your head on the table, Rose fell asleep. Nodded off just for a minute or two, and I took them then" Scott said. "Why didn't you just take the gun?" Asked Lucy puzzled. "Because I needed Rose to trust me. I had to know she was working alone" Scott said with a wry smile.

When Lucy arrived home later that night, she fell into bed exhausted. Mrs Armstrong had made her a sandwich and a mug of cocoa, whilst Ben ran her a bath. The next morning, she was awoken early by the sound of her bedroom door opening and two little voices screaming "Surprise!", as they charged across the room. "Jake, Emily, how did you get here?!" She cried, throwing her arms around them. "Bob and Sue brought us back! We got up really early and it was still dark!" Exclaimed Jake. "Oh that's wonderful! I've missed you so much" said Lucy, hugging them both even tighter. "I spoke to Sue while you were in the bath last night" confessed Ben with a grin. "The kids are staying with their grandparents for the weekend, so I suggested Bob and Sue might like to stay with us. You don't mind do you?" Ben asked. "Mind? Of course not that's a lovely idea" cried Lucy happily. "DCI Fields also mentioned yesterday that Ray and Pete are in court today, he thought you would have enough on your plate" said Ben. "Oh okay" said Lucy, the reality of everything that had happened coming back to her again. "Do you know what time?" She asked quietly. "DCI Fields said that he should think there will be news by lunch time" Ben told her. She nodded solemnly, "Right you two go and find Leah, I'll get dressed and I'll be straight down." Lucy said. "Leah!" They both chorused, rushing for the door.

Lucy and Ben dressed and were sitting enjoying a late breakfast by the time Jake and Emily came through the back door, followed by a puffing Sue and a rather red faced Bob bringing up the rear. "We've been playing football!" Cried Jake happily. "Well they've been playing, we barely got near the ball" laughed Sue, collapsing onto a chair. "Yes, definitely not as young as we used to be" agreed Bob. The kitchen door opened and Janet rushed in, "Oh Lucy thank goodness you're okay" she cried, locking her in a tight embrace. "I'm fine honestly" Lucy said. "Tom's just filled us in on everything that happened" DCI Fields had been keeping him up to speed,

"I just can't believe it" said Frank. "Lucy, I'm going to get off to the court. I want to hear what happens" Tom told her. "Okay" she replied. "Do you want to come?" Tom asked. She shook her head, "No thank you, I want to be with the children. Those people are in my past" said Lucy determinedly. "That's exactly right, they are" Tom agreed.

"I made up a bed for your guests" said Mrs Armstrong, coming back into the room. "Thank you Margaret, Ben would you show Bob and Sue where to put their things please?" She asked. Before he had chance to answer, there was the sound of running feet in the hallway, the door burst open and Nick appeared. "Lucy!" He cried, giving her a hug. "What happened to mum?" She grinned. "I didn't know after everything that has happened you'd still be comfortable with that" said Nick shyly. "Of course I would, it's a lovely gesture I think" said Lucy. "So do I" said a female voice from the doorway. Everyone turned to see Nick's real mum Julie standing there. "Julie?" Gasped Ben. "I'm sorry to intrude, but Nick's been so worried. We set off first thing" she said. "That's very good of you" Ben replied. "I won't stay. I just wanted to tell you I'm really glad you're okay Lucy" said Julie earnestly. "Nonsense, please stay for a while. Why not have lunch with us later? I feel we owe you an explanation" said Lucy. "No of course you don't, and from what Nick's been telling me on the way here, you've certainly had very good reason" Julie declared. "Thank you for understanding" Lucy said.

Julie did decide to stay, and as she and Lucy sat on the patio 15 minutes later, watching everyone else compete in a mammoth game of football, "I'm really glad things have come good in the end, it's important to me that Nick's happy and I can see he is with you all" smiled Julie wistfully. Lucy shifted uncomfortably in her seat, "He's a lovely boy. A real credit to you. I hope you realise I meant nothing by that mum business earlier" she said. "No I know you didn't" Julie replied, hugging Nick who had just joined them with all the other thirsty players, for a well earned half time drink. "You're both very important to me, mum for bringing me up and being there for me, and Lucy for being there for me ever since we've met. You've become very special to me over the years, my two favourite girls" said Nick, putting an arm round each one of them. "What about me?" Asked Emily. "Oh no, you're my very very favourite" said Nick, picking her up and swinging her round as she giggled happily. Lucy explained the goings on of the last few weeks to Julie over lunch, with everyone else adding in the details that she might have missed. "Oh my god!" Julie exclaimed when she'd finished. "Yes it certainly has been a very hard time" said Lucy nodding.

Just then, her mobile rang, "Excuse me, it's DCI Fields" she said, hurrying out into the hallway. When she returned five minutes later, everyone was looking at her expectantly. "DCI Fields has just come from the court room, Pete was given a 2 year suspended sentence, providing he undertakes a drink and drugs rehabilitation programme" she said. "Drugs?" Asked Nick. "Yes, apparently he has been mixing prescription anti-depressants and drink since his wife left him. And they feel that although his involvement wasn't big, it could have had catastrophic consequences" said Lucy. "Thankfully it didn't!" Declared Janet, voicing what everyone was thinking. "Ray on the other hand received a 10 year prison sentence for his involvement, with the scaffold lorry incident, hitting Jeff and Tom, and for trying to run us off the road" said Lucy. "Good" said Frank approvingly. "DCI Fields said that the judge accepted that he had been so worried by his father's behaviour, that he had been at his wit's end. Ray had said that his father never had any money, they were behind with their rent and other bills, they had no food in the house. Pete had spent money on other things, with Ray not finding out until debt collectors came knocking and utilities were disconnected. Ray had been desperate for money" Finished Lucy. "Oh I almost feel sorry for him" said Mrs Armstrong. "So do I" Janet agreed. "The judge insisted on a custodial sentence, saying that however desperate Ray had been, there was no excuse for endangering life. He said this way Ray would hopefully have some much needed time away from the pressures of supporting his father, and that Pete would learn to cope again when he comes out of the residential help course they were sending him on" said Lucy. "Well at least you now have closure on two of them" said Ben. "Yes I know, DCI Fields said Avril is in court on Monday" she said quietly.

The rest of the afternoon passed uneventfully, and just after four, they waved Julie off down the driveway. Lucy and she had got a lot of things sorted over the last few hours, she'd always liked Julie, but still kept that step back, not wanting to interfere where Nick was concerned. Julie had explained that in her opinion, she and Ben were always more like best friends than husband and wife. They had just been too young, she felt. Julie had told her that she was so glad that Lucy and Ben were so happy, and that she loved her new husband Phil very much. Although he was often not the easiest man to understand, even he and Nick had seemed to have found some common ground. They had spent a long time discussing their differences last night, hearing what had happened to Lucy really seemed to have brought this into perspective for them. Both men had shook hands and agreed to wipe the slate clean and start again. Lucy and her family, with Bob and Sue, spent a lovely weekend, just enjoying each other's company. Lucy and Ben visited Jonathan on Saturday and he was extremely pleased to see them. Although his sad eyes clouded when he realised Phyllis wasn't there, but he was ecstatic when he and Ben sailed the Phyllis Rose together. Sunday lunch was had by all at the Yew Tree, it was very strange going back in there, but Lucy knew this was another demon from her past that she had to overcome. On Monday morning they waved goodbye to Bob and Sue, they were calling in at Sue's parents to retrieve their offspring, who they were sure would have been suitably spoilt by their grandparents all weekend.

That afternoon, Lucy sat in the courtroom holding Ben's hand, waiting for the judge's summing up and sentencing. Avril looked so small and lost, she looked terrified. Everyone rose as the judge entered the room, "Miss Snow" he began. "I really hope he understands what she's been through" whispered Lucy worriedly. Ben squeezed his wife's hand and smiled proudly. She really was the most amazing woman. Even after everything she had been through, she still had compassion, her first thought was for someone else. The judge cleared his throat and continued. "I have given great consideration to everything you have been through and even after all the evidence your defence have put before this court, you cannot change the fact that you attempted to abduct a child. So it was my initial view, a custodial sentence was the only way forward" he said. Avril let out a sob, "Please no" whispered Lucy. "However, I cannot ignore the remarkable compassion and understanding shown to you by the Reid family. Especially Lucy Reid. Even offering you a place to stay. Their understanding has shown no bounds. I also feel that you were of previous good character, and it was your fear of Fred Reid and his accomplices, and your fear for the safety of your mother and uncle, that brought you to act in the way you did. It is with this in mind, that I am sentencing you to 12 months imprisonment, suspended for 2 years" said the judge. "Thank god" said Lucy in relief.

Avril just stood there shell-shocked, staring ahead. "Miss Snow, you are free to go" said the judge, a little more softly this time. When Lucy got outside, Avril and her barrister were waiting. "Mrs Reid, how can I ever thank you enough?" Said Avril. Lucy took both of Avril's hands in hers, "The only thanks I need is to see you make something of yourself" she said. "My legal team have all the keys and documentations of Primrose Hill, be happy there" said Lucy kindly. "Thank you" said Avril again. Lucy nodded, put her arm through Ben's and turned and walked away. "Oh a surprise came for you when you were out, I put it in the living room" said Mrs Armstrong, as they came through the front door of Hilltop Manor. Lucy hurried down the hallway to the living room, and opened the door. "Amira, Paul!" She cried happily. "Hi Lucy" said Amira, coming to give her a big hug. "Hi Lucy" smiled Paul, giving her a kiss on the cheek. "I wasn't expecting you so soon, I thought you'd be unpacking" Lucy laughed. "Paul rang the station as soon as we landed and after Suzanne told us what happened, we came straight here" said Amira. "Yes, it's so hard to believe isn't it?" Said Lucy. "Even harder for you to have to live through it" said Amira earnestly. The door opened and Jake and Emily came running in. "Mummy!" They cried together, "Amira!" Exclaimed Jake, spotting her. "Paul!" Squealed Emily, seeing him standing behind her. Poor Jake and Emily were so excited they didn't know who to hug first.

Everyone settled into life at Hilltop Manor, it was normal and uneventful, just how Lucy liked it, with time to do things as a family. Two weeks later, Lucy found herself sitting back in the courtroom. This time staring at a much less remorseful character, as everyone stood when the judge entered the room, Fred Reid remained seated. He was grinning wildly around the court and as his gaze met Lucy's he blew her a big kiss. She shuddered with distaste. Fred had made everyone take the stand to relive the whole ordeal, as he was still maintaining his innocence, they had all been called to give evidence.

Most people in Fred's situation would have been terrified, but not him. He seemed to view it all as a game. The policeman standing by Fred was saying something to him, while he just continued to grin and sat fast in his seat. Eventually he rose, and slouched sullenly on the wooden ledge in front of him. "Stand up!" Ordered the judge, taking Fred so much by surprise that he actually did what he was told at last. "Are you Frederick Arthur Reid?" The usher asked. "If I say no can I go home?" Asked Fred, roaring with laughter. "Silence!" Shouted the judge. "Okay, okay keep your wig on" said Fred grinning. "That's enough. If I have to tell you again, you will be held in contempt of court, and I shall delay your hearing" roared the judge. That soon made Fred sit up and take notice. Lucy was stunned to realise that Fred actually still believed that he would be walking free today. Fred kept up this devil may care attitude throughout the trial, but was always very careful not to try the judge's patience too much. Fred didn't seem quite so sure of himself when the jury retired to consider their verdict. In just two hours, the foreman of the jury rose to his feet back inside the courtroom. The list of charges were read out and the court usher addressed the foreman. On every charge, when asked "How do you find the defendant?", the foreman replied, "Guilty". A murmur of agreement went round the courtroom. Each jury member had agreed that Fred was guilty, Lucy let out a huge sigh of relief. The Fred that was lead away to await sentencing, whilst the judge waited for all the relevant reports, was a different man. Still self-assured, but not quite so opinioned. Lucy still got the feeling though, he still hadn't let himself consider that he was going to prison.

Lucy did have to admit, that the Fred Reid that stood before the judge waiting to hear his fate a few weeks later, was a shadow of his former self. Instead of the loud, obnoxious comments, Fred sat silently in the dock, head bowed. When the judge began to address him, he barely glanced up. "Mr Reid, I have read with great interest all the reports and evidence put before me, and it is my opinion that you behaved how you did deliberately. You continually broke the law, endangered lives and terrorised the Reid family and its acquaintances willingly and without any thought for them, or even showing any signs of remorse for your actions" the judge continued. Everyone in the court listened in silence, as the list of charges Fred had been found guilty of were read out. Everything seemed to go in slow motion for Lucy, she began to shake, her ears felt like she was listening under water, her vision began to blur, she could feel herself falling…"Lucy, Lucy" she heard Ben's voice as she opened her eyes. "Oh thank god" said

Tom. Lucy looked around slowly, she was sitting in an armchair in what looked like an office. A paramedic stood over her, looking down at her with concern, "Where am I?" Lucy asked quietly. "You're in an office at the court Mrs Reid, you fainted. How are you feeling?" Said the man. "Much better thank you, I'm so sorry to put you to any trouble" Lucy said. "Not at all, with what you've been through, this was a natural reaction to the news I should think" said the paramedic kindly.

"Fred, they've not let him out have they?" asked Lucy, suddenly remembering and sitting up in panic. "Take it easy" said Ben, easing her back down into the chair. "No Lucy, they've not let him go. Fred Reid was sentenced to 10 years" said Tom. The weeks ticked by and although Lucy tried to function normally, life was still overshadowed by the forthcoming sentencing of Rose, Sean and of course Phyllis. There had been some sort of delay in receiving one of the reports in Phyllis' case, so the next sentencing she found herself back in court for was Sean's. As they sat waiting for the judge to enter, Lucy glanced sideways to where Scott was sitting. He had thankfully made a full recovery from his ordeal with Rose. She couldn't help thinking how hard this must be for him, after all, when all was said and done, Sean was his relation. She looked at his handsome face, his perfectly chiselled jaw set in a straight line, giving nothing away to how he was feeling.

"All rise" said the court usher. Lucy looked at Sean sitting hunched in the dock, he hadn't said a word when he had appeared in court previously, only to confirm his name and say how he was pleading. Sean appeared equally silent today. "Mr Lewis" the judge finally addressed him. "I'm sorry" said Sean, promptly bursting into tears. Lucy was shocked, she certainly hadn't expected that. His barrister passed him a box of tissues and the judge remained silent, giving him a few moments to compose himself. Finally Sean's sobs subsided and the judge continued, "Mr Lewis, it is to your credit that you have shown remorse for your actions, and all reports and evidence put before me backs that up. However, I cannot ignore the seriousness of the crimes you have committed" he said. Sean's charges were read out to him again and at the end he raised his head, looked directly at Lucy and said "I'm so sorry". She looked back at this man, and again he just looked like the small boy that he had done when he was awaiting instruction from Rose back at Hilltop Manor.

The judge cleared his throat and continued, "It seems to me that however remorseful you may be now, you were still part of an organised ring of crime. I do accept though, the psychiatric opinion that you found yourself led by a more forceful third party" he continued. "Rose" whispered Lucy. She had seen for herself just how powerless Sean was against her, she was a much brighter character academically than him and he did everything she said. Rose seemed to use Sean's love and admiration of her to get him to do everything she wanted. The judge went on to explain that Sean was found to have been involved in a fight when he was in prison previously, he had been beaten to a pulp by a fellow inmate, and no one had ever admitted why. Sean had suffered mild brain damage as a result of the attack, but not one of the inmates had revealed who the perpetrator of this vicious assault was, and Sean said he couldn't remember. That was, not until he had undergone a new form of intense questioning by a young psychiatrist emerging in this field. Lucy recoiled in horror as the judge revealed that this man had helped Sean remember his attacker had in fact been Fred Reid. The psychiatrist further revealed it was likely that Sean had subconsciously blocked this out, but it was always there in the background of his mind. "Oh my god" gasped Ben. "Taking all of these things into account, I sentence you to 8 years imprisonment, take him down" Finished the judge. "No, I'm not going back there" cried Sean, struggling for all he was worth against the two prison guards that lead him away. Lucy breathed a sigh of relief, allowing herself to believe just one more little bit that this really was almost over.

CHAPTER 20

WHERE'S PHYLLIS?

Another two weeks passed with still no sign of a trial date for Phyllis, Lucy couldn't understand why she hadn't been mentioned. It was as if she had been forgotten. There was a knock at the living room door, "Lucy, DCI Fields is here to see you" said Mrs Armstrong. "Oh hello, I wasn't expecting you" said Lucy, as the DCI came into the room. "Hello Lucy, I need to speak to you. Is Ben here?" He asked uncomfortably. "Yes, he's upstairs. Is something wrong?" Asked Lucy. "Shall I call him?" Asked Mrs Armstrong. "Yes please" Nodded the DCI. "Take a seat" offered Lucy worriedly. "DCI Fields" said Ben, coming into the room and shaking his hand. "Hello Mr Reid, I just wanted a quick word with you both" said DCI Fields. "We heard back today from the authorities about Avril's application to have Jonathan home to live with her. I'm afraid it was turned down" he said. "Oh no, why?" Exclaimed Lucy. "It was decided that Jonathan has been away from life outside the care home for so long that he would need time to readjust. With Avril still seeing her psychiatrist, it was felt that at this point, she would struggle to cope with his needs alone" the DCI continued. "That's a real shame, what does that mean for them now?" Asked Ben. "For now, Jonathan will remain where he is whilst Avril continues her therapy" DCI Fields added. "Maybe the authorities will rethink it when Phyllis' case comes to court, if she doesn't receive a custodial sentence?", suggested Lucy. DCI Fields looked decidedly uncomfortable, "Rose is in court tomorrow, I can't stop you Lucy, but it's my advice that you don't attend the hearing" he said. "Psychiatric reports have deemed Rose perfectly fit to stand trial, and in a nutshell they've confirmed she is a hundred per cent responsible for her actions. It's just, in my opinion again, Rose hasn't mellowed at all in her time on remand. She has a vicious tongue and doesn't miss an opportunity to use it. I just feel that as a family you have been through enough, why relive it all unnecessarily?" The DCI finished.

"DCI Fields has a point Lucy" said Ben in agreement. "We know that Rose is going to prison, it's just a question of how long." "Well we were planning to go out for the day tomorrow, and I have to be honest I wasn't looking forward to seeing Rose again" said Lucy with a shudder. "Then don't go. DS Lowe and I will be there anyway" said DCI Fields. "Won't Lucy have to give evidence?" Asked Ben. "No, as Rose is pleading guilty, the CPS are happy to proceed using Lucy's statement for her part" he said. "Okay, I won't go" Lucy concluded. "Now DCI Fields, what about Phyllis? Everyone else has come to court apart from her" Lucy said. DCI Fields looked uncomfortable again. "Lucy, we don't know if or when Phyllis will stand trial" he said solemnly. "But why?", she asked. "It was decided not to tell you as it was felt you had a lot on your plate, we didn't want to worry or cause you any more stress" said the DCI. "What's happened? Is Phyllis okay?" Lucy exclaimed. "Phyllis is very ill and has been for some time now. She caught a strain of a viral infection, the doctors have said. It turned to flu, and then pneumonia. We thought Phyllis was beating it, but I'm not a medical man, I don't understand how, but the infection has spread to her blood" said DCI Fields. "Oh my god no, poor Phyllis" said Lucy.

Despite all that had happened, she had a soft spot for her. Lucy had told Ben over and over again that she didn't believe Phyllis was a bad person, and that she had done all that she had through intense fear and desperation. "Will she be okay?" Asked Ben. "The honest answer is, I don't know. All I know is that we've been told the next few hours are crucial" said DCI Fields. "What about Jonathan, does he know?" Asked Lucy in concern. "Yes he does, Jonathan was told a few days ago, and has taken it very badly. He is refusing to come out of the residential home with any of us to see her. The nurse says it's fear that he doesn't know us, and confusion over what has happened to Phyllis" he said. "Oh my god, poor Jonathan, he must be terrified" Lucy said. "Let me try" said Ben suddenly. "Sorry?" Said the DCI, looking at Ben questioningly. "Let me try. Jonathan and I have started to build a good relationship in the times I've seen him. Let me see if he will visit Phyllis with me" Ben said. "Ben, that's a wonderful idea" Lucy declared. DCI Fields thought for a minute, "It's worth a try" he said with a nod. "Are we going to be allowed to see Phyllis, as we've both done statements for the prosecution?" Said Ben suddenly. "Yes, I'm sure I can get that agreed under the circumstances. Phyllis is hardly in any fit state to cause any issues" said DCI Fields grimly.

"Is Phyllis alone?" Asked Lucy in concern. "No, Avril is with her permanently. She's refusing to go home, we've had to send an officer to collect some clothes from Primrose Hill and the hospital are letting her use the facilities there. Understandably, Avril is taking this very hard" said DCI Fields. "The poor girl" said Lucy in despair. "When can I see Jonathan?" Asked Ben. "Let me make a phone call, I need to see when I can arrange it and get it logged what we're doing" said DCI Fields. Lucy watched as he took his mobile out of his pocket and walked out onto the patio. He was soon deep in conversation. "Are you okay?" She asked Ben, putting a hand on his arm. "Yes, I just can't believe all this. It just never stops does it?" Sighed Ben. "That's all settled" said the DCI, coming back into the living room. "The residential home have said that as soon as you can make it, at any time, is fine. They said Jonathan is in a really bad way, and he has not eaten for two days now either" added DCI Fields. "We'll go there now" said Ben, standing up. "Now? Are you sure?" Asked the DCI in surprise. "Quite sure" nodded Ben determinedly.

It was just after lunch when Lucy and Ben walked into the reception at Whitelea. "Mr and Mrs Reid, thank you for coming" said Lily after the receptionist had called her. "How's Jonathan?" Lucy asked. "He's no better I'm afraid. Not eating and barely speaking. It is heart breaking seeing him so sad" said Lily. "Can we see him please?" Asked Ben. "Of course" said Lily, leading the way. She stopped outside Jonathan's door, knocked, but receiving no answer, opened it and went in. He was sitting by the window in the same position as when Lucy and Ben had first met him. It was almost as if time had stood still, he didn't look up when they came in. Ben walked slowly over to him and placed a hand on his shoulder, "Hello mate" he said softly. Hearing a voice he recognised, Jonathan looked up, those big sad eyes gazing into Ben's. "Ben" said Jonathan. "How are you?" Asked Ben, sitting down next to him. Jonathan didn't answer. "Hello Jonathan" said Lucy, sitting down in the chair opposite. He looked at her briefly and smiled. "What's this I hear you're not eating Jonathan?" Asked

Ben brightly. "No point" he replied quietly. "Of course there's a point. You don't want to end up ill do you?" Ben said. Jonathan turned his head and began to stare out of the window again.

Ben took a deep breath and tried again, "Lily tells me you won't let them take you to see Phyllis. Why's that mate? Don't you want to see her?" He asked gently. "They don't want to take me to see Phyllis, they want to take me away from here. Phyllis is dead" sobbed Jonathan. Ben leapt from his seat and hugged Jonathan to him, "Phyllis isn't dead mate, whatever made you think that?" He asked. "She is, she is. I heard Lily talking to the police" Jonathan wailed inconsolably. Ben knelt down in front of Jonathan and took both of his hands in his, "Look at me" he said softly. Jonathan raised his head slowly, until his tear glazed eyes met Ben's. "She's dead" he whispered. "Jonathan, I don't know what you think you've heard, but Phyllis is not dead. She's not very well at all, but she is definitely alive" said Ben firmly. Jonathan stared at Ben, pain, confusion, hurt all crossing his face at once. "Really?" He asked. "Really" said Ben with a smile. "Can I see her?" Asked Jonathan. "Of course you can, I'll take you to her now" said Ben. Lucy and Lily breathed a sigh of relief. "Can we go in your car? Is it blue?" Asked Jonathan. "Yes we can go in my car, and it's blue" laughed Ben. "Good, I like blue. Where's my coat?" Asked Jonathan smiling. "Not so fast mister, I need you to do something for me first" said Ben. "What?" Asked Jonathan in surprise. "The lady has just put your dinner on the table, I want you to eat it before we go" said Ben.

Jonathan looked unsure, "But I want to see Phyllis" he protested. "You will see her, but I don't want you making yourself ill. What would Phyllis say if she knew you hadn't been eating?" Ben said. "She would be very cross with me" Jonathan smiled. "Exactly" said Ben. "Okay, I'll eat it. You won't tell Phyllis I've not been eating will you?" Asked Jonathan, his eyes wide. "Our secret mate, I won't say a word. Now eat up, it's shepherd's pie and apple crumble" Ben said, pushing Jonathan over to the table and taking the cover off of his meal. "My favourite" Jonathan declared, starting to eat. "Mine too" smiled Ben, giving Lucy and Lily the thumbs up over his head.

After Jonathan had eaten, Ben helped him into the car and put his wheelchair into the boot. Lily was coming as well, so that way at least Jonathan had someone familiar with him. When Ben pulled up outside the hospital, he switched off the engine and turned round to look at Jonathan.

"I'm going to see Phyllis" said Jonathan excitedly. "You certainly are, but I need to explain something to you first" Ben said gently. "What? It's Phyllis isn't it? She's dead" Cried Jonathan, his eyes filling with tears. "No, no, no, Phyllis is not dead but she is very ill. When you see her she won't be able to speak to you because she's asleep" Ben told him. "Yes but she can wake up when I get there" said Jonathan. "I wish it were that simple mate. No, Phyllis is asleep to try and help her get better, and she can't wake up until she's feeling better." Ben said, hoping Jonathan understood. Jonathan nodded, "Phyllis always says sleep is the best thing for you when you aren't feeling well" he declared. "Yes that's exactly right, but when you see Phyllis she's not only going to be asleep. There will probably be a lot of pipes and tubes connected to her and machines around her making lots of different noises. I don't want you to panic though, as these things aren't hurting Phyllis, they're trying to make her better." Said Ben softly. "Okay" said Jonathan, nodding again.

Ben wasn't quite sure if Jonathan completely understood, but he had done his best to prepare him as much as he could. "Come on then, let's go and see Phyllis" said Ben cheerily. Jonathan chattered happily about all the things he was going to tell Phyllis as Ben pushed him along. Lucy and Lily walked behind, "I can't thank you and Ben enough. I know how difficult it must be under the circumstances" Lily said. "Jonathan's become very important to me since I've been at Whitelea, he's a lovely person" "He certainly is" agreed Lucy. Ben buzzed the buzzer at the entrance to the ward. "Yes?" Asked the lady that answered. "I have Phyllis Kramer's brother Jonathan here to see her. "I believe you've been expecting us" he said. "Yes we have, please come in" said the lady.

As they stepped inside the door, a nurse came to meet them. Lucy recognised her voice from the buzzer, "Follow me please. Phyllis is in here" she said, stopping outside the door at the end of the corridor. Ben opened it and wheeled Jonathan inside, "Are you going to say hello to Phyllis?" Asked Lily gently. "She's sleeping" said Jonathan. "The doctor said we should all talk to Phyllis as she can probably still hear us" said the nurse. "Even when she's sleeping?" Asked Jonathan doubtfully. "Yes" said Ben with a smile. "What should I say?" Asked Jonathan shyly. "I'd tell her about how much you've missed her and what you've been doing at Whitelea. Oh and don't forget to tell her how good the Phyllis Rose is looking" said Ben. Jonathan looked at Phyllis, "Can I hold her hand?" He asked. "Of course you can, I'm sure she'd like that" Ben smiled. Jonathan gently took her hand between both of his. "Hello Phyllis, it's me Jonathan. I've really missed you. No one told me why you didn't come to see me. I thought you were dead but Ben said you're not. He said you're just sleeping, you can wake up now though. I want to tell you about my drawing" he said, raising his head expectantly, as if waiting for Phyllis to open her eyes. "That's it mate, you're doing great. Keep talking to Phyllis as if she were awake" Urged Ben.

"Okay Phyllis, you sleep for a bit longer if you're still tired. Because I know you're not going to die, you can wake up soon and we can all go home" said Jonathan. Lucy turned and looked out of the window so that Jonathan couldn't see her crying, this was so hard to listen to. It would break Jonathan's heart if anything happened to Phyllis, or even if she just goes to prison. Lucy knew that Jonathan could probably visit, but nowhere near as much as he had been used to seeing her in the past. This was why Jonathan was taking not seeing Phyllis so hard whilst she had been on remand and then ill. "Shall we let Phyllis sleep some more now?" Lily asked gently, placing a hand on Jonathan's shoulder. "No not yet, I want to tell her about my drawing" Jonathan insisted. "Okay" Lily said softly. "I've been doing a drawing for you Phyllis, it's not very good but it's of you, me and Avril when I come home to live with you soon" said Jonathan with a beaming smile. Lucy bit her lip hard, this was heart wrenching. "This is so sad, someone needs to try explaining all this to Jonathan again, he needs to understand" whispered Lucy to Lily. "I know, I'll try later" she nodded.

As Ben settled Jonathan back into his wheelchair from the car later that day at Whitelea, Jonathan turned to him. "Thank you" he said, giving him a hug. "What for?" Ben laughed. "For letting me see Phyllis" he smiled. "No problem, and you can go and see her tomorrow as well. Lily is going to arrange for someone to drive you" Ben said. Jonathan's face fell, "I thought you would take me" he said to Ben. "No Jonathan, Ben can't take you every day" said Lily gently. "Why not? He's my friend" Jonathan said. "Of course I'm your friend, but I took you today and now you know where everything is you'll be fine" said Ben brightly. "I don't want to go with anyone else, please take me Ben, please" said Jonathan. Ben looked at Lucy and she smiled back, "Okay, I'll be here at 12 tomorrow" he told Jonathan. "Oh thank you, thank you" he cried.

As Lucy and Ben drove home, he was very quiet. "What's up?" Lucy asked. "Do you know I don't understand entirely about Jonathan's condition, but he's a very remarkable man. One minute he seems to be very hard to get close to, void of emotion and doesn't seem to take anything in and avoids physical contact at all costs, then the next he seems wordly wise and able to understand everything" Ben replied. "Yeah I know exactly what you mean" said Lucy nodding. The next day, as Jonathan sat at Phyllis' bedside, he was much more self-assured, chatting away to Phyllis as if she were awake. "How much longer is it going to be until you wake up Phyllis? You can't still be tired" Jonathan said. "Phyllis still needs her sleep, remember what we talked about" said Lily. "Oh okay, you sleep. I know you're listening anyway. Lily said that some people made you do some bad things and you might have to go to prison for a while. She said I could still see you sometimes though" Jonathan reached out and took Phyllis' hand. "Doesn't matter though, because I know you won't go to prison. You aren't bad, you're kind and I love you. The man with the wig that Lily told me about will see you're kind too" finished Jonathan.

Lucy, Ben and Lily looked at each other in despair, they hated seeing Jonathan set himself up for a fall. They had tried to explain though and were at a loss of what else to do. Jonathan chattered away happily for the next hour, then kissed Phyllis' hand tenderly as he said goodbye. Lucy switched on her mobile again as she got back into the car, looked at it and frowned. "I've missed a call from DCI Fields" she said, glancing at Ben worriedly. Lucy knew that DCI Fields would be ringing to tell her the outcome of Rose's court appearance. "Ring him back" said Ben quietly. Lucy flipped the phone back to open and scrolled through the contacts until she came to DCI Fields' number. Taking a deep breath she pressed dial and listened as the phone began to ring at the other end.

"Hi Lucy" said the DCI. "Hello, I'm sorry I missed your call, we were at the hospital with Jonathan." She answered. "How is Phyllis?" Asked DCI Fields. "No change I'm afraid" she replied. "The judge decided to do all sentencing today, and reports had already been sought on Rose due to the seriousness of the crimes and the callous unpredictable way in which she was acting. Lucy, Rose was given 15 years" said DCI Fields. "Thank you for letting me know, I appreciate it" Lucy said. When she and DCI Fields said goodbye, she placed the phone back in her handbag. "Lucy?" Said Ben taking her hand. "15 years" she said softly. "That's good news, Rose was a very dangerous woman" said Ben squeezing her hand comfortingly. As the days passed, Ben took Jonathan to visit Phyllis every day. He just got too upset at the thought of having someone else take him. Phyllis had started to respond well to treatment and although there were very short periods when she was awake, they just never seemed to coincide with when Jonathan was there. One Sunday afternoon a week later, Jonathan was sitting at Phyllis' bedside, telling her all about the apple crumble that Lily had helped him make the day before, when Phyllis opened her eyes. "Jonathan" she said slowly. "Phyllis, look Ben, Phyllis is awake! She's not tired anymore!" Said Jonathan excitedly. "That's great news mate. How are you Phyllis?" Asked Ben, coming to stand beside Jonathan. "Mr Reid, it's lovely to see you" said Phyllis in a low voice. "Mrs Kramer, please don't try to talk too much. You need to rest" said the doctor who Lily had gone to tell Phyllis was awake.

"Hello Phyllis" said Lucy, who had been sitting in the armchair in the corner. "Lucy, I'm so sorry" said Phyllis, a tear escaping down her cheek. "I'm sorry but I really think we should leave Phyllis to rest now, she needs to regain her strength" said the doctor. "But Phyllis isn't tired anymore" protested Jonathan. "Come on now, we can come and see Phyllis again tomorrow" coaxed Lily. Jonathan looked at Phyllis who nodded her head gently at him, "Go on" she whispered. "Okay, I'll be back tomorrow, and I'll bring the Phyllis Rose too" said Jonathan. Phyllis smiled weakly as Ben pushed his wheelchair out of the room. The next few days passed quite uneventfully, with Ben spending his mornings with his family, and his afternoons taking Jonathan to visit Phyllis. Now that she was growing stronger, Ben thought it was best for him to wait for Jonathan in the hospital waiting room. He didn't feel it right to be as close to Phyllis, in view of her forthcoming court appearance. Ben had tried to explain to Jonathan that it would be better to let Lily bring him now, but he didn't seem to want to let go. Lily had tried to talk to Jonathan about it as well, but all to no avail.

Ben had explained his worries to Lucy, and she could see how uncomfortable her husband was with things. When they arrived at the hospital the next day, Lucy asked Ben to take Jonathan to the hospital shop to get Phyllis some magazines. She wanted chance for a word with Phyllis alone. When she arrived at Phyllis' room, she was sitting up in bed. "Lucy" she smiled broadly. "Hello Phyllis" said Lucy. "How lovely to see you" Phyllis replied. "I need to talk to you about Jonathan" Lucy said. "Is he okay?" Asked Phyllis looking worried. "He's fine, it's just we don't think Ben should keep bringing him to visit. DCI Fields overlooked things when you were ill and because of Jonathan's difficulties, but in view of the court case, we shouldn't still be seeing you. Ben and Lily have tried to explain things to Jonathan, but he doesn't understand. He feels that Ben is his friend and wants him to bring him to visit you each day. Ben's very fond of Jonathan, but he doesn't feel it's fair on him to be becoming so reliant on him. He's worried because we have no way of knowing how things will turn out. Do you understand what I'm trying to say Phyllis?" Asked Lucy earnestly. Phyllis was silent for a moment, "Yes of course, I'll speak to him" she said quietly.

At that moment, the door opened and Jonathan appeared with Ben and Lily. "Phyllis, you're awake!" Cried Jonathan. "I'll leave you to it" said Ben, making for the door. Ben, Lucy and Lily walked down to the hospital canteen together. "I'll get us some teas" Lily said. "Do you know I think I'll try one of those roast dinners that Ben keeps telling me are so amazing as well" said Lucy laughing. "Three roast dinners as well then" said Lily. "What did you want to talk to Phyllis about?" Asked Ben, as they waited for Lily to return. "I've tried to explain to Phyllis that we need her to talk to Jonathan about Lily bringing him to visit in future" Lucy said. "Any luck?" Ben asked. "She said that she would speak to him, so I think we'll have to play it by ear" Lucy replied. When they all returned to Phyllis' room an hour later, Jonathan was still chattering happily. "Are you ready?" Asked Ben chirpily. "Oh but I don't want to leave yet" said Jonathan. "No, I'm tired now. You go with Ben" insisted Phyllis. "Okay" said Jonathan in defeat. "Before you go, what have you got to say to Ben?" Asked Phyllis, squeezing Jonathan's hand. Jonathan gazed from Ben to Phyllis, then nodded his head slowly, "Phyllis said I need to be brave and let Lily bring me in future, she said you need to spend some time with your little boy and girl because they need you more than I do as they're only little" said Jonathan. "That's right, they do. But I'll still phone you and come and see you sometimes" said Ben. Jonathan didn't seem at all sure, but said okay. When Ben dropped him off that day, he realised just how close he and

Jonathan had become. He was going to miss him a lot, but really thought this way was best for Jonathan.

Ben rang him each Sunday, but didn't visit during the next month. He didn't want to confuse him. Jonathan seemed okay, he chattered excitedly about what he had been doing, until one day Lily rang, sounding very worried. "Hi Lily, is everything okay?" Ben asked. "No I don't think it is, we've just got back from the hospital. The doctors told Jonathan Phyllis is being moved back to the prison tomorrow. The infection caused a lot of problems with Phyllis, and she's spent a lot of time in bed. The doctor said they have done all they can for her now, and she needs specialist help from the physiotherapists, to build up her muscles" she said. "Well that bit's good news isn't it? Surely it must mean she is getting better" said Ben. "Yes it does, but the only prison with the facilities Phyllis will need nearby is over 200 miles away" finished Lily. "Oh no, surely there's something closer" said Ben in dismay. "No, it's the only prison with space available with a specialist facility that close, to allow Phyllis to attend as an outpatient" said Lily. "Poor Phyllis will never get any visitors and poor Jonathan, he must be so confused. How is he?" Asked Ben. "He's very down. The doctors said the Phyllis will only get to have a visitor once a fortnight" Said Lily. "That's terrible. Can I speak to Jonathan please?" Asked Ben. "Yes of course, I'll get him for you" said Lily. "Hello" came Jonathan's voice on the phone a few minutes later. "Hello mate, it's Ben. How are you doing?" He asked cheerily. "They're sending Phyllis to prison a long way away and I won't be able to see her" said Jonathan sadly. "I know, but Phyllis has to see special people to make her better, and they live a long way away" Ben said. "But I won't see her" wailed Jonathan. "Yes you will, just not as often" Ben reassured him.

"Phyllis has to go to prison. Phyllis is kind, she shouldn't be where they put the bad man. He'll hurt her" sobbed Jonathan. "No, she's not with any bad man, only ladies. She won't be hurt. But Phyllis does have to wait in the special part of the prison until she's well enough to see the judge. Do you remember the man with the wig that Lily told you about?" Asked Ben soothingly. "Yes, then when she sees him he'll know Phyllis is kind and she can come home and I can live with her and Avril" babbled Jonathan in one endless breath. Ben swallowed hard, "Yes, I'm sure there will be a time when you can all live together again" he said, hoping he was right for Jonathan's sake. "Lily said even though I can't see Phylis very much, I can write to her lots and send her drawings" said Jonathan. "Of course you can, I'm sure Phyllis will love that" Ben said. "Okay, I'll go and start my drawing for Phyllis now. I want her to go to see the special people, because I want her to get well and come home soon. I love her" Jonathan declared. "I know you do mate, and she loves you. Now you get off and do that drawing" said Ben. Jonathan said goodbye and handed the phone back to Lily. "Hello, thank you so much for talking to him Mr Reid. He's really brightened up just from speaking to you" she said gratefully. "Never a problem. Let me know how he is won't you?" Said Ben. "I will Mr Reid" Lily promised, putting the phone down.

CHAPTER 21

JUDGEMENT DAY

It was a long, hard road to recovery for Phyllis, but a year to the day from when she was charged, she finally appeared in court. Lucy looked over at Phyllis in the dock, and their eyes met. Phyllis eyed Lucy warily, then smiled for a moment. Lucy didn't know for a second how to react, then suddenly she realised she had no grudge against Phyllis, and smiled warmly back. She truly believed that Phyllis wasn't a bad person, she had naively allowed herself to become involved with a group far more manipulative than she had bargained on. "All rise" said the court usher as the judge entered the courtroom. "Are you Phyllis Rose Kramer?" The usher asked. "Yes" she replied. The usher read out what Phyllis was charged with, then everyone held their breath waiting for the answer to the next question. "Guilty" said Phyllis without any hesitation. As Lucy and the rest of the Reid family had given statements in the case, they would not normally have been permitted to sit in the court room until they had been called to give evidence, but as Phyllis had pleaded guilty there was no need for anyone to take the stand.

The judge cleared his throat, "Mrs Kramer, you have been involved in some serious crimes here, but it is to your credit that you have immediately admitted your guilt in them. This admittance has saved the recipients of these acts having to give evidence in court. I also understand from DCI Fields that you have been nothing but helpful during their investigations. I have had presented to me a number of reports about you, including one from a highly trusted psychologist in his field, prison and also ones from your medical teams. The psychology report states you to be a timid woman with low self-esteem, but perfectly understanding of right and wrong. The prison describes you as an exemplary inmate, both before your illness and after you returned from hospital, it states you were always friendly and helpful to the other prisoners, taking time to guide some of them with their reading and writing. The hospital doctor describes your illness in full complexity and feels that many months of physiotherapy are going to be needed to allow the maximum recovery possible. Finally, your physiotherapist says that although much of your treatment so far has been very intense, you have worked with them without complaint. They also feel that the walking stick you have with you in court today is likely to be something you will need for the rest of your life" he said.

The judge paused for a sip of water and re-sorted his notes. "How do you think it's going?" Whispered Ben. "I don't know, I honestly don't" whispered Lucy. "I've read the report from Whitelea Care Home where your brother resides, and of his wish to return home to live with you now that, shall we say, outside influences, are no longer present. I have also taken into consideration the statements of all the Reid family, and acquaintances that were involved, I don't think I've ever read such surprising findings. Each and every one of those statements are full of positive comments about you, that also includes statements from the officers involved in the case who came to know you well. I take my hat off to the sheer understanding and generosity of the entire Reid family, especially Lucy Reid. This woman has shown you nothing but compassion. I have received a letter from Lucy Reid offering you a job reference and a property to stay in, rent free, for a year. I believe your daughter is already residing at this property that Mr and Mrs Reid own. Is that still the case?" Asked the judge, glancing at the usher.

"Yes your honour" he replied. The judge looked through some papers on the desk in front of him, "The surprises still keep coming here. I have also a letter here from a Miss Lily Simms, who I believe is the main carer for your brother at Whitelea, is that correct?" Asked the judge, addressing Phyllis directly. "Yes she is sir" said Phyllis quietly. "Miss Simms has managed to arrange things with her employers to be able to work with Jonathan at home, if he were to be returned there, for three days a week for the first six months, which I should imagine would be a great help to you" "Yes" said Phyllis emotionally. "However, I have also received a letter passed to me by your counsel just this morning, from a Mr Frank Reid. Mr Reid is offering to pay a salary arranged on a live-in basis, for a daily carer to help with Jonathan for the next year, should you be released and Jonathan be allowed to return home. Mr Reid has spoken to Miss Simms, and she has agreed" said the judge. "Oh I can't believe it" said Phyllis, clasping her hand to her mouth in shock. Lucy glanced sideways at Frank, who caught her eye and gave her a wink. She smiled to herself, Ben and Frank were so alike, both perfect gentlemen and big softies at heart. She loved them both very much.

"Mrs Kramer, I shan't ask you to stand in view of your health, but you may if you wish" said the judge. Phyllis took a deep breath, gripped the sides of the box she was sitting in and pulled herself to her feet. "I'll stand sir" she said determinedly. "Very well, in my opinion Mrs Kramer, you are a very lucky woman. You have a family that love you and a clear network of support put in place by people who could so very easily have turned their back on you, which no one could blame them for. I do hope you realise that" said the judge. "I do sir" said Phyllis nodding. "However, I cannot ignore the seriousness of what you have done. I have given this a lot of thought and have taken into account your fear for the safety of yourself, your daughter and your brother, but still feel it only appropriate to issue a custodial sentence" said the judge gravely. Phyllis let out a sob, "No!" Cried Avril. "Please be quiet" ordered the judge. "I can't believe this" whispered Lucy quietly.

"In view of the complexity of this case, I have decided to issue a more fitting sentence. Phyllis Rose Kramer, I sentence you to 2 years imprisonment. This period will be served by means of a combination order, the first part you have already served awaiting trial, the second part, you will undertake a hundred hours of community service and be required to report to your probation officer or a local police station, three times a week. This method allows you to give something back to your community and allows your whereabouts to be noted for the remainder of your sentence. Mrs Kramer you must understand though, any breach of the law, or these terms and conditions will result in your return to prison" said the judge. Phyllis just stood there looking shell shocked, not seeming to be taking in what was going on around her. "Thank god" sighed Ben with relief. "Mrs

Kramer, you are free to go" said the judge. Avril burst into tears whilst Phyllis was being helped from the stand by her barrister.

As Lucy and Ben stood in the foyer of the court waiting for Frank, who was on his mobile telling Janet the outcome, Phyllis came out of the courtroom with her barrister. Avril clung to her arm still weeping, but this time tears of joy. Phyllis said something to Avril, then slowly walked towards Lucy and Ben. "Mr and Mrs Reid, I don't know how to thank you for all you've done. After everything, you've still been so kind, I don't deserve it" said Phyllis, her voice quivering with emotion. Lucy turned to look Phyllis square in the eyes. "Yes you do, don't ever think you aren't worthy Phyllis. Because that's what helped to get you into problems in the past. Think of this as a new start and don't let anyone force you back where you were. Take this chance Phyllis, and be lucky." Said Lucy, smiling to herself as she realised she had just used one of Great Aunt Maud's favourite parting phrases. "I will and thank you so much, both of you. Please thank your father for me Mr Reid" said Phyllis, her eyes glistening with tears. "I will do" nodded Ben. "Goodbye Phyllis" said Lucy as she and Ben began to walk away. "Lucy" called Phyllis. "Yes?" She said, turning back. "Do you think that maybe some day you could ever forgive me enough for us to be friends?" Asked Phyllis hopefully. Lucy looked at this frightened woman, unsure of her future, setting out for the first time in a very long while without someone dictating her movements, "Who knows Phyllis, who knows" she said with a smile. Lucy put her arm through Ben's as they went to find Frank.

3 weeks later, Ben received a phone call, "Hi Ben, it's Lily" said the voice. "Lily, how are you? How's Jonathan?" Ben asked. "It's Jonathan I'm calling you about, he has something he wants to tell you. Hang on and I'll put him on" said Lily. "Hello Ben" came Jonathan's voice down the line. "Hi mate, how are you?" Ben said. "I'm packing, I'm packing!" Cried Jonathan. "Packing? Why, where are you going?" Asked Ben in confusion. "I'm going to live with Phyllis! The man with the wig said I could. See, I knew he'd see what a nice lady Phyllis is!" Cried Jonathan excitedly. "That's great news mate, I'm really pleased for you" Replied Ben. "Lily's coming to live with us too!" Added Jonathan happily. "That's brilliant! Can I speak to Lily again please?" Asked Ben. "Will you come to see me at my new house?" Asked Jonathan. "Well I'm not sure about

that, but Lily has my new number so you can ring me any time" replied Ben chirpily. "But I want to see you" said Jonathan, his voice suddenly sad. "Maybe Lily can bring you to my house sometime" said Ben, trying to keep things cheery. "Yes, I'd like that. Lily wants to talk to you now. I've got to go and do some more packing" Jonathan said, sounding happy again. "Bye Jonathan" said Ben. "Hi Ben" said Lily coming back on the phone. "That's fantastic news for Jonathan, I'm sure Phyllis and Avril must be thrilled" said Ben. "They're over the moon, and as you can hear, Jonathan's so happy" Lily replied. "When are you going?" Ben asked. "In an hour" replied Lily. "Good luck, please let me know how Jonathan is" Ben said. "Of course, bye Ben".

Life for the Reids was a whirlwind of events for the next few months, Frank and Janet's house was finished on the plot next door, and they finally moved in to Maud's Manor. The family had spent ages discussing ideas for the name for their new home, but everyone was taken by surprise at the housewarming party. Frank said it was a down to earth name, in memory of a real down to earth lady. He said that people say home is where the heart is, and Maud will always have his heart. Nick and Leah got engaged and moved into Swallow Lodge, right beside Frank and Janet. That was Emily's choice, she had insisted on it, after seeing a swallow sitting on the driveway the first time she had gone to visit. Everyone liked that, it was such a pretty name. Nick was working towards setting up a business, trading in fine arts, he had found an advisor to help him in this field quite by chance, Mrs Armstrong's brother in law was a retired art dealer and auctioneer. Jake and Emily started school. Jeff was fully back on his feet now, but Bruce hadn't returned home. He kept extending that holiday by…just another few weeks. Lucy and Ben still saw a lot of Amira and Paul, especially as Amira was now on maternity leave. Hilltop Manor was seeing a lot more of Mr Benson now too, he and Mrs Armstrong were 'stepping out together' rather a lot, as Frank put it. He and Ben got great enjoyment out of teasing Mrs Armstrong mercilessly about Mr Benson being her boyfriend.

Lucy and Ben had refurbished the little cottage up in the top field, it looked lovely now, and they soon found a new tenant in Tom. Emily spent the whole time telling everyone that Tom lived at the bottom of her garden. As for Phyllis, Lily told Lucy and Ben that she'd arranged for her to do her community service at Whitelea, she was no threat to the residents there, and most of them knew her anyway from her time visiting Jonathan. Lily said that Mrs James, who ran Whitelea, was so pleased with her she had offered Phyllis work there two days a week, when Jonathan attended their drop in days. Lucy and Ben settled down to life at Hilltop Manor, and the days ticked peacefully by. One morning at breakfast, Ben noticed that Lucy was very quiet, she clearly had something on her mind. "Are you okay?" He asked, resting his hand on hers. "Not really, I didn't sleep well. I had a lot to think about" she said quietly. "Anything I can help with?" Ben asked concerned. "There's something I need to do today, will you come with me please? I've thought about this, and I really mean thought about it, and I know it's the right decision. It's time to move on, time to face my past head on" said Lucy determinedly. "Okay" said Ben nodding.

Although Lucy hadn't actually told him what she'd been thinking, there was no need for words. She could see he already knew. "Well, this is it" said Lucy, as they arrived at their destination an hour later. "Are you sure you want to do this?" Asked Ben. Lucy nodded, "Quite sure. But do you mind if I go in alone at first?" She asked. "Of course, I'll wait here" Ben replied. Taking a deep breath, Lucy opened the door and got out. She gazed up at the house, her mind a whirlwind of memories, she walked slowly up the drive towards the door, the gravel crunching under foot, Lucy reached up and took hold of the door knocker. For a second, it crossed her mind to turn and run, but no, she knocked. Seconds later, the door opened, "Mrs Reid!" Said the shocked voice. "Hello Phyllis" said Lucy. "What a lovely surprise, please come in" said Phyllis, stepping back out of the way and opening the door wide. Lucy smiled and stepped inside.

"Would you like a cup of tea?" Asked Phyllis, leading the way into the living room. "Thank you, tea no sugar please" said Lucy, taking a seat on the sofa. "I remember" said Phyllis, smiling uncertainly. As Lucy looked around the room, memories flooded back, the furniture may be different, but this place still felt warm and welcoming. The front door slammed, "Mum we're here!" Called a woman's voice that Lucy instantly recognised as Avril's. "Oh, Mrs Reid, h-h-hello" said Avril, stopping short as she came into the room. "Hello Avril" Lucy smiled. She looked so different to the last time that she had seen her, Avril was wearing jeans and a smart red baseball jacket, but above all, she looked happy and relaxed. "This is

Harrison" she said, introducing the shy looking young man who's hand she was holding. Harrison was wearing black jeans and a leather jacket, "I'm pleased to meet you" he said with a nervous smile. "You too" Lucy replied.

At that moment, Phyllis returned with Lily carrying a tea tray. "Hi Lucy" Lily smiled warmly. Lucy returned her grin "Hello Lily". "Mum I've just come back to get changed, then we're going into town for the afternoon cinema showing. Is is okay if Harry has tea with us please?" Asked Avril. "Of course it is" Phyllis beamed. "Thanks mum" said Avril, giving Phyllis a hug. "Thanks Mrs K" said Harrison bending to give her a kiss on the cheek. Phyllis grinned broadly, she clearly approved of Harrison, "He's such a lovely boy and so good to Avril" said Phyllis after they'd gone. "He certainly seems very nice" agreed Lucy. "Oh he is, he's the perfect gentleman and treats Avril like a princess. He works at the estate agents near the park, right next door to the bakers that Avril works in" said Phyllis. "Avril's working now? That's wonderful news" said Lucy. "It's only three afternoons a week, but it's really been the making of her" said Phyllis proudly. "That's fantastic, I'm very pleased for her" Lucy added. "Where's Ben?" Asked Lily. "He's in the car" Lucy replied. "Oh I'm sorry, I didn't realise. He could have come in" said Phyllis. "Yes I know, but I wanted to come in on my own at first as you weren't expecting us" Lucy told her. "Shall I go and get him?" Lily asked. "Yes please, if you wouldn't mind" Lucy nodded.

Lily returned a few minutes later with Ben in tow, "Mr Reid" said Phyllis with an uncertain smile. "Hi Phyllis" said Ben brightly. Lucy smiled at her husband, she was so proud of how he was making such an effort to start on the right foot. "Sit down Ben, I'll get you a coffee" said Lily. "Thank you, black with two sugars please" Ben replied, taking a seat next to Lucy. "Wont be long" Lily said hurrying off. "So how's Jonathan?" Ben asked. Lucy smiled to herself, she wasn't surprised that Ben's first question was about Jonathan. She knew how worried Ben had been about him. "He's very well thank you. Still attending Whitelea for their drop in days, and he goes swimming as well now. Avril and Harrison take him after work on Wednesdays. Jonathan loves being in the water and Harrison is amazing with him, so kind and caring" said Phyllis, her whole face lighting up at the mention of her younger brother. "Harrison?" Asked Ben puzzled. "Avril's boyfriend" Lucy told him. "Awh that's great!" Ben said. "I'll put your coffee down here" said Lily, placing it on the table for him. "Lily" called Jonathan's voice. "Coming" she called back, rushing out of the room "How are you then Phyllis?" Ben asked. "I can't complain Mr Reid, I'm grateful for every day and I'll always have you and Lucy to thank for that. My physio's going well and I even managed to walk along the corridor without my stick at the hospital the other day." Phyllis replied. "That's fantastic" remarked Ben, genuinely pleased for her. "I don't mind telling you I was worn out at the end of it though" said Phyllis with a laugh. Lucy looked at her intently, realising that's something she had never heard before. In all the time she had known Phyllis, she'd never actually heard her laugh. It just shows how Phyllis' new life was agreeing with her. No one to boss her about, intimidate or bully her. Happiness definitely seemed to agree with the new Phyllis, Lucy thought.

The living room door opened, "Ben!" Cried Jonathan, his whole face alight at seeing his trusted friend again. "Hello mate!" Said Ben, jumping to his feet and going to give him a hug. "Have you come to see me?" Asked Jonathan excitedly. "Of course" Ben replied. "Hi Jonathan" said Lucy, smiling warmly. "Hi Lucy" said Jonathan giving her a wave. Lucy laughed, she was used to coming second to Ben in the friend stakes where Jonathan was concerned. "Come and see my bedroom Ben!" Cried Jonathan, still brimming with excitement at his surprise visitor. "Is that okay?" Ben asked, looking at Phyllis. "Of course it is" she smiled back. When Ben, Jonathan and Lily had gone, Phyllis turned to Lucy, "Please don't think me rude, but can I ask you something?" Asked Phyllis warily. "Yes" replied Lucy, already guessing what she was about to ask. "Don't get me wrong, you turning up here today was a lovely surprise, and you are always welcome. But in honesty Lucy, you were the last person I expected to see when I opened the door" Phyllis said. Lucy nodded, "Yes, I can understand that, and if I'm truthful, it was a spur of the moment decision to finally come here. It crossed my mind a number of times, but I have always firmly pushed it away" Lucy said. "What made you decide?" Asked Phyllis quietly. Lucy took a deep breath, "I found out I was pregnant today" she said with a smile. "Oh my god Lucy, that's wonderful news! I'm so pleased for you both, congratulations!" Phyllis gushed. "Thank you, it's been a very difficult 18 months, but I feel that we are all gradually putting things behind us" Lucy stopped, noticing tears in Phyllis' eyes.

"I'm sorry Lucy, I've put you through so much" said Phyllis sadly. Lucy got up, walked over to Phyllis and sat down on the sofa next to her, she took the older woman's hand gently, "Phyllis, my intention is not to make you feel bad. Please don't keep apologising, this baby is a new start and for me to draw a line under the old I felt I needed to come and see you. I truly believe you are sorry" said Lucy. "I am" Phyllis said, wiping a tear from her cheek with the back of her hand. "I know, I thought that maybe next time Jonathan comes to visit Ben, you might like to come with him" said Lucy softly. "Oh Lucy, I'd like that very much" said Phyllis. "Okay, that's settled then" Lucy said. "I'd love for us to be friends" said Phyllis hopefully. "Let's take things slowly, see how things go" Lucy replied. "Okay, I understand. You're an amazing woman Lucy Reid, and you're giving me far more than I deserve. I know that" said Phyllis nodding sadly. "Anyway, I must be going" Lucy said, standing up. "Are you sure you wouldn't like to stay for lunch?" Phyllis asked. "No thank you" said Lucy, shaking her head, "Maybe next time". "So there will be a next time?" Phyllis asked hopefully. "Never say never, Phyllis, never say never." Smiled Lucy.

In bed later that evening, Ben drew Lucy close, "Are you still sure today was the right decision?" He asked. "I didn't think I blamed Phyllis for what went on, and seeing her today I know I don't" Lucy said. "For what it's worth Mrs Reid, you are a very wise woman, and I think today was the right decision too" said Ben, kissing the top of her head. The next day, Lucy and Ben invited all the family to lunch. They had decided to tell them all about the baby together. When everyone had finished eating and was seated back in the living room, Ben cleared his throat, "I have an announcement to make" he said. Everyone looked at him expectantly, "There's no other way to say this but come straight out with it, Lucy and I are expecting a baby" said Ben. "Oh that's wonderful news!" Exclaimed Mrs Armstrong. "I'm going to be a nanny again!" Cried Janet excitedly. "Congratulations!" Said Frank, clearly thrilled. "Nick are you okay?" Asked Lucy, noticing her step son was very quiet. Nick looked over at Leah who nodded shyly, "You're not only going to be a nan again, you're going to be a great grandma as well" said Nick smiling. Janet clasped her hand to her mouth in shock, "Well I think this deserves a toast" said Bruce, grinning broadly. "I'll help you get some glasses" said Jeff, following him out of the room. "I'm so happy for you both" said Lucy, hugging Nick and Leah in turn.

"That's fantastic news, and you know what this means Lucy?" Said Ben, suddenly looking serious. "What?" Asked Lucy in concern. "You're going to be a nanny at 27!" Ben replied, roaring with laughter. Everyone laughed at that. "Do you know, I don't mind a bit" Lucy smiled. "So do we know when these babies are due then?" Asked Mrs Armstrong. "We make it around easter" said Nick. Ben let out a hearty laugh, "So do we!" He cried. When Jake and Emily returned later that afternoon from their day out at the adventure park with Amira and Paul, they told them about their new brother or sister and their new niece or nephew. "How old do they have to be to play football?" Jake asked, his face a mask of seriousness. "Ooo we can have one each!" Emily told Jake happily. That night, as Lucy and Ben said goodnight to everyone and waved them all off down the drive, Ben laughed as Jake, Emily and Morph raced back up the steps together towards the house. He smiled happily as he threw his arm around Lucy's shoulders and once again turned to face his future. As he bolted the door on Hilltop Manor, he was sure he heard Great Aunt Maud's voice whisper, "Stay lucky, be happy" and Ben knew he would be.

Lightning Source UK Ltd.
Milton Keynes UK
UKHW040340160421
381768UK00030B/274

9 781665 580755